Invent
with Invent**or**

Yoofi Garbrah-Aidoo

authorHOUSE®

AuthorHouse™
1663 Liberty Drive
Bloomington, IN 47403
www.authorhouse.com
Phone: 1 (800) 839-8640

Published by AuthorHouse 02/24/2016

ISBN: 978-1-5049-8107-1 (sc)
ISBN: 978-1-5049-8108-8 (e)

Library of Congress Control Number: 2016903062

Print information available on the last page.

Invent with Inventor

YOOFI GARBRAH-AIDOO

About the Author

Yoofi Garbrah-Aidoo graduated from the University Of Houston College Of Technology with a bachelor's degree in Mechanical Engineering.

Yoofi has been working for different Oil & Gas companies since 1999, before joining the school system.

He taught Engineering design graphics at Lonestar Community College, in Houston and currently employed as an Engineering design Instructor at North Harris college of the Lonestar College Systems.

Foreword

The goal of writing this book is to enable the user to be more productive and get things done accurately and on time.

To introduce the user to tips of the trade, short cuts and innovation to make working with Inventor easier and fun.

Chapters in this book walk the user through the Model stage from 2D sketches. Each chapter is loaded with practical examples, which reflect exact location of tools for specific design.

Using this Book will enable the user and designer to be able to produce Models like it is second nature in no time at all.

Acknowledgments

The author would like to thank Autodesk for creating this state of the art software.

The author would also like to thank his family for their patience and support.

The author and publisher would like to thank all the professionals who reviewed the manuscript.

A special acknowledgement is due the following instructors and professionals.
Ibrahim ElSamahy, North Harris Community College, Houston, for his style of teaching.
David Mott, Lonestar College-North Harris Houston, the one who gave me a chance when no one would.

In the memory of Dr. Ahmed Nassef, my Dynamics professor, University of Houston, who broke it down to simple terms when it became complicated.

Ghassan Khalil, University of Houston, who gave me refresher course on calculus.
To all my students for, bringing the best out of me through, their diverse questioning.

Dedication
In loving memory of my Mother Eva Victoria Garbrah-Aidoo for seeing to it that I obtained the basic foundation of formal education.
To my wife and children, for their understanding and especially to Mia, for her unconditional love.
To my son, Omahn, for helping bring the best out of me as a parent and a father.

TABLE OF CONTENTS

Preface

Designers and students alike will find these valuable step by step examples of Inventor easy to follow and understand. The book will guide the user through the technical aspect of designing and 3D modeling and students and designers familiar with any of Microsoft packages will hit the floor running.

Inventor is loaded with all the tools you will need for designing a part and has an enhanced intelligent capability known as parametric design, a self-correcting tool which will help you make immediate changes to wrong designs and not lose a drawing or time. By so doing, changes made to the part will automatically reflect in other areas of the drawing and update accordingly.

Assembled parts can be checked for perfect fit using Interference Detection under the Tools palette and get corrected before manufactured.

There are different uses of the 3D package allowing the user to design complex shapes with *sweep* as well as *loft,* otherwise would be impossible or difficult to achieve.

This book is written for the novice as well as the advanced designer who would like to explore further into Inventor by combining *FEA* for calculations and analysis.

Introduction to Inventor

Inventor is 3D model application software, used in designing different types of parts and assemblies, from electrical, civil, architecture and piping to mechanical. Certain design software, required the designer to draw all over again when minor changes had to be made. Inventor has built-in parametric capabilities, meaning changing a dimension changes the part and upgrading of the model. Sequencing used in the model is also captured. With all these capabilities added on, the designer gets his work done more quickly and accurately, thus improving production and service. There is also the Internet commerce connection to share drawings across with clients. Drawings could be started in CAD software and saved as a DWG, DXF or jpeg file and opened up in Inventor for editing and parametric added on. With the help of this book users would be able to:

- Start basic 2D drawing add all necessary dimensions and convert it to 3D model
- Build on existing parts and make changes
- Use the built in capabilities to calculate the inertia of a beam, find the mass property of a part and determine interferences.
- Automatically generate bill of materials, balloons as well as parts lists; and with the aid of the equation function update files as dimensions changes accordingly.
- Generate production drawings using the assembly files or drawing files
- Use external referenced files in an assembly
- Create configuration to enable the user speed up production with a tied-in Excel program.

User Interaction

A complete set of visual display and mouse-driven control capabilities reduces design steps and minimize the need for dialogue boxes. It is assumed that you are familiar with Windows and worked with the menu and its tools, start programs, move windows, select various commands from menus as well as edit features, copy and paste save and print.

New Windows users can pick up a 'How to Book' on Windows for a crash course to bring them up to speed.

It is also assumed that you have access to a mouse and know how to use it, for most of the sketches are performed with the aid of a mouse. The keyboard is mostly used to enter certain values when called for by a dialogue box.

Feature-Based

In Inventor different objects make up a model and these objects are known as elements. Put together to form assembled parts, the elements are classified as features.

Certain geometric features such as bosses, cuts, holes, ribs, fillets, chamfers and draft are invoked and utilized in the application to the parts you create, when you use Inventor software. There is the transformation of the work piece into a finished part enhanced by the application of the elements and features directly to the model.

Welcome to State of the Art Software:

Welcome to Inventor design. After reading and practicing the first few chapters of this book, you will become very knowledgeable in the CAD environment world and design like a professional.

Note on Exercises:

The exercises given after each lesson, is to provide the student or designer, an opportunity to try out similar examples just covered and to offer hands on experience for each topic. It is advised that all necessary effort be put forth in completion of such exercises. This will give you hands-on experience as well as build your confidence.

Make sure you cover all the given exercises at the end of each chapter.

Who is This Book For?

- This book is supported under the Microsoft Windows graphical interface and users who have used Windows before or similar operating system and eager to know more about designing faster and easier.

- If you are a newcomer to designing parts and gadgets, and do not want to mess around sitting in long lectured classrooms and itching to plunge straight in at the deep end.

- You would like to learn the basics and start using your knowledge for better and challenging design, and then you have certainly got hold of the right book.

- Alternatively if you have been working in any CAD environment and would like to know what Inventor could do differently, strap on your seatbelt, for you are about to set aside the one you are with, Inventor can do what you do even better and easier. What you already know is going to be reinforced, letting you get to the real thing straight away.

- There is the Final Project that covers most of the topics in the book and the student/design is to create it from start to finish.

Design Skills:

It is very essential to review previous material as you continue to learn new topics. By so doing, you will be able to obtain a general concept of the material ahead, since each chapter is built on the ones already covered.

Why Inventor?

This software is user friendly and contains all the capabilities of CAD software in the market, which incorporates everything from 2D drawings to parametric design, to links on the Internet as well as conversions to and from other CAD software like Pro-E and AutoCAD. Those familiar with AutoCAD will find familiar features like the Command Line to make keyboard entries as well as draw in an AutoCAD environment. The Drawing Sheet offers the capabilities of Layers as found in other CAD programs.

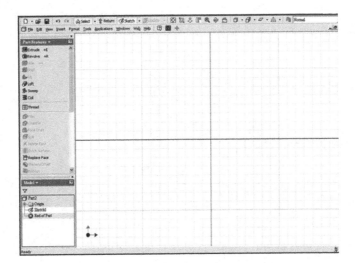

Graphics area

Chapter I

After completing this chapter the student will be able to:

- Set up a Project folder
- Draw a line
- Use the *Offset* entity to make copy of the line
- Create another line perpendicular to the two lines.
- Use the *Extend* entity to extend a line perpendicular to another line
- Place a circle from the center of all the intersecting lines.
- Use the *Trim* tool to remove certain parts of the sketch
- Use the *Undo* button in restoring the sketch again
- Move the whole sketch with the *Move* entity.
- Start a new drawing to get familiar with some of the tools and draw a sketch using basic tools and saved it.

Begin Inventor: -

The Inventor program could be started in one of two ways, click on Start button, to the bottom left of the screen, highlight Programs, and choose *Inventor* from the programs menu. A dialogue box pops up, click on File, New and OK to start a new drawing file.

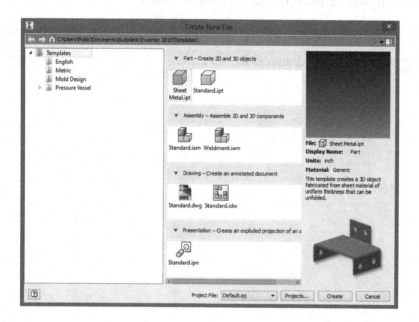

Create New File

Alternatively one can click on the *Inventor icon* on the windows desktop and click on new and in the New File, one has the option of double-clicking on *Standard.Ipt*

1. If the designer/student has worked with Microsoft office application before, most of the steps will look familiar, if not, just hang in there and I will bring the student up to speed. I realize that the student has just started and very anxious to go on the freeway, but let us build a strong foundation, and move on by steps.

2. On the desktop, double click on the Inventor icon to load the program. Alternatively one can click on start, usually at the bottom left corner of the monitor, highlight all programs, move on Inventor and click on Inventor icon to launch Inventor.

3. Open Dialogue box pops up and you have the option of working in English units or Metric, just by clicking to select one of the Titles; to work with.

4. The screen will show a graphics area depending on the Version of **Inventor** and system in use.

Setting Up a Project:

Planning how the end product would look like is very important in *Inventor*; thus one will be able to incorporate Parts and Assemblies into a projects comprising of electrical, bolts and nuts with other related components for a particular client or a company.

By so doing created parts could be built with folders containing Files tied into that particular Project.

Before creating the New Project, let us make available a Folder to save all Drawings into.

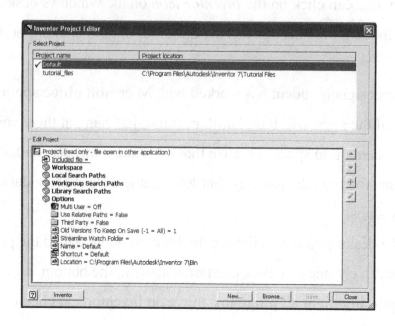

Inventor Project Editor

Follow these steps to create a New Project for MyProject.

1. Create a folder on the C: or an alternate drive to hold the project drawings and name it *Inventor Projects*.

2. From the Microsoft Windows, click on the *Start Menu, Programs* and *Inventor* select the version to load the program.

3. Alternatively double-click on the Inventor icon on the desktop to start the program.

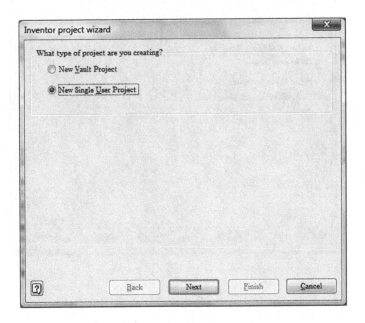

Inventor Project Wizard

4. Expand the arrow by *'I'PRO* on the top left of the graphics area, highlight Manage and click on Project.

5. The Projects dialogue box should open up.

6. Click on the *New* button to open up Inventor project wizard and click inside the Radio Button besides, *New Single User Project.* This will specify the same library definitions with the selected project. This action will also activate the Project for existing Inventor files.

7. Click on the *Next* button Inventor project wizard opens up with Name and other text boxes to fill.

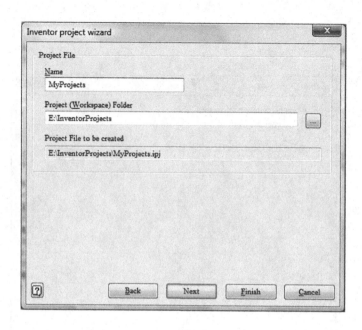

Inventor Project Wizard

8. Click on Browse for project location tab at the end of the middle text box, locate the *Inventor Projects* created earlier on and click on open to be placed in the text box, under *Project (Workspace) Folder.*

9. Click on the Finish button to exit the setup and double-click on MyProject under Project name to make it current by placing a check mark by the name.

10. Click on Done button at the bottom of the Project setup and click on New to open up the New File dialogue box to select an option.

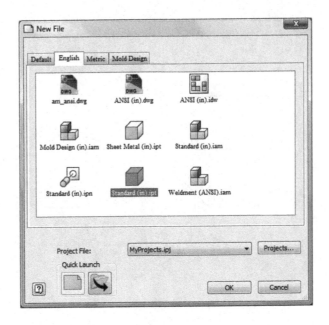

New File dialogue box

Now that a Project File has been added, the student will start creating basic drawings. Engineering designs and natural structures, all have shapes comprising of lines, circles, spline and polygons as such we will begin learning how to draw these basic shapes and move on to advanced drawings.

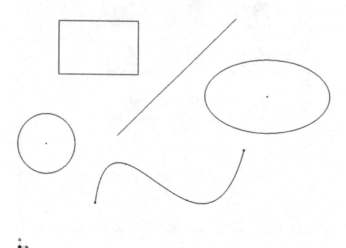

Geometric Sketches

Shapes:

1. Click on the English (in).ipt tab under New File and click on OK.
2. Select the *Line* tool from the Ribbon under the Sketch tab.
3. Click on the graphics area release the fore finger from the left mouse button, move the mouse pointer away from the first point, click on the Graphics area again to draw a line and hit the *'esc'* key on the keyboard.
4. Follow the steps above and select *Ellipse*.
5. Click on the Graphics area, release the fore-finger, move the mouse pointer *vertically* up and click again.
6. Release the fore-finger, move the mouse pointer *horizontally* to the right click and hit the 'ESC' key. Draw the rest of the Shapes.
7. To draw a Circle, select the Circle tool, click anywhere on the Graphics area,

release the fore-finger from the left mouse button, move the mouse pointer to another location and click again to place a circle on the screen.

8. Hit the ESC key on the keyboard to exit the circle tool.

9. To draw a Spline, select the spline tool click up and down on the graphics area whiles spacing the points, right click on the mouse when finished and select Create.

Note that the arrows besides various tools indicate that there are more tools to be selected. All one has to do is click on an Arrow to reveal the next Tool, under the Sketch tab.

Note: When the Mouse pointer is left to rest over an Icon for few seconds, a *Tool Tip* reveals what that particular icon is used for, at the bottom left corner of the screen.

Lines and Circles could be used to create patterns like the one in Pattern below.

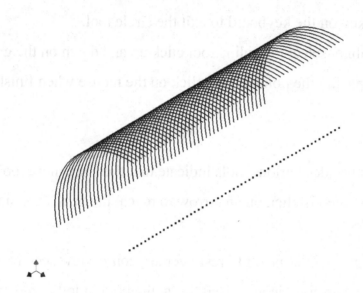

Pattern

Editing:

(This will be explained further in detail later on in the chapter)

All projects, no matter how well planned, will be changed one way or the other during the course of the design. The student will therefore be introduced to editing and modifying drawings.

1. Start a new file by clicking on the *Inventor* icon from the desktop or click on *start* on the desktop, click on All Programs and select Inventor from the list of software.

2. Click on *English,* select *Standard (in).ipt* and click on OK.

3. Select the *Line* tool from Sketch, click on the graphics area, and release the fore-finger from the left mouse button.

4. Drag the pointer away from the first point and click again to complete the operation. Hit the escape (*esc*) button.

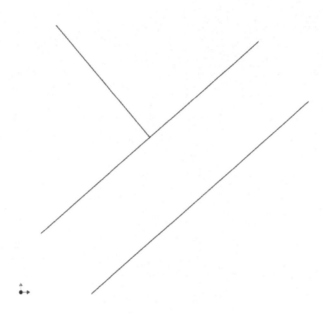

5. Click on the line just drawn and hit the *'delete'* key by the *keyboard,* then click on the undo icon, which is a *curved arrow* pointing towards the left, on the main menu and hit on the escape button (*esc*) to complete the first edit.

6. Click on *Offset* in the *Panel Bar* and click on the line in the graphics area.

7. Move the pointer to another location and click on the Graphics area again, a copy of the line should be placed a distance from the Original sketch.

8. Follow the procedure for drawing a Line above and draw a line perpendicular to the two lines as below.

9. Notice a *perpendicular sign* at the base of the pointer as the mouse pointer gets closer to 90°.

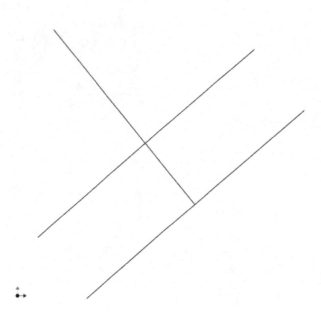

Extended Line

Extend:

Extends a line to the next intersecting line, or selected boundary geometry.

To extend a line, do the following:

1. Click on the *Extend* tool in the Panel Bar and select Extend.
2. Next click on the line to extend and it automatically moves to the next closer line.
3. Select the *Center point circle* from the Panel Bar, click on the intersection of the first two lines, and release the fore-finger from the left mouse button.
4. Move the pointer and click on the intersection of the second lines to place the circle. Use the *Trim* tool to remove certain portions of the Lines.

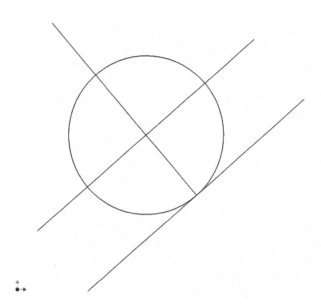

Circle tangent to Line

Trim:

Trim a curve/line to the next intersecting curve/line or selected boundary geometry.
To trim lines, do the following:

1. Click on *Trim* from the *Panel Bar* and click on the lines inside the Circle to remove them.

2. Click on *Undo on the Main Menu* several times after that, to restore the original drawing.

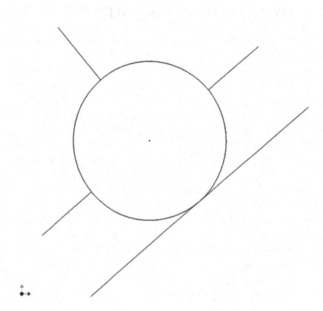

Trimmed Line

Move:

Move selects sketch or geometry from one point to the other as specified, with an option to copy.

To move sketches do the following:

1. Click outside the sketch hold down the left button on the mouse and drag an *invincible rectangle* around the sketch.

2. Release the fore-finger from the left mouse button. The entire sketch should now be highlighted.

3. Click on the highlighted sketch, hold down on the left mouse button and move it across the Graphics area.

4. Release the forefinger to drop the sketch in a different location.

Creating first drawing

Tool Tip:

Remember to leave the mouse pointer on top of an icon to reveal of what it does when in doubt.

1. In this exercise, simple geometric tools will be used to create basic sketches, like lines, circles, and learn how to place dimensions on drawings and save a part.

2. Click on *File* and select *New* from the toolbar, then click on *English* and select *Standard (in).ipt* this will be the first step the student will take every time to start a new drawing, therefore be conversant with it.

3. Notice that, this action activates the *Origin* icon, with the *'Y'-colored green* pointing vertically in the positive direction and *'X'-colored red pointing horizontally* the positive direction and a *'Z'-colored blue in the positive direction*.

4. Next click on *Line* tool from the *2D Sketch Panel*.

5. Click on any place on the graphics area with the left mouse button, release the forefinger, move the mouse away and drag the pointer *vertically up*.

6. Next move the mouse pointer *horizontally* to the right and watch the increase in *Length* at the bottom right of the screen, as pointer moves away from the base.

7. Finish the Sketch and add all the dimensions.

Dimensioning:

Dimensions control the size of a part. Dimensions can be expressed as numeric constant, variable equations or in parameter files.

Follow the steps below to add dimensions to the sketch.

1. For now click on the *General Dimension* tool from the 2D Sketch.

2. Click on the first vertical line, release the fore-finger from the left mouse button, drag the mouse to the right and click on the graphics area.

3. Edit Dimension: *d0* dialogue box pops up.

4. Enter 4 on top of the given value and click on the *check mark*. Finish placing the rest of the dimensions in a similar fashion.

5. The finished sketch should look like the Geometric Sketch.

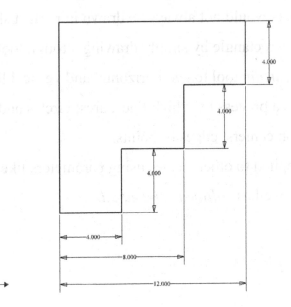

Geometric Sketch

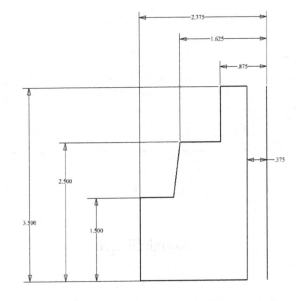

Outline of a Sketch

Adding/Deleting Constraint:

Two dimensional objects would not always be drawn in perfect shapes; for an example, one can start a rectangle by simply drawing a rough looking sketch and use the *Geometric Constraint* tool to add horizontal and vertical lines to the sketch. Geometric constraint is a process by which lines; arcs; circles and or ellipse are forced to share common centers, edges or points.

Constraint could be applied to other shapes using parameters like *concentric, coincidence, and fix* as well as *collinear and equal.*

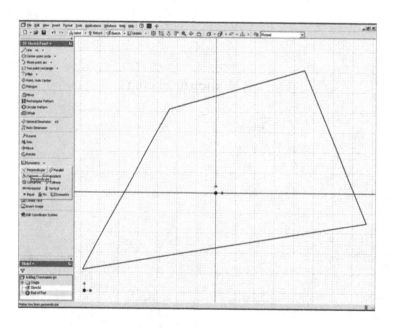

Rough Sketch

Adding Constraint:

- Start a new file and draw a rough sketch of a polygon using the line tool as in Rough Sketch.
- Click on Horizontal under *2D Sketch Panel* and select *Horizontal.*
- Click on the first top line then the bottom line to change into horizontal lines.
- Select the *Vertical Constraint* and click on the left and the right lines in the sketch to change into vertical lines.

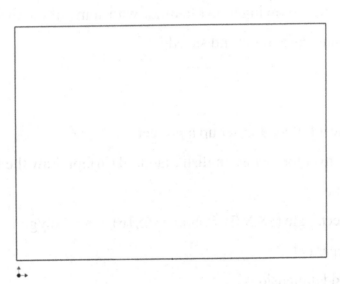

Rectangular Sketch

34

Summary

In this chapter topics covered included but not limited to:

- Setting up a Project folder
- Drawing a lines and circles.
- Using the *Offset* entity to make copy of the line
- Creating another line perpendicular to the two lines.
- Using the *Extend* entity to extend a line perpendicular to another line
- Placing a circle from the center of all the intersecting lines.
- Using the *Trim* tool to remove certain parts of the sketch
- Using the *Undo* button in restoring the sketch again
- Moving the whole sketch with the *Move* entity.
- Starting a new drawing to get familiar with some of the tools and draw a sketch using basic tools and saved it.

Exercise:

1. Create a Folder and set up a project
2. Start Inventor, using English Standard (in).ipt draw the following sketches
   - ❖ Rectangle (18 X 7), Square (16x16) and a Polygon with 6 sides separately.
   - ❖ Add dimensions
   - ❖ Save it as Proj. Rectangle, Proj. Square and Proj. Polygon.
3. Draw the sketch below with all the necessary dimensions and save as Project1

Chapter II

This chapter will cover Part Features:

- Boss-Extrude
- Extrude-Cut
- Revolve
- Revolve-Cut
- Sweep
- Loft
- Fillet / Variable / Setback
- Chamfer
- Ribs
- Shell
- Taper / Draft
- Holes
- Linear / Circular Pattern
- Mirror
- Wrap
- Coil
- Engrave

The *3D Model* contains different features used in creating *3D* objects. This includes but not limited to the following: Extrude; Revolve; Loft; Sweep; Rib; Coil; Emboss; Decal; Hole; Fillet; Chamfer; Shell; Face Draft; Thread; Split; Combine; Copy Object; Move Bodies; Grill; Boss; Rest; Snap Fit; Fillet; Thicken.

All these *Features* will be covered one after the other but not necessary in this order.

After completing this chapter the student will understand the different options in features from the 3D Model tab.

Boss-Extrude:

Adding numerical value to a 2D drawing sketch to give it depth is known as extrude feature.

1. Start Inventor place an Ø2.00 inch circle on the **XY Plane** and click on the Finish Sketch checkmark.

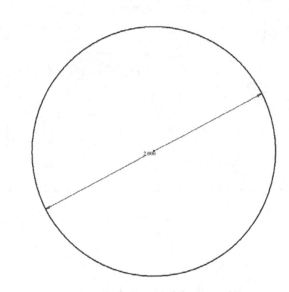

2 inch Circle Sketch

2. Click on the *Extrude* icon under the *3D Model* tab on the Ribbon change the value under Distance to 2 and click on OK to exit.

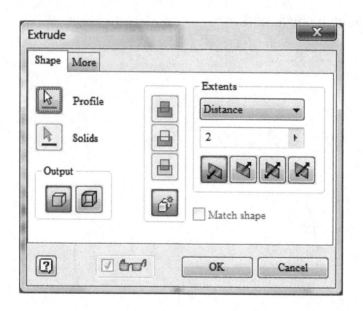

Extrude dialogue box

3. Right-click on the graphics area and select Home view.

Extruded Circle

Extrude-Cut:

This is a process in which material is removed from a solid part.

1. Click on the flat face of the extruded circle and select create sketch.

2. Create a rectangular sketch with the dimension text as shown below.

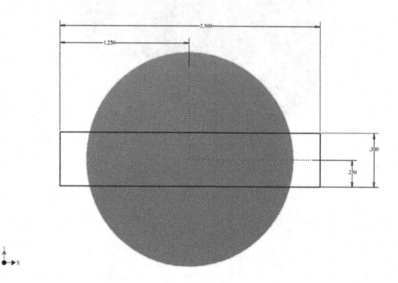

Rectangular sketch on extruded Part

3. Right-Click on the graphics area, select Home view and click on the Finish Sketch check mark to exit the sketch.

4. Click on the extrude icon under the Model tab, change the condition of the feature to Cut with 1 inch distance.

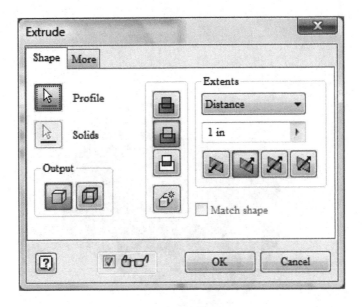

Extrude Cut dialogue box

5. Click on the rectangular shape on top of the Part on the graphics area and select OK to create a cut on the cylinder.

Extruded Cut

Revolve:

Revolve creates a feature or body by revolving one or more sketched profiles about the axis.

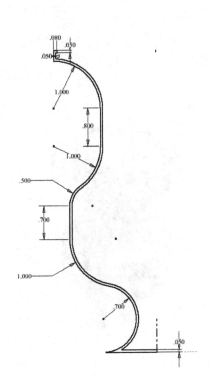

Vase Outline

1. Use the line tool together with arc to create the Vase Outline and exit the sketch.

2. Click on the Revolve icon under the Model tab and click on the centerline by the bottom sketch.

Revolved Sketch

Revolve-Cut:

Revolve cut creates a feature that adds or removes material by revolving one or more profiles around a centerline. The feature can be a solid, a thin feature, or a surface.

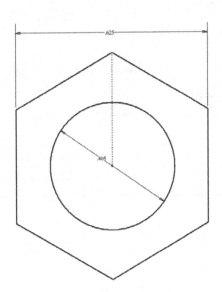

Hex nut sketch

1. Draw a 6-sided polygon and add dimension text, 0.625 across flats and 0.405 ID as in Hex nut sketch.
2. Click on the Finish Sketch check mark to exit.
3. Add a depth of 0.188 using the extrude feature, click on OK.

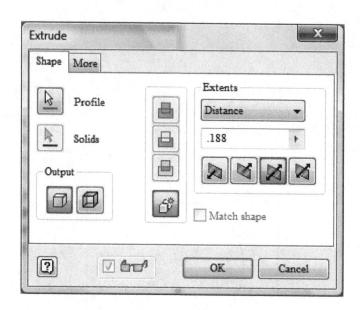

Extrude dialogue box

4. Click on the YZ Plane in the Browser and add a new sketch.

5. Draw a triangle on each top corner of the Hex Nut and place a dimension text of 0.031 X 0.031 and a centerline from the Origin.

6. Click on Finish Sketch check mark to exit the sketch and click on the Revolve icon under Model.

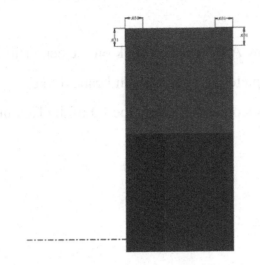

Triangular Sketch with a Centerline

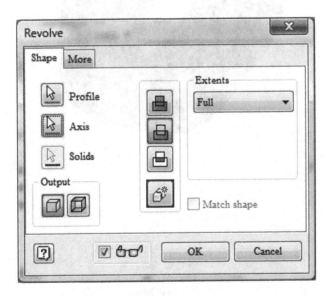

Revolve dialogue box

7. Select the Cut option and click on the two triangular outlines to highlight both objects.

8. Click on the Arrow by Axis text and click on the centerline on the Hex nut.

9. Click on OK to complete the operation and cancel to exit.

10. Click on the Threads icon and click on the ID of the Hex nut.

11. Save the Hex nut.

Hex Nut

Sweep:

Sweep creates a base, boss, cut, or surface by moving a profile (section) along a path, according to these rules.

1. Draw a spline on the graphics area and click on the Finish Sketch check mark to exit the sketch.

2. Click on the *Work Plane* under the Model tab and click twice on the endpoint of the spline.

Spline

3. Right-click on the work plane at the tip of the spline and add a new sketch.

4. Create a circular pattern with a 0.5 inch diametric circle with 16 instances and exit the sketch.

5. Click on Sweep under Model tab and click inside the 0.5 inch circles one at a time using the Profile button, to highlight each one and click on the Spline when finished to create the Sweep.

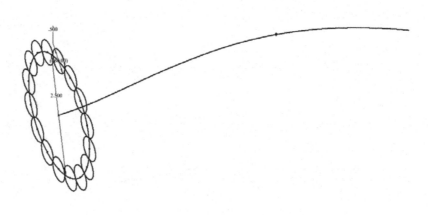

Circular pattern of 0.50 inch circle

Sweep dialogue box

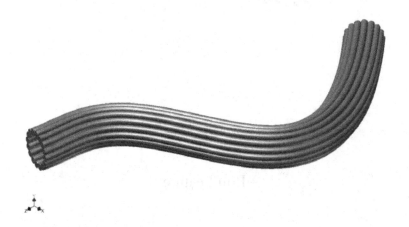

Sweep Feature

Loft:

Loft creates a feature by making transitions between profiles. A loft can be a base, boss, cut, or surface.

Loft Feature

1. Draw a 0.75 inch circle on the origin and exit the sketch.

2. Use the work plane to offset another plane from the first sketch at a distance of 0.25 inch.

3. Add a new sketch to this plane and place a 1.00 diametric circle on the plane. Exit the sketch.

4. Offset another work plane from the last sketch and add a new sketch.

5. Place a 0.563 inch circle on the plane and exit the sketch.

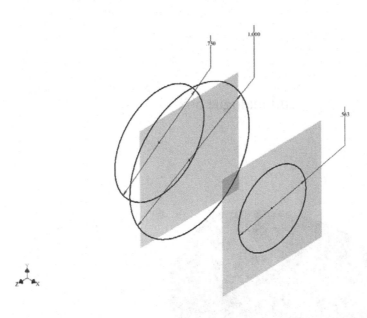

Offset Circles

10. Click on the *Loft* icon under Model and place a check mark by Closed Loop.

11. Click on the circumference of each circle one after the other to create the Loft feature and save the Model.

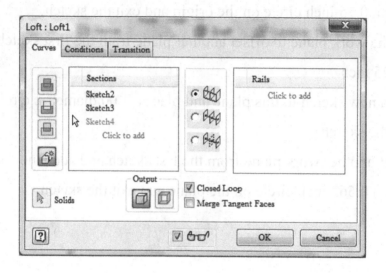

Loft dialogue box

Closed Loop Loft

Fillet:

One can create different types of fillet, from variable radius, to face, full and multiple radii.

Constant Fillet:

The constant Fillet keeps the same radius along the entire length of the Model.

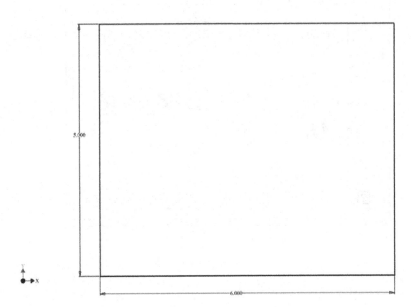

6 X 5 Rectangle sketch

1. Start a new file using English.ipt and place a 6 X 5 inch rectangle on the graphics area.

2. Click on the check mark by Finish Sketch to exit the rectangular sketch and click on the Extrude icon under the Model tab.

3. Change the distance to 5 to add and click on OK to add depth to the sketch.

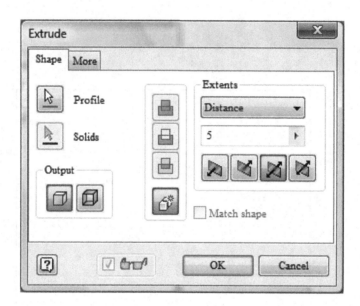

Extrude dialogue box

4. Click on the Fillet icon under the Model tab and select the *Constant* tab.

5. Change the Radius to 0.25 and click on '*click to add*' and click on one of the edges on the block.

6. Click on the *Apply* tab and *Cancel* to exit the Fillet feature.

Extruded Rectangle

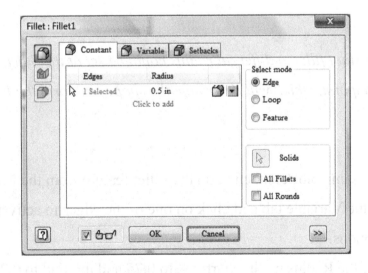

Fillet dialogue box

Fillet Edge

Variable Fillet:

Unlike the constant fillet, a different radius could be set at the Start, Intermediate as well as the Endpoint, which will determine the shape and form the Fillet will take on the Part.

1. Use the same block and click on the Fillet feature from the Model tab.
2. Select the Variable tab and click on one of the edges to activate the Start and End options.
3. Change the Radius by the Start text to 0.75 and the End to 0.25
4. Click on *Apply and Cancel* to exit the Fillet feature.

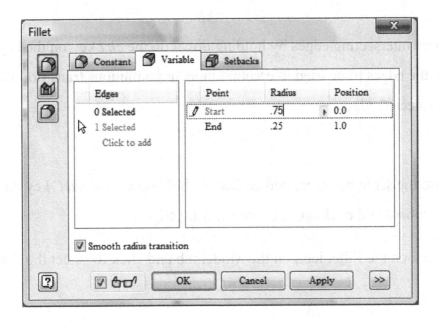

Fillet dialogue box

Variable Fillet

Setbacks:

Select three intersecting edges by holding down on the *ctrl* key on the keyboard, to highlight the edges to be used in creating tangent continuous transition fillet between selected edges.

1. Use the same block created earlier on, hold down the *'ctrl'* key on the keyboard and click on three intersecting edges.

2. Click on the Fillet icon on the Model tab and click to select the Setbacks tab.

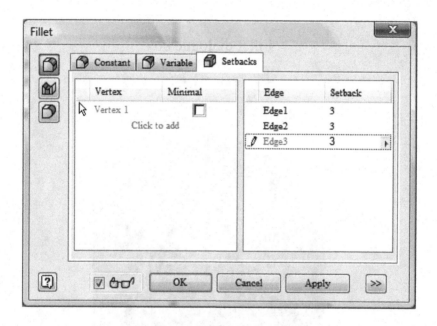

Fillet with selected Setbacks tab

5. Click on the intersecting *Vertex* to highlight it and change the Setback values to **3** on all three edges and click on Apply and Cancel to exit the Fillet dialogue box.

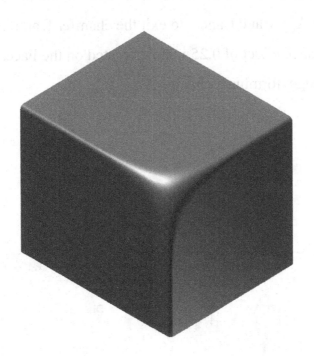

Setback Fillet on three edges

Chamfer:

Chamfer will create a beveled feature on selected edges or a vertex, with angle and distance, distance and distance.

1. Using the same block created earlier on click on the Chamfer icon under the Model tab and select the Distance option.
2. Change the Distance value to 0.25 and click on one of the edges to highlight it, click on Apply and Cancel to exit the chamfer feature.
3. Equal-distance offset of 0.25 will be created on the Faces that share the common edge, forming a chamfer.

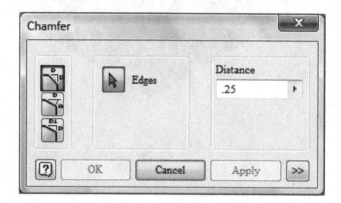

Chamfer dialogue box

Distance Chamfer

Distance and Angle

1. Use the block created earlier on and select the Chamfer icon under the Model tab and click on *Distance and Angle* option.

2. Enter the decimal number 0.50 in the Distance box and 45 degree under Angle.

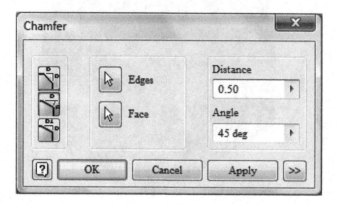

Chamfer dialogue box

6. Click on the Edges arrow and click on the required edge on the block.

7. There should be an offset of 0.5 from the edge to the face of the block with an angle of 45°.

Distance and Angle Chamfer

Two Distances Chamfer:

The distances on the faces could vary with the *Two Distance* option.

1. Uses the same block created earlier on and click on the Chamfer icon under the Model tab.
2. Select the Two Distance tab and enter 0.75 in Distance1 box and 0.25 in the box under Distance2.

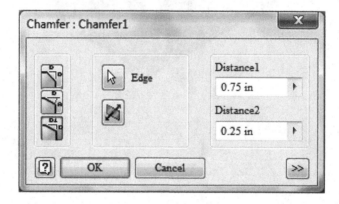

Chamfer Feature

3. Click on one of the edges click on Apply and Cancel to exit the Chamfer dialogue box.

Two Distances Chamfer

Ribs:

Ribs are used in creating rigidity in plastic parts and also to prevent warping of parts.

The student can create a rib using either single or multiple open, or closed sketches.

1. Start a new file in English.ipt and use the Line and the 3Point arc tool to create the outline below.

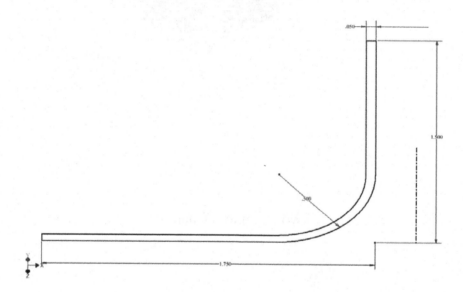

Outline

2. Click on Finish Sketch check mark to exit the sketch and select the Revolve icon under the Model tab.

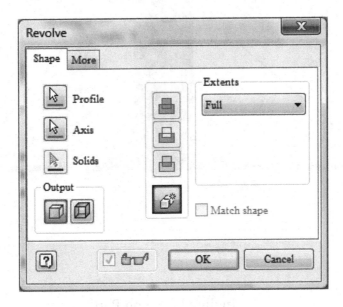

Revolve dialogue box

3. Select Full under Extents and click on OK the outline should revolve around the centerline.

4. Right-click on the *XY Plane* and add a new sketch and draw a line at an angle of 40°.

5. Exit the sketch and click on the Rib icon under the Model tab.

6. Click on the inclined line change the Thickness as required and click on OK button to place a Rib on the Part.

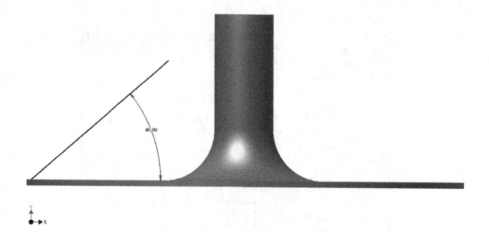

Inclined Line on Part

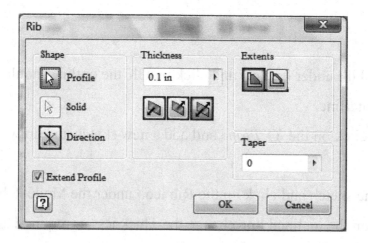

Rib dialogue box

7. Use the Circular Pattern tool to add six ribs on the Part.

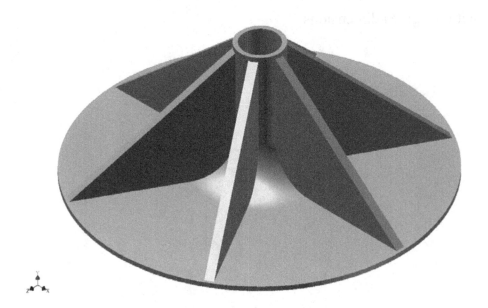

Rib Pattern

Shell:

Shell removes material from the interior of a part, creating a hollow cavity with specified wall thickness.

The smaller the Thickness value of the shell, the thinner the edge of the Model.

1. Start a new file on the *XY plane* using English.ipt and draw the sketch below with the given dimensions.

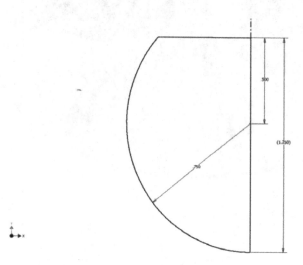

Shell Outline

2. Click on the check mark by Finish Sketch to exit sketch and click on Revolve icon under the Model tab.

3. Click on the Shell icon click on the flat face of the Model and change the default Thickness of 0.10 to 0.0125 by click on the OK button.

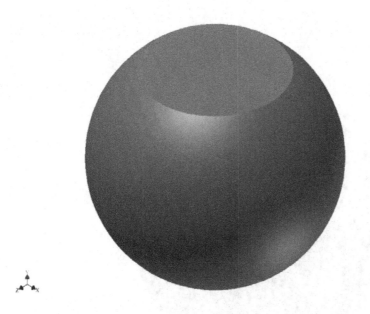

Revolved Sketch

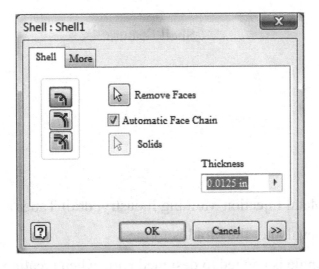

Shell dialogue box

Shell Feature

Taper:

In the Plastic & Metal Injection Molding Industry, draft Taper is applied to parts to enable easier retrieval after the Mold is formed.

Specified Taper angle is applied to designed parts when creating extrusion, sweep or lofted parts. This is a Tapered Nozzle.

1. Start a new part on the XY Plane using the English (in).ipt and draw a 1.50 X 2.00 inch rectangle from the origin.

2. Click on the check mark by the Finish Sketch to exit the sketch.

3. Click on the Extrude feature, change distance value to 6 and click on the *More* tab.

Tapered Nozzle

4. Replace 0.0 under Taper to 5 degree and click on the OK button.

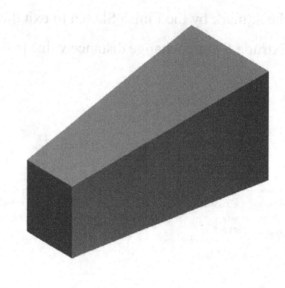

Model with Taper

Add fillet to the edges as well as a Shell feature.

Fillet and Shell

Draft:

Another use of a Taper is to apply it to the surface of a mold part to form a Draft in order for a part to be retrieved from the Mold.

Draft could be applied in the design stage to Parts to be used in Molds, with a positive or negative angle for an extrusion depending on the shape of the part.

78

1. Start a new part and place a 2 X 2 inch rectangle on the graphics area from the origin.
2. Exit the sketch and add a depth of 3 inches using the Extrude feature.
3. Click on the Draft feature under the Model tab and click on the top face of the block to be used as the direction pull.

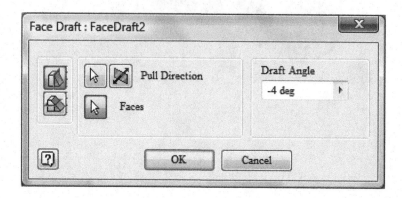

Face Draft dialogue box

5. Change the Draft Angle to (-4 degree) and click on the right and left faces of the block.
6. Click on Ok to apply the Draft to the block and the Cancel button to exit.

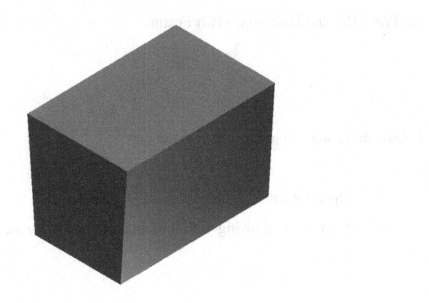

Draft Model

Holes:

In this project the student will add holes to a part using the Point Hole Center from the Panel Bar and Hole under Part Feature.

Follow these steps to insert a hole in the part.

1. Open Inventor, double-click on English.ipt.
2. Start a new drawing with the Line tool and draw the sketch below.

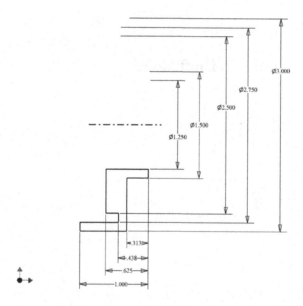

Geometric Outline

3. Add all the necessary dimensions and revolve the sketch to turn it into 3D Part.

4. Click on the Inside Flat face of the Model and add a new Sketch.

5. Click on *Point* from the Sketch tools and add a point on the inside face of the dish and exit the sketch.

6. Click on *Hole icon* under *Model tab* and in the Hole dialogue box, select *Drilled, Counterbore or Countersink.*

7. Repeat the above process to add different holes to the dish and save the Model.

Revolved Feature

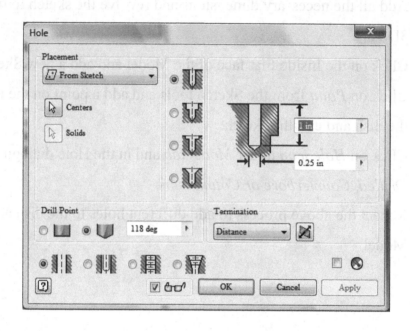

Holes Feature

Drilled

1. On the Hole dialogue box should read 1 in and 0.25 in, depending on the Version of Inventor in use when Drilled is selected.
2. One could edit the values by clicking on the number and changing the entries.
3. Click on Ok to finish placing the hole.

Counterbore / Countersink

1. When *Counterbore* is selected one has the Option of changing the values under *Threads, Size and Options.*
2. Under *Termination* the user could select *Distance, Through All and To.*

3. Under *Tool Geometry* click in the box by *Tapped* to activate more options.

4. Under *Threads Type*, choose *Right Hand* or *Left Hand* depending on the application.

Holes

Type	Threads	Size	Option

Centers   Termination   Distance

Threads

Tool Geometry

Tapped   Full Depth

Thread Type

ANSI Unified Screw Threads

Right Hand   Left hand   SIZE

Nominal 0.125	Pitch 5-40 UNC / UNF
Class 2B	Diameter Minor
Options Drill Point Flat Angle	118 Measure Show Diameter

Countersink:

This option has similar entries. Below is an example of the Three Types of Holes. The student has just learned how to create a 3D part and add different holes to the Model.

Part with different holes

Linear:

This feature is used to pattern multiple instances of selected features along one or two linear paths.

1. Start a new part on the XY Plane using the English (in).ipt and place a 3 X 3 inch rectangle on the graphics area and exit sketch.
2. Add a depth of 4 inches using the Extrude feature and click on OK and Cancel.
3. Click on the top face of the block add a new sketch and exit.
4. Place a Point on top of the block and 0.5 dimensions from both edges and exit.
5. Select the Hole feature under the Model tab and click on the radio button by the Spot face option.

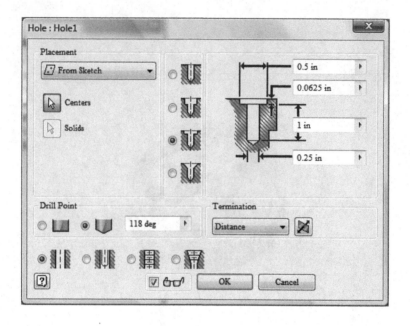

Hole on Part

6. Make the following entries as in the Hole on Part and click on OK.

7. Click on the Rectangular Pattern icon and select the Hole1 under the Browser.

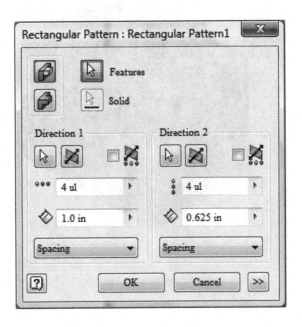

Rectangular Pattern

8. Click on the arrow under Direction 1 and click on the longer edge of the block.

9. Enter 4 in the text box under Direction1 and 1.0 in.

10. Click on the arrow under Direction2 and click on the shorter edge of the block.

11. Enter 4 in the text box under Direction2 and click on the 0.625 in and click on OK and Cancel to complete the process.

Rectangular Pattern

Circular Pattern:

The circular pattern is used to create multiple instances of one or more features, which can be spaced uniformly around an axis.

1. Start a new part using English.ipt and place a 1.50 inch circle on the graphics area.
2. Exit the sketch and add a depth of 1 inch using the Extrude feature.
3. Place a Point on a Bolt Circle diameter of 1.125 and exit the sketch.
4. Click on the Hole icon and make the following entries and click on OK

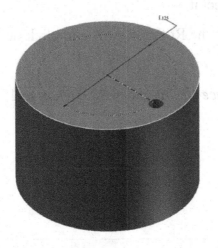

Hole on Cylinder

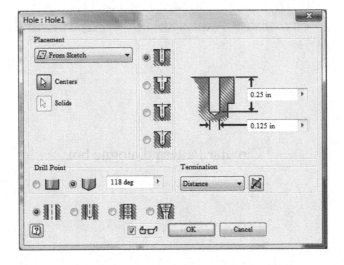

Hole dialogue box

5. Click on the Circular Pattern icon under the Model tab and click on the Hole in the Browser to select it.

6. Click on the arrow by the Rotation Axis and click on the circumference of the cylinder.

7. Change the *Occurrence Count* under *Placement* to 12 and click on the OK button.

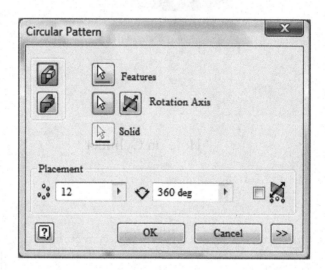

Circular Pattern dialogue box

Circular Pattern

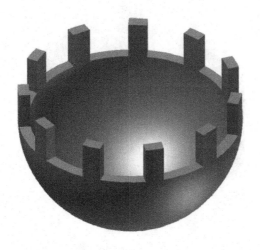

Circular Pattern

Inventor Help file contains tons of information and examples. It is very necessary to consult with the help files anytime the student needs enforcement on a particular topic. For an example whiles working on the *Shell* option, the student can hit the F1 key and it automatically opens up the help file with examples to follow.

Mirror:

Creates a copy of a feature, (or multiple features), mirrored about a plane. The student can select the feature or select the faces that comprise the feature.

1. Draw a 2 X 2 inch rectangle from the origin and exit sketch.

2. Add a depth of 3inch using the Extrude feature and click on OK button to exit.

3. Add a new sketch on top of the flat face of the block and add a 1.75 diametric circle from the midpoint of the edge.

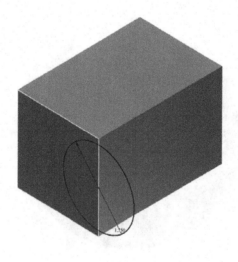

1.750 diametric circle on Midpoint of block

4. Exit sketch and use the cut extrude feature to add a cut of 1.5 in on the block.

5. Use the Mirror feature under the Model using the top of the block as the *Mirror Plane.*

6. Click to select Extrusion 1 and Extrusion 2 as Features to mirror and click on OK and Cancel to exit.

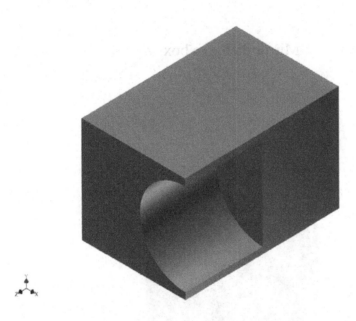

Model

94

Mirror dialogue box

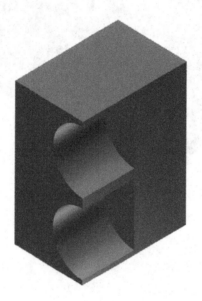

Mirrored Part

Curved-Driven Pattern

1. Start a new part using English.ipt and create a quarter circle with 1.00 in radius from the Origin adding dimension text.

2. Offset the arc a distance of 0.05 inch as in sketch below.

3. Using the Revolve feature under the Model tab, click on the centerline and change Full to Angle under Extents and enter 180.

4. Click on OK button to exit the revolve feature.

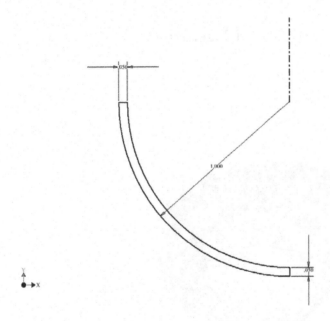

Sketch

Revolve dialogue box

Revolved Sketch

5. Click on top of the flat face and add a new sketch and offset the edge a distance of 0.025.

6. Place a 0.025 in diametric circle on the endpoint of the offset line as shown below.

7. Exit sketch and extrude the circle 0.5 inches.

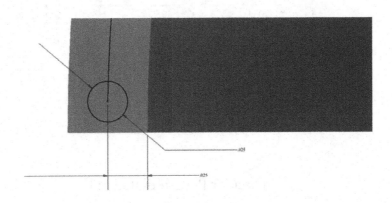

Circular Sketch

8. Expand the plus sign by *Extrusion1*, right-click on *Sketch2* and select Share Sketch; the offset line placed earlier on should be visible.

9. Click on Axis under the Model tab, click on the curved edge of the model to place a vertical axis on the center.

10. Select the Circular Pattern under the Model tab, click on the Extrusion as the Feature.

11. Click on the arrow by *Rotation Axis* and click on the *Work Axis1* in the browser.

12. Enter the number *20* for Placement and *175* for the angle and click on OK.

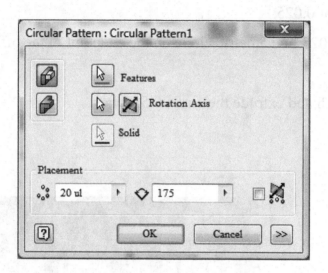

Circular Pattern dialogue box

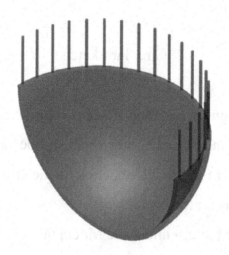

Threads

This feature is used to create threads inside holes and outside of studs, bolts and shafts.

1. Create a 0.25 inch circle on the Top XZ Plane and add a depth of 2 inch using Extrude boss.

2. Expand the arrow under Hole icon and select Threads.

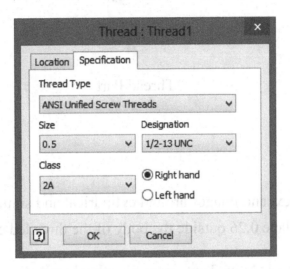

Thread dialogue box

3. With the selection arrow adjacent to Face highlighted, click on the body of the cylinder.

4. Click on Specification tab and select ¼ -20 UNC under Designation and the Apply button.

Thread Part

Wrap:

This used to wrap text and images around cylindrical and similar objects.

1. Offset XY plane 0.26 outside the body of the threaded cylinder.

2. Select the letter 'A' by Text under Sketch tab and click on the Work plane just added.

3. Type ½ -13 UNC in the Format textbox and click on OK button.

4. Expand the arrow under Sweep icon, select Emboss and click on the text placed on the work plane.

5. Select Engrave from face, place a check mark in Wrap to Face text box, change the depth and click on OK button.

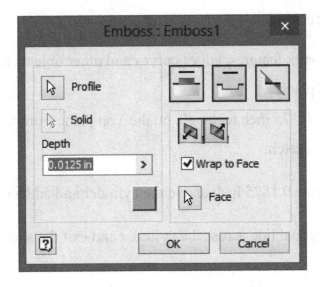

Engrave dialogue box

Wrap to Face

Project to Surface

This will project work features, edges curves and other objects from current objects to the new sketch plane.

1. Draw a 1 x 0.175 inch rectangle on the Top plane from the Origin and revolve the sketch.

2. Offset a Plane 0.1875 inch above the cylinder and add a new sketch.

3. Draw a diagonal line across the cylinder and exit the sketch.

Diagonal Line on Cylinder

4. Click on Create 3D Sketch to open up 'Project Curve to Surface' dialogue box and select the Wrap to Surface tab.

5. Click on the arrow by Faces and click on the body of the cylinder to highlight it.

6. Click on the arrow by Curves and click on the line on the Work plane.

7. Click on *Apply* and *Cancel* to exit the 3D Sketch and click on Finish Sketch.

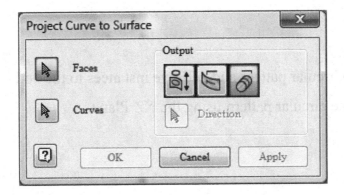

Project Curve to Surface dialogue box

8. Click on Plane and click on the endpoint of the line twice to plane a work plane at the end of the projected yellow line.

9. Add a new sketch and place a 0.05 inch at the tip of the endpoint.

10. Exit the sketch and click on Sweep-cut to add a groove on the cylinder.

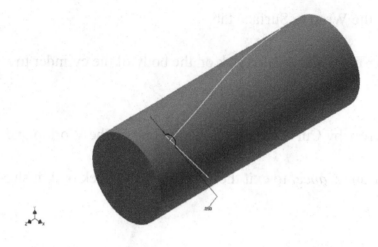

11. Use the Circular pattern and add five instances to the body of the cylinder.
12. Mirror the circular pattern using the XZ Plane.

Designing a Helical Spring Lock Washer:

1. Draw a rectangle together with a Centerline and add all dimensioning as in shown.

2. Click on Finish sketch to open up the Part Features and click on Coil.

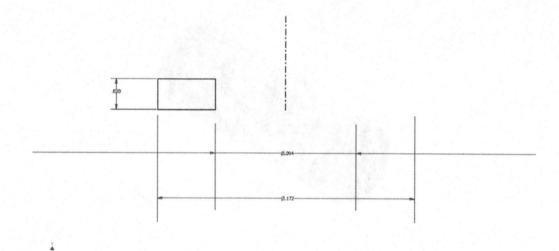

Coil Sketch

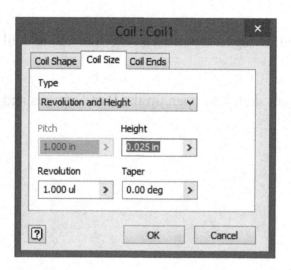

Coil dialogue box

3. Make the following entries as in the Coil dialogue box and click on OK complete the coil design.

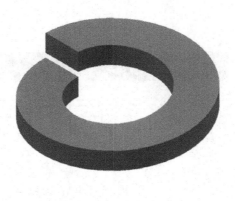

Spring Lock Washer

Engrave

This is used to engrave text and other information to the body of a part for an example model and serial numbers.

1. Start a new part document click on Box and select XY plane to place a box on the graphics area.

2. Accept the default setting of 1 and click on OK button to exit.

3. Click on the front face of the box and add a new sketch.

4. Select the letter *A Text* from the Ribbon tab and click on the face of the block to open up Format Text.

5. Type the Word *'Engraving'* and click on OK button and the *esc* key on the keyboard.

6. Expand the arrow by Sweep under 3D Model and select Emboss.

7. Click inside the middle button to select Engrave.

Emboss

8. Select the Profile arrow and click on the Engraving letters on the face of the block.

9. Change the Depth to 0.05 and click on OK button to engrave the block.

10. Add fillet to the edges of the block.

Engrave

Summary

Topics covered included:

- Boss-Extrude
- Extrude-Cut
- Revolve
- Revolve-Cut
- Sweep
- Loft
- Fillet / Variable / Setback
- Chamfer
- Ribs
- Shell
- Taper / Draft
- Holes
- Linear / Circular Pattern
- Mirror
- Wrap
- Coil
- Engrave

Exercise

Without using the book select a part from an engineering book and create it from scratch using all the topics covered in this chapter.

Chapter III

After completing this chapter the student will be able to:

- Visualize the proper Plane to start a drawing on for the best orientation.
- Select the right tools to draw from scratch and add all dimensions to create the Base Part.
- Add Features to the sketch to form a 3D Model
- Place additional cuts and or boss as needed on the base part
- Save the model
- Start a new drawing using the Drawing Sheet
- Create 3 basic views the Front, Top and Right side using Projection option
- Add dimensions, centerlines to circular parts and all needed annotations
- Select the Third Angle for the ANSI (American National Standard Institute) Drawings and enter data in a Title Block
- Add Geometric Tolerances

At this point, the student should begin to notice certain general rules and in what order, in creating drawings. For an example, the user will select *New* from file; choose *English or Metric* and OK, in starting a new drawing.

3D Modeling takes the outline of a Sketch and adds depth to it. Alternatively pieces of blocks and cylindrical shapes are removed or carved into different shapes to form a finished part.

This session will introduce the designer to solid modeling, an easier approach to accomplishing a particular goal and the correct planes to use in drawing Sketches. After completing the tutorial the designer will be able to:

1. Start a new part using English.ipt and use the line tool to add a sketch on the Origin.

2. Add all required dimension text and click on Finish Sketch.

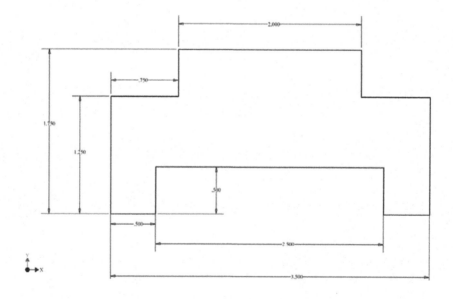

Block Sketch

3. Add a depth of 6.50 inches using the Extrude feature and click on OK button.

4. Click on the flat top of the block and add a new sketch.

5. Place two circles of 1.00 inch diameter with 3.750 distances apart and 1.375 from both edges. Save the Model.

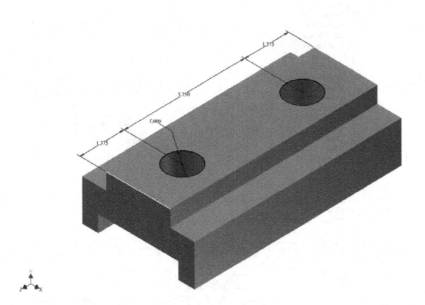

Block with through hole

6. Expand the arrow by IPRO and click to select *iProperties.*

7. Click on the Physical tab expand the arrow under Material and select Alloy Steel, click on Apply button and Close.

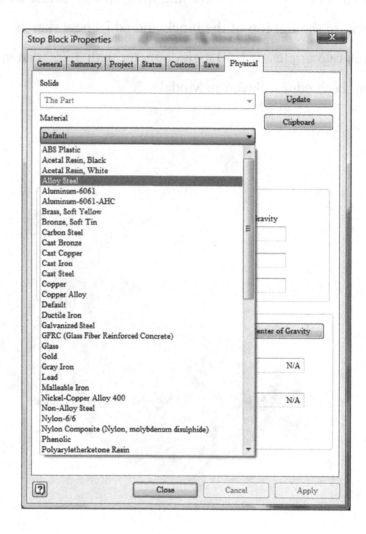

iProperties dialogue box

8. Expand the arrow by New and click to select Drawing, this action opens up a drawing sheet.

9. Click on Base under the Place Views tab to open up the Drawing View dialogue box.

10. Move the mouse pointer to the graphics area and click to place the Front first view.

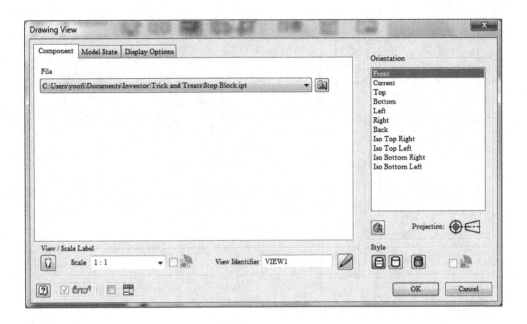

Drawing View dialogue box

11. Click on Projected under Place Views, move to the graphics area and click inside the base Front view placed on the graphics area to highlight it.
12. Move the mouse pointer just above the Front view and click to place the Top view.
13. Move the mouse pointer directly across from the Front view and click to place the Right view.
14. Move the mouse pointer diagonally to the top right and click to place the Isometric view.
15. Right-click on the graphics area and click on Create to complete the operation.

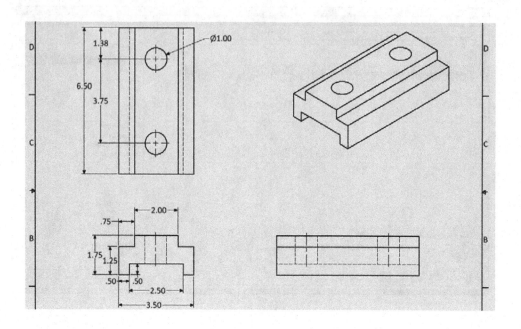

Drawing Views

16. Expand the arrow by ANSI–Large right-click on Field Text and click on Edit Field Text.

17. This action opens up Edit Property Fields dialogue box.

18. Click on a field and click on the iProperties button on the top right corner of the Edit Property Fields dialogue box.

Edit Property Fields

19. In the iProperties dialogue box that opens should have several tabs that include General; Summary; Project; Status; Custom and Save headings.

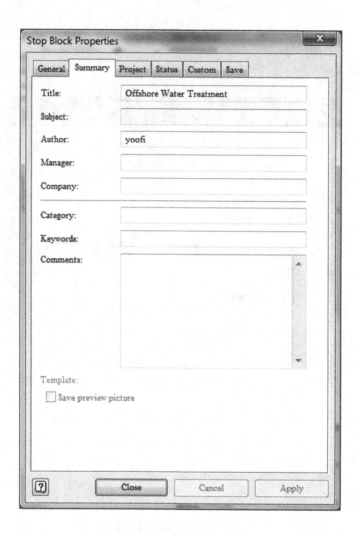

iProperties dialogue box

20. Click on each heading to explore other options.

21. Click on Summary for an example and type *Offshore Water Treatment* in the text box by Title and click on Apply and close to exit.

22. Clicking on the OK button again will place the text just entered under Title on the Drawing Sheet.

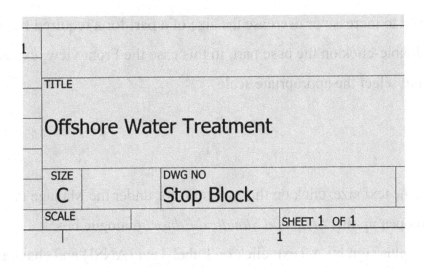

Section of Drawing Sheet

To add another sheet size after placing one on the graphics area, expand the plus sign by Drawing Resources. Expand the plus sign by Sheet Formats and double-click on the required size under Sheet Formats. In the Select Components box, click on OK button to accept.

Select Component

Scale

Scale is used to increase or decrease the size of a part for a required fit. To change the scale double-click on the base part, in this case the Front view, expand the arrow by Scale and select the appropriate scale.

Text Size

To change the text size, click on the Styles Editor under the Manage tab on the Ribbon, to open up the *'Style and Standard Editor'* dialogue box.
Expand the plus sign by A Text, click on Label Text (ANSI) and change the Text Height as well as the Font. Click on Done button and Yes when asked to save edits. Click on Note Text (ANSI) and repeat this process.

Style and Standard Editor

Precision

Click on Dimension and Default (ANSI) and change the decimal places as well as Precision, click on Done button and Yes when asked to save edits.

Style and Standard Editor

Arrow Size

To change the Arrow size of the dimension text, click on the Styles Editor and expand the plus sign by Dimension in the Style Editor, click on Default (ANSI) and click on the Display tab.

Change the *Size and Height under Terminator* and click on Save.

Click on Done button when finished to see the changes.

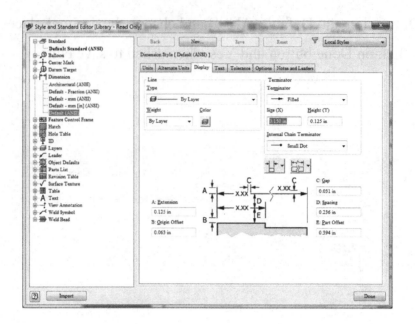

Style and Standard Editor

Block A

1. Start a new part using English.ipt and place a 6 X 4 inch rectangle on the graphics area.

2. Add a depth of 4 inches using the Extrude feature.

3. Add a new sketch on the right face of the block and create a triangle with dimension text as illustrated below.

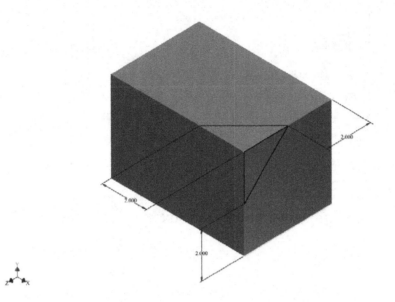

Model with Sketch

4. Click on the Top face and add a new sketch and use the line tool to add a diagonal line with dimension text.

5. Exit the sketch tools and use the Sweep cut Feature with the Triangle as the Profile and the line as the Path.

Sweep dialogue box

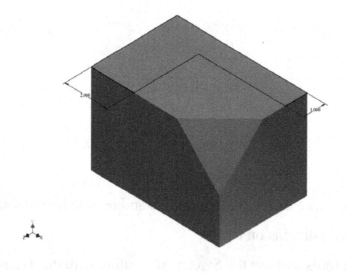

L-Shape sketch on top face of block

6. Use the Cut Extrude option to remove a depth of 2 inches from the block, using the L-Shaped sketch.

7. Click on OK and Cancel and save the part.

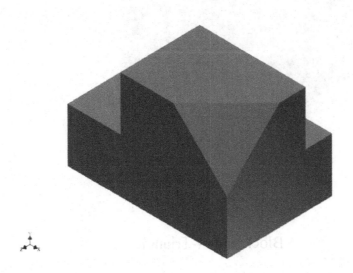

Finished Model

Block B

1. Start a new Part using English.ipt and place a 6 X 4 inch rectangle on the graphics area and exit the sketch.

2. Use the Extrude Feature to add a depth of 4 inches and click on the OK button and Cancel.

3. Add four different sketches and create triangles with dimension text as shown in the drawing below.

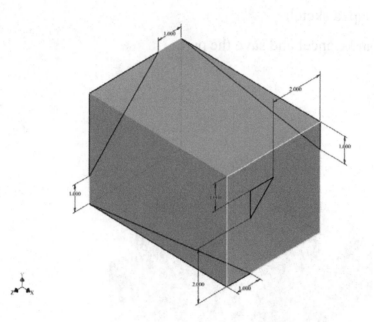

Block with 4-Triangles

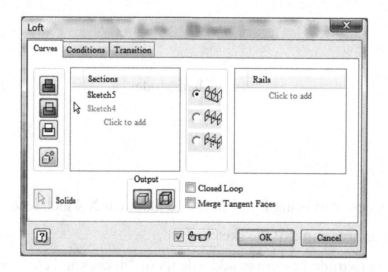

Loft dialogue box

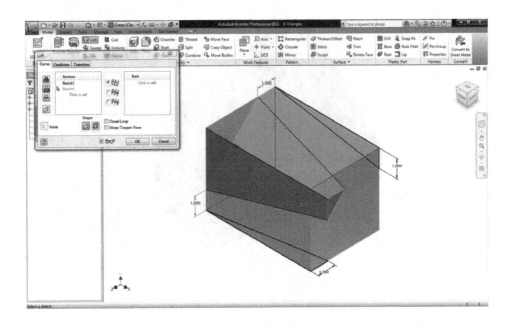

Sweep Cut outline

4. Click on the *Loft* Feature under the Model tab and click on the *'Click to add'* text under Sections.

5. Click on one of the lines on the smaller triangle, rotate the block and click on a line on the larger triangle.

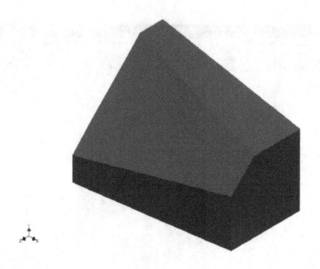

Block with Cuts

6. Select the *Cut* option under *Curves* and click on the OK button.

7. Next click on Extrude Feature, select the *Cut* option and click on one of the remaining triangles.

8. Click on the OK button and Cancel to exit.

9. Repeat this action for the last triangle to cut off the rest of the outline.

10. Save the Model.

Block C

1. Start a new drawing using the English (in).ipt and place a rectangle with dimension of 6 X 4 inch on the graphics area and exit the sketch.

2. Using the line tool create the outline as in the drawing below and exit the sketch.

3. Use the Cut Extrude feature and the *All* option, under the Model tab to remove the outline of the triangle on the top face of the block.

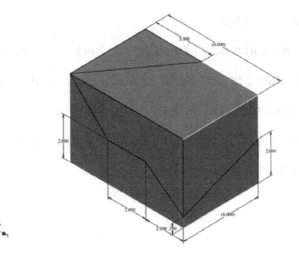

Block with sketches and dimension text

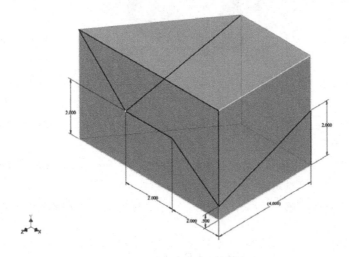

Diagonal line from a point to vertex

4. Use the 3D Sketch tool to add a diagonal line from a point to the vertex of the block and exit the sketch.

5. Rotate the block and add a new sketch on the back face and exit the sketch.

6. Select the Sweep feature under the Model tab, click on the Cut option and click inside the front outline to be used as the Profile.

7. Click on the diagonal line to represent the Path and click on the OK button to complete the operation.

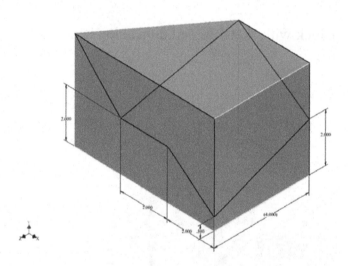

Outline of Sketch

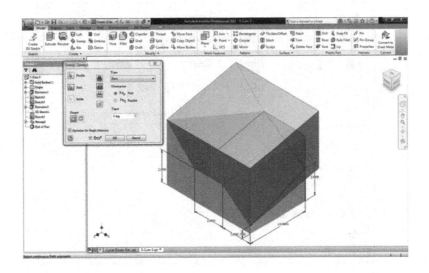

Sweep Cut

8. Click to select Sweep from the Model tab and select the Cut option.
9. Click inside the remaining triangle to be used as the Profile and select the diagonal line as the Path.
10. Click on the OK button to complete the operation and Cancel to exit.
11. Add a new sketch on the Front plane and add a circle of 0.50 diameter.
12. Use the Cut Extrude feature to place a through hole on the block and save.

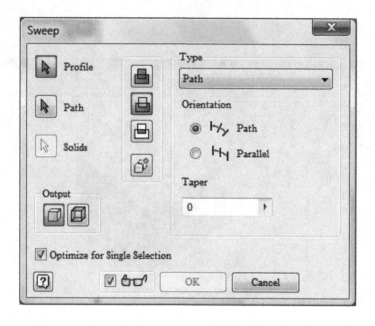

Sweep dialogue box

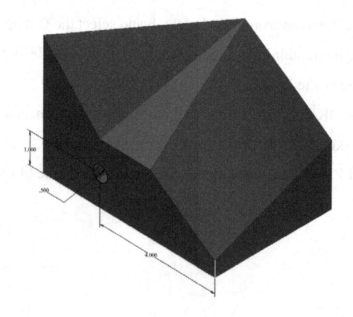

Finished Model

1. Start a new Part from using the English.ipt and select the XY Plane.

2. Create a 3.50 X 2.06 inch rectangle starting from the origin and click on Finish Sketch.

3. Add a depth of 2.50 using the Extrude feature.

4. Click on top face of the block and add a new sketch.

5. Place a diagonal line from the right most vertex and add two more lines to turn it into a triangular-shaped sketch.

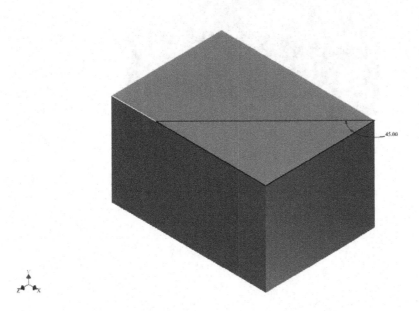

Triangular Sketch on Block

6. Use the Extrude feature with the Cut option and change the distance to 1.310.

7. Click inside the triangular-shaped sketch and click on OK to add a cut on the block.

8. Click on top of the block add another sketch and draw a rectangle with dimension text as shown below.

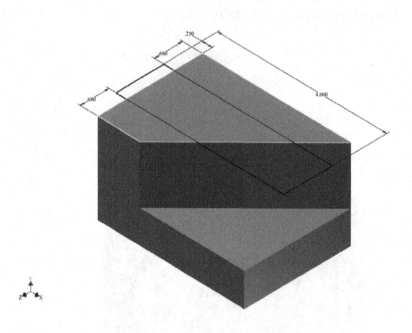

Rectangular-Sketch on top face

9. Use the Extrude feature with the Cut option and change the distance to **0.62.**
10. Click inside the rectangular-shaped sketch to highlight it and click on OK button to complete the operation.
11. Click on top of the block add another sketch and draw a rectangle with dimension text as shown below.

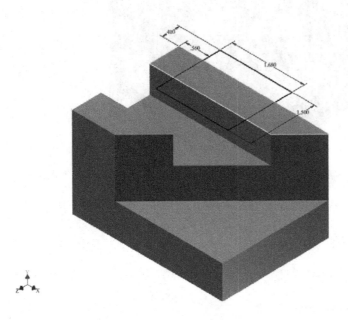

Rectangular-Sketch on top face

12. Use the Extrude feature with the Cut option and change the distance to *0.31*.

13. Click inside the rectangular-shaped sketch to highlight it and click on OK button to complete the operation.

14. Click on top of the first cut add a new sketch and draw a circle with a diameter of *0.75* and all dimension text.

15. Click on Finish Sketch and use the Extrude feature with the Cut option and change the distance to *All*.

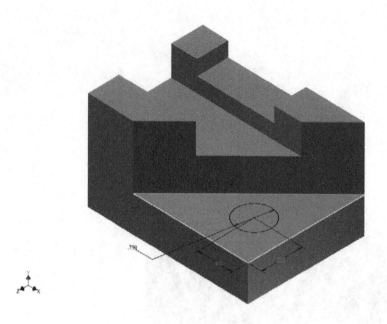

Circle on Cut Face

16. Click on the OK button to complete the cut.

17. Save the model and add Drawing Views.

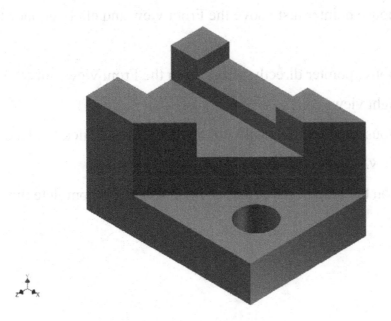

Completed Model

Adding Drawing Views

1. Expand the arrow by New and click to select Drawing, this action opens up a drawing sheet.
2. Click on *Base* under the Place Views tab to open up the Drawing View dialogue box.
3. Move the mouse pointer to the graphics area and click to place the base view that of the Front.
4. Click on Projected under Place Views, move to the graphics area and click

inside the base Front view placed on the graphics area to highlight it.

5. Move the mouse pointer just above the Front view and click to place the Top view.

6. Move the mouse pointer directly across from the Front view and click to place the Right view.

7. Move the mouse pointer diagonally to the top right and click to place the Isometric view.

8. Right-click on the graphics area and click on **Create** to complete the operation.

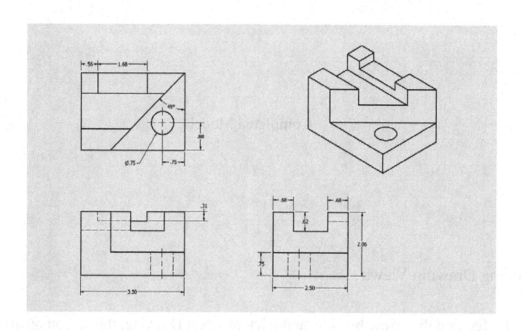

Drawing Views

Exercises:

Use the following Drawing Views to complete the models below

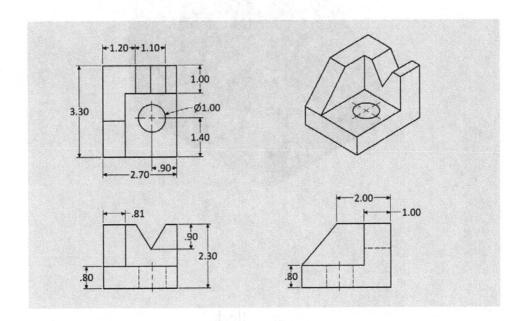

Drawing Views

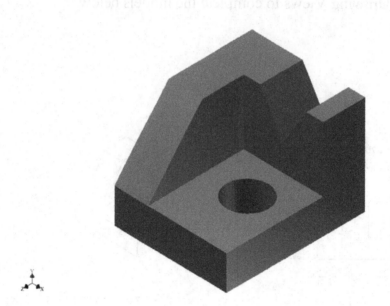

Guide Block

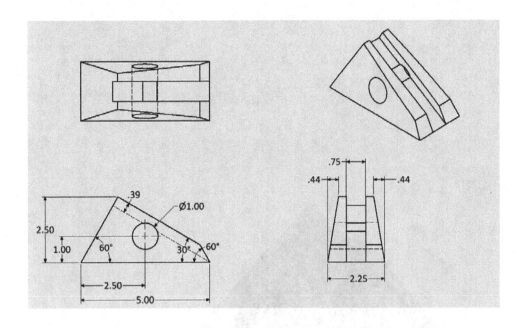

Drawing Views

Wedge

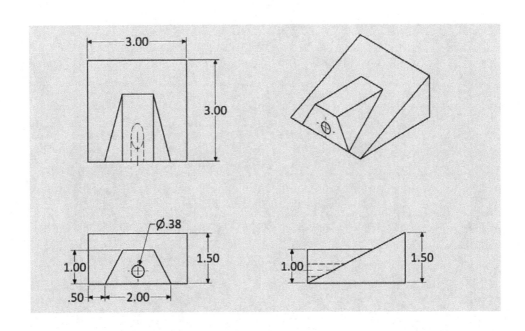

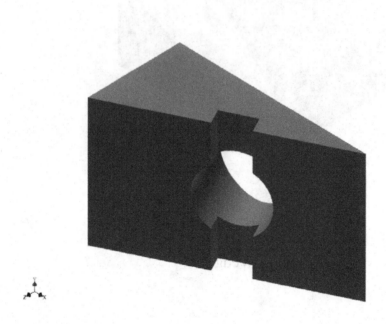

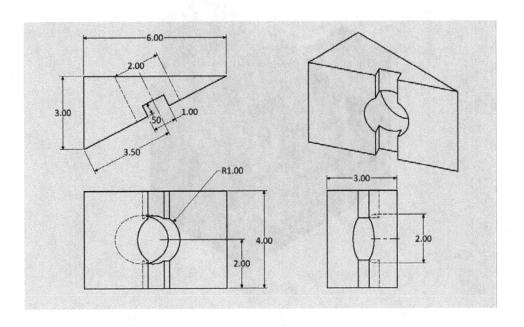

Drawing Views

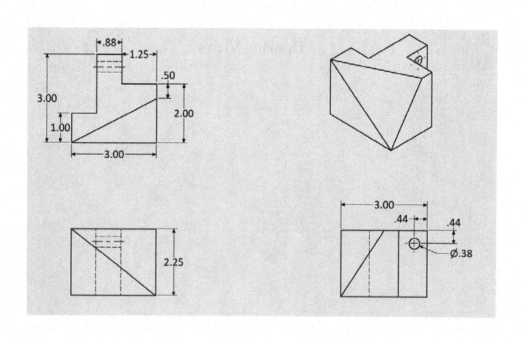

Drawing Views

Inlet Model

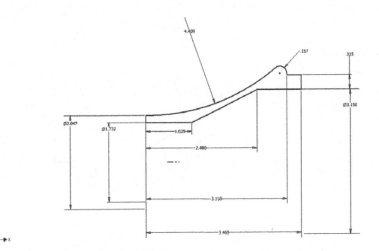

Inlet Outline

1. Start a new part on the XY plane and create the outline as shown and exit sketch.
2. Use the Revolve feature to turn the sketch into a 3D Model.
3. Select the XZ plane and add a rectangular sketch as shown.
4. Create a Path Sketch for Sweep as shown and exit the sketch.
5. Use the Sweep feature, select the rectangular profile and click on the arc-shaped outline.
6. Select the work plane, click on three corners of the rectangular shape to place a plane on the sweep feature.
7. Add a new sketch to the new plane and create the cutout sketch as shown.
8. Use the Cut-extrude feature to create the cutout on the side of Model.

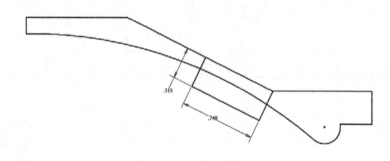

Rectangular Profile for Sweep

9. Use the Fillet feature to add 0.125 inches to the corners.

10. Save the Model.

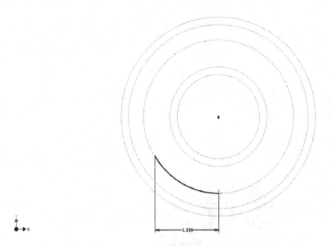

Path Sketch for Sweep

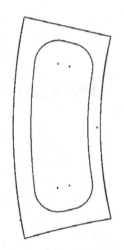

Cutout Sketch

Inlet Model

Summary:

In these Tutorials the student/Designer was guided to be able to:

- Visualize the proper Plane to start a drawing on for the best orientation
- Select the right tools to draw from scratch and add all dimensions to create the Base Part.
- Add Features to the sketch to form a 3D Model
- Place additional cuts and or boss as needed on the base part
- Save the model
- Start a new drawing using the Drawing Sheet
- Create 3 basic views the Front, Top and Right side using Projection option
- Add dimensions, centerlines to circular parts and all needed annotations
- Select the Third Angle for the ANSI (American National Standard Institute) Drawings and enter data in a Title Block
- Add Geometric Tolerances

152

Chapter IV

After completing this session the student will be able to:

- Start a new Part using Sheet Metal
- Learn to use Bend
- Turn the line into a part using Contour Flange
- Learn the uses of Sheet Metal Styles
- Draw a rectangle and use the Face tool to turn it into a plate
- Create Hem on the edges of the Part
- Create Contour Roll
- Learn how to use Fold
- Use Cut and Cut across Bend
- Lofted Flange
- Hem
- Punch

Sheet Metal:

Imagine a piece of steel rolled into sheets for further manufacturing. There are so many uses of Sheet Metal that includes, forming, packaging building enclosures for various components.

Designs could be generated either in an Assembly or as stand-alone parts. The designer will be introduced to Sheet Metal design in this Tutorial. There are several ways to draw in Sheet Metal environment. There are several tools under the *Sheet metal* Toolbar and we will cover most of the tools under the Sheet Metal. The designer will be guided in using each tool to create a part for better understanding of how the tool works.

Sheet Metal Design

1. Start a new Part using English Sheet Metal.ipt and draw a 2 inches horizontal line from the Origin.
2. Click on Finish Sketch and select *Sheet Metal Defaults* under the Sheet Metal tab on the Ribbon.

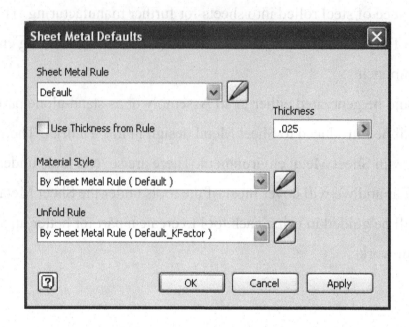

Sheet Metal Defaults dialogue box

Contour Flange

1. Uncheck the text box by *'Use Thickness from Rule'* change Thickness value to **0.025** and click on Apply and Cancel to exit

2. Click on Contour Flange icon to open up a dialogue box, change Distance to 2 and click on the line just drawn.

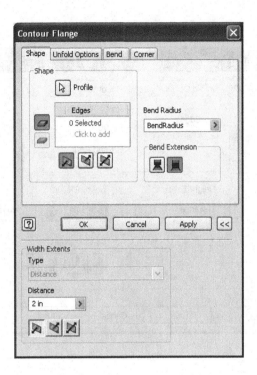

Contour Flange dialogue box

3. Click on Apply and the Cancel button to exit and hit the Home key on the keyboard.

Flange Feature

1. Click on Flange icon and click on an edge on the sheet metal plate and let go off the finger on the left mouse button.

2. Click on the next three edges one after the other using the same process and change the distance in the dialogue box to 1.50.

3. Click on Apply and the Cancel button to exit.

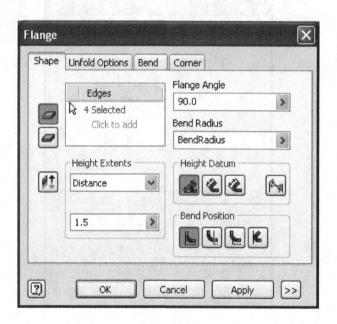

Flange dialogue box

HEM Feature

1. Select Hem from the Ribbon and click on the outside edge on the box and click on Apply button.
2. Repeat these steps for the rest of the edges with the Apply button each time.

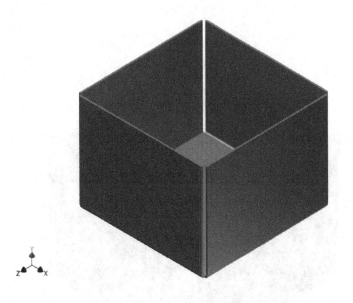

Sheet Metal with Flange

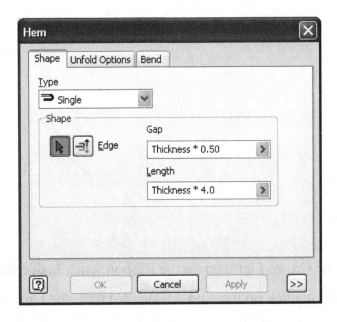

Hem dialogue box

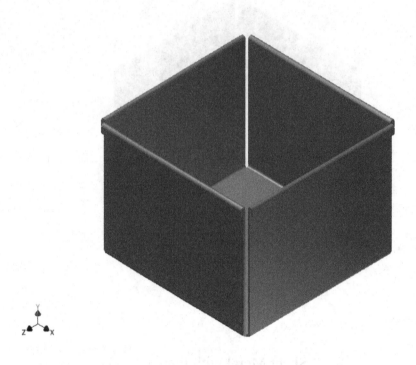

Edges with Hem Feature

Unfold Feature

1. Click on the Create Flat icon on the Ribbon, click inside the flat bottom of the model and click on the Add All Bends tab in the Unfold dialogue box.
2. Click on Apply to flatten the model.

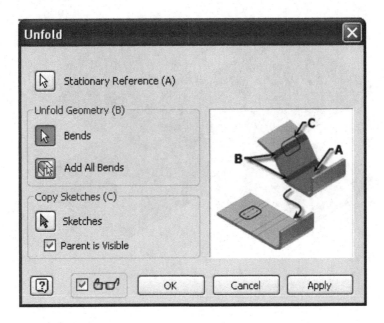

Unfold dialogue box

3. Click on top of the flattened sheet metal and add a new sketch.

4. Place four 0.250 inch circles as shown below and exit the sketch.

5. Click on the Cut icon and click inside the circles one at a time to highlight each one and click on Apply button.

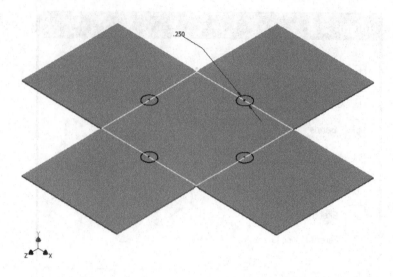

.250

Unfolded Sheet Metal

Refold Feature

1. Select the Refold icon on the Ribbon, click on top of the Flat plate to highlight it and click on Add All Bends button under the Refold dialogue box.

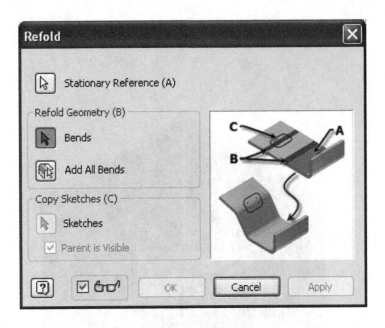

Refold dialogue box

2. Click on Apply and the Cancel button to exit.

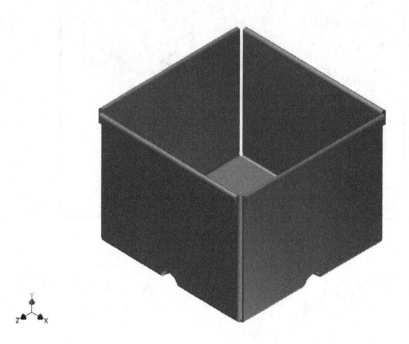

Refolded Box

Create Flat Pattern

1. Click on Create Flat Pattern and click on the Model.

2. Save it and add a Drawing Sheet.

3. Bring in the Flat Pattern as the base the folded model next.

163

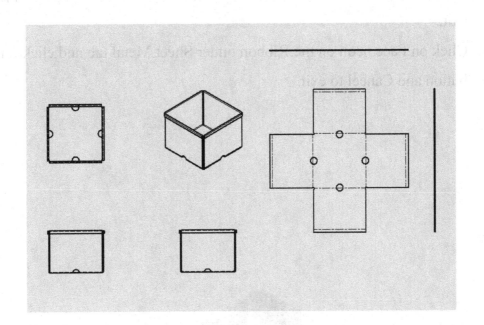

Drawing Sheet

Fold Feature

1. Start a new Part using Sheet Metal option and place a **2 X 2** inch rectangle from the Origin.

2. Click on Sheet Metal Defaults and change the thickness to 0.025 Apply and exit.

3. Click on Face icon on the Ribbon under Sheet Metal tab and click on Apply button and Cancel to exit.

Plate with Fold

4. Click on top of the sheet metal plate and add a new sketch.

5. Draw a diagonal line from one edge to the other 0.5 inch from endpoint of the line to the edge.

6. Select the Fold icon from the Ribbon, click on the Line just drawn and click on Apply button and Cancel to exit.

Contour Roll Feature

1. Start a new Part using Sheet Metal and use the Line tool as well as Arc to reproduce the sketch below.

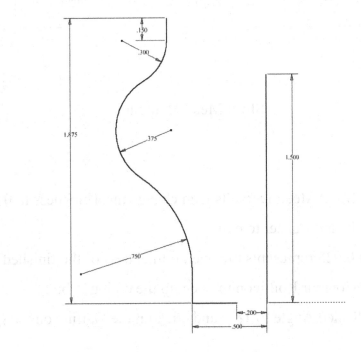

Sketch for Contour Roll

2. Place a Line from the Origin add dimension text and exit the sketch.

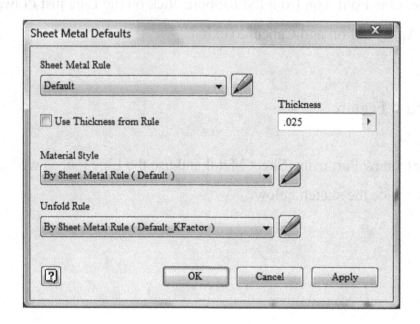

Sheet Metal Defaults

3. Click on the Sheet Metal Defaults icon change the Thickness to 0.025 and click on Apply and Cancel to exit.

4. The decimal 0.025 represents the overall thickness of the finished model.

5. Click on the Contour Roll icon to open up the dialogue box.

6. Change the Rolled Angle to 180° and click on the Outline on the graphics area.

7. Click on the arrow by Axis to highlight it and click on the vertical line to roll the outline into a contoured shape.

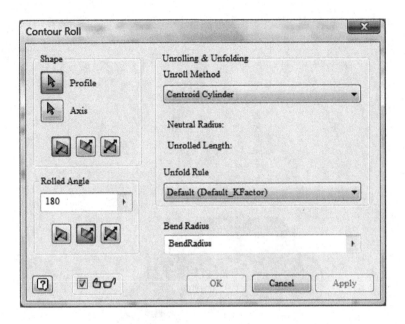

Contour Roll dialogue box

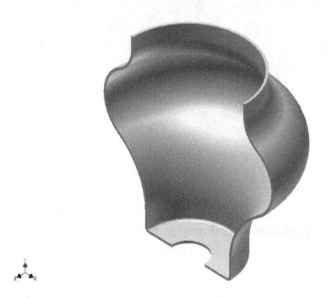

Contour Rolled Model

169

Use the Mirror tool to add a copy to the model

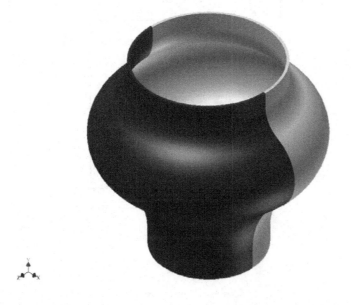

Mirrored Model

Cut Across Bends

1. Start a New File and click to select English Tab and the Sheet Metal icon, click on OK to exit.

2. Select the Line tool under the 2D sketch panel and draw the sketch below and add all dimensioning.

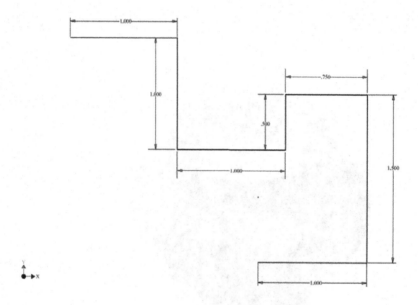

Cut Across Bends Sketch

3. Click on *Sheet Metal Styles* and change the thickness to 0.05 and click on Save and then on Done.

4. Right-Click on the Graphics area and click on Home.

5. Next click on *Contour Flange* and change the distance to 3.50.

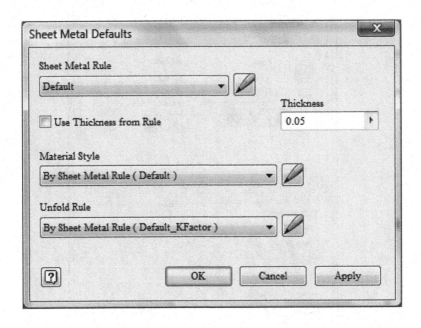

Sheet Metal Styles

6. Select *Distance Mid-Plane* icon under Distance and click on the arrow by *Profile under Shape*.

7. Click on the Line sketch created earlier on, click on Apply and hit the *'Esc'* key on the keyboard.

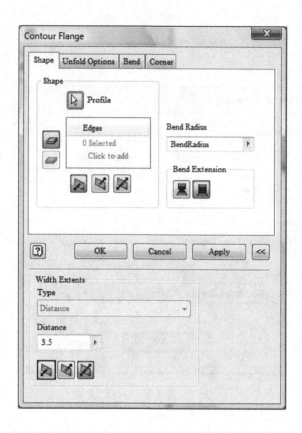

Contour Flange dialogue box

8. Right-Click on top of the Sheet Metal part just created and click on New Sketch.

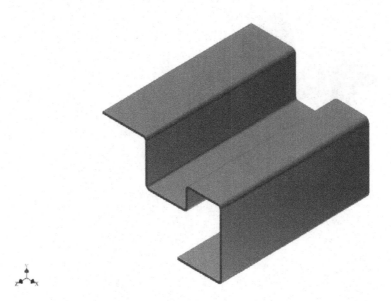

Contour Flange Model

9. Expand the arrow by *Project Geometry* under the *2D Sketch Panel* and click to select *Project Flat Pattern*.
10. Click on the subsequent flat faces in sequential order one at a time, using Free Orbit to orient the part.
11. Using the Line and Arc tools draw the sketch as shown below with all the dimensioning text.

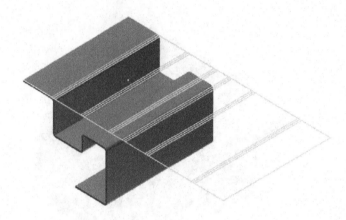

Project Flat Pattern

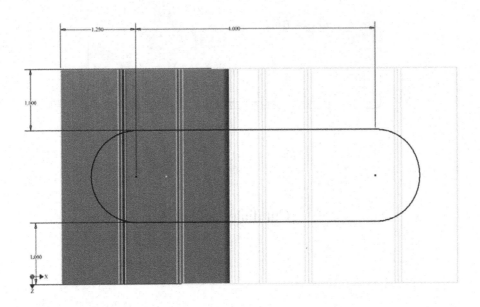

Outline of a Slot on Model

12. Click on *Cut* under Sheet Metal and place a check mark by *Cut Across Bend.*

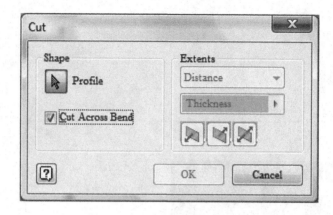

Cut dialogue box

13. Click inside the Slot profile just created to highlight it and click on OK.

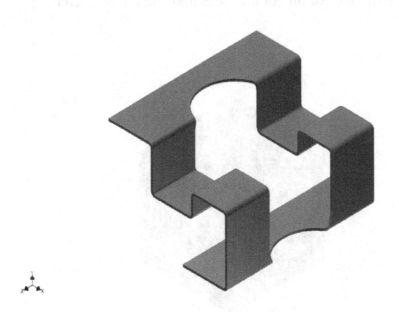

Cut Across Bend Model

14. The next step is to click on *Create Flat Pattern* under the *Sheet Metal Feature* to flatten the Feature just created.

15. Click on *Go to Folded Part* icon under the *Sheet Metal* tab to fold it again when needed.

16. Save the drawing.

Using the Punch Tool

1. Draw a 5 X 5 inch rectangle and add a depth of 5 inch using the extrude feature.
2. Shell the top with a thickness of 0.125 and save the model.
3. Click on the flat face of one of the sides and add a new sketch.

Points on Box

4. Add a couple of points and exit the sketch.
5. Click on Convert to Sheet Metal icon on the top right of the ribbon and click on the Punch Tool.
6. Select Round Emboss and click on Open button and Finish to place the punch part on the box.

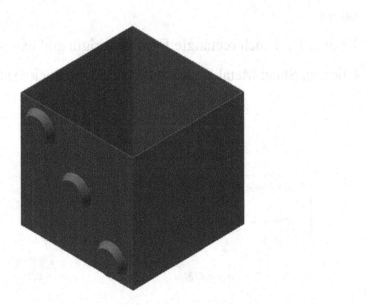

Box with Punch tool

Creating an iFeature

1. Start a new part and click on English, Sheet Metal.ipt and click on the OK button.

2. Draw a 1 x 1 inch rectangle form the origin and exit sketch.

3. Click on Sheet Metal Styles and change the thickness to 0.025.

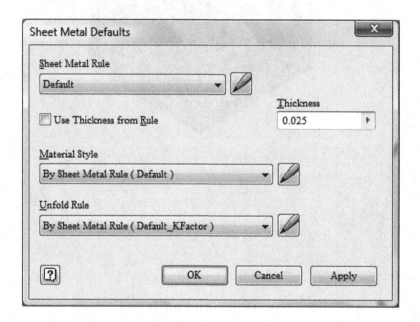

Sheet Metal Styles dialogue box

4. Click on Face under Sheet Metal tab and OK to give the sketch a thickness.

5. Right-click on top of the plate just created and click to select New Sketch.

6. Draw an outline to be used as a cutout for a Punch Tool.

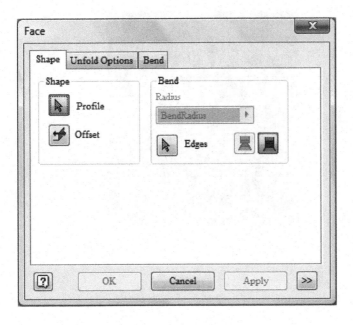

Face dialogue box

7. Add a Point approximately 0.10 from the base of the sketch.

8. Click on Finish Sketch to move to the *Sheet Metal Features*.

182

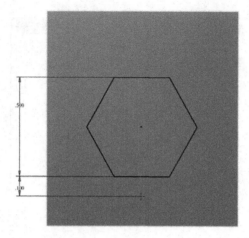

Punch Tool

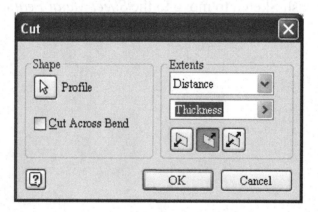

Cut dialogue box

9. Click on Cut from the main menu bar, click inside the polygon to highlight it and click on OK to add a hole in the plate.

Extract iFeature:

1. Click on the *Manage* tab and click on ***Extract iFeature*** to open up a dialogue box.
2. Click on Cut1 inside the Browser under *Model* to populate the dialogue box and click in the radio button by *Sheet Metal Punch iFeature.*

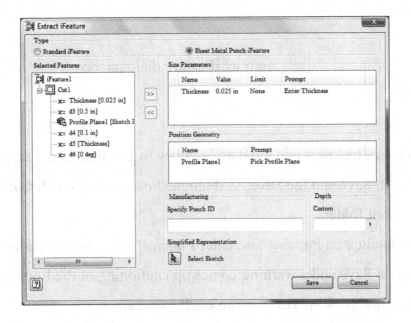

Extract Feature dialogue box

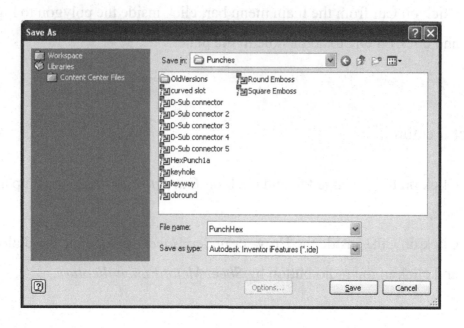

Extract iFeature dialogue box

3. Click on Thickness and the double-arrow to populate Size Parameters.

4. Click on Save and the Save As dialogue box opens up with *Catalog* showing as current folder.

5. Double-click on Punches and enter *Punch Hex.ide* as File name.

6. Click on Save and a warning comes up cautioning of the Location not being active, just click on *Yes* to complete the operation.

7. Draw a rectangle 5 x 5 inches with Sheet Metal and change the Sheet Metal Defaults value to a thickness of 0.025.

8. Click on Face icon Apply and exit.

9. Add flange of length 2.5 to the four sides and save it.

10. Add a New Sketch to the box and place several *Points* as indicated in Figure and exit sketch.

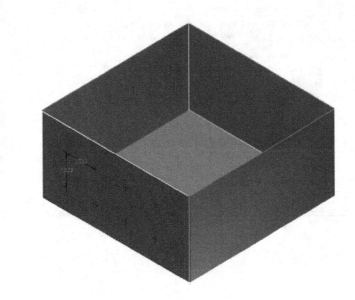

Points on Box

11. Click on the Punch Tool under the Sheet Metal, locate the Punch Hex saved earlier on in Tutorial and click on Open.

12. The Punch Tool dialogue box opens up with a preview of the outline and all the points covered on the box.

13. Click on Finish and save the Part.

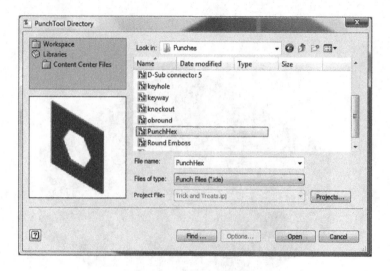

Punch Tool Directory

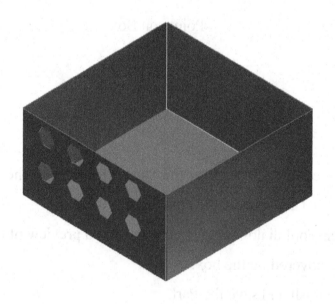

Box with Punch holes

Drawing Views Setup

1. Expand the arrow by the New Sheet and click on Drawing a new drawing sheet opens up on the graphics area.

2. Click to select *Base View* from the list of options to open up Drawing View dialogue box.

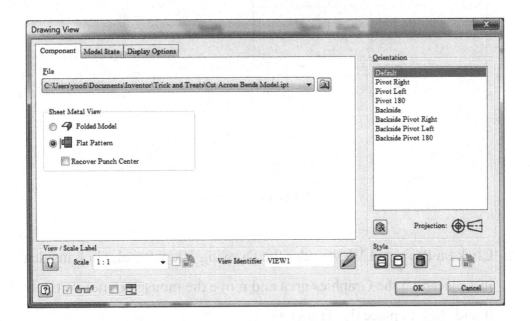

Drawing View dialogue box

3. Click inside the Radio button to the side of *Flat Pattern* and with Default highlighted under Orientation, click on OK button to place the first view on the Graphics area.

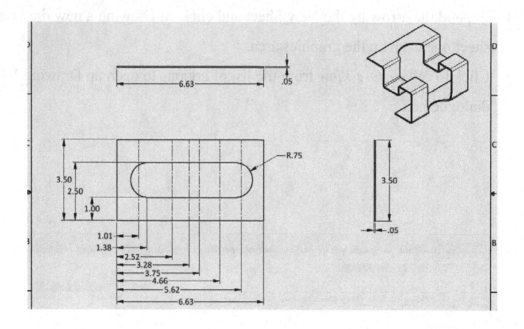

Drawing Views

4. Click on Projected View under the Drawing View Panel, click inside the part just placed on the Graphics area and move the mouse pointer vertically above it and click to place the Top view.

5. Move the mouse pointer to the Right of the Base part to place the Right view.

6. Click on the *Base View* again but this time click to select Iso-Top Right, from the Drawing View dialogue box and place it at the top right corner of the Graphics area as shown in the Figure above.

Dimensioning:

1. Click on the *Annotate* tab and select *Baseline Dimension* from the list, click on the vertical lines on the base part on the Graphics area, one after the other.

2. Right-click when finished and click on *Continue* to generate the dimensioning text.

3. Click on the *Manage* tab and select Styles Editor, make changes for the text height, the Font as well as Dimensions and arrow size and click on Done.

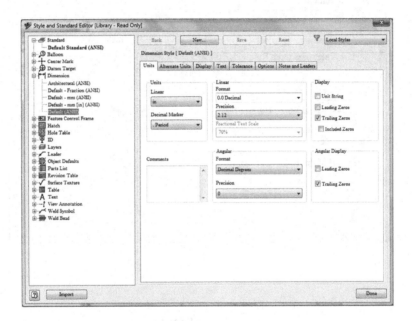

Style and Standard Editor

Corner Round:

1. Open Sheet Metal Part and draw three connecting perpendicular lines with the Line tool. Refer to Figure in the drawing.
2. Click on *Sheet Metal Styles* and change the thickness to 0.075 save and exit.

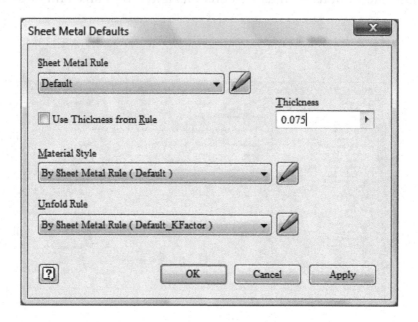

Sheet Metal Defaults

3. Click on *Contour Flange* change distance to 2 inch, select Midplane and click on the line just drawn as the Profile.
4. Click on Apply and Cancel to exit.
5. Right-click on the graphics area and click on Home View.

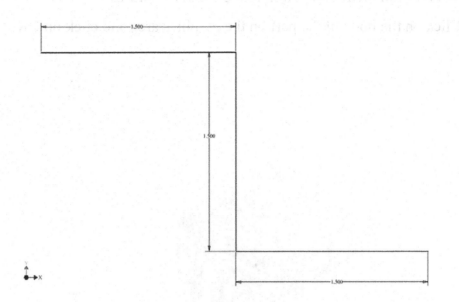

Line Sketch

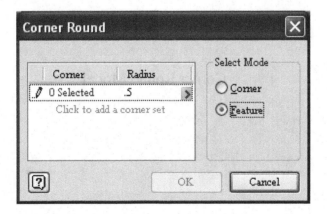

Corner Round dialogue box

6. Click on *Corner Round* under the Sheet Metal Feature, change Radius to 0.5 and click on the Radio button to the side of *Feature*.

7. Click on the body of the part on the graphics area and click on OK.

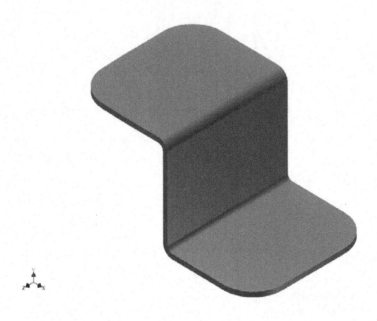

Corner Round Model

8. Mirror the Feature using the back rest as the *Mirror Plane* and save the drawing.

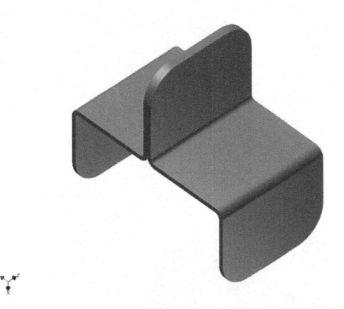

Mirrored Feature

Exercise:

Using the Tutorials just covered, create the Sheet Metal Part below and add all dimensioning Text. Figure A and B are mirror images.

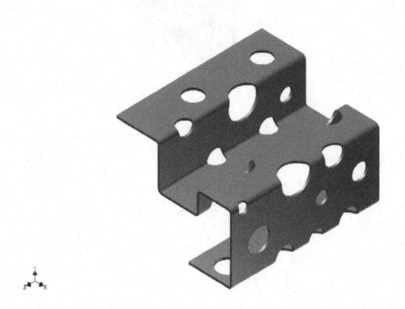

Figure A

Figure B

Summary:

Topics covered in this chapter included:

- Starting a new Part using Sheet Metal

- Drawing a simple line and added dimension text

- Turning the line into a part using Contour Flange

- Learning the uses of Sheet Metal Styles

- Creating Flat Pattern with Fold and Unfold options

- Drawing a rectangle and using the Face tool to turn it into a plate

- Creating Hem on the edges of the Part

- Creating Contour Roll

- Learning how to use Fold

- Using Cut and Cut across Bend

- Creating Drawing Sheet with different views

- Using Corner Round

- Creating Punch Tool.

- Creating iFeature

Chapter V

This module covers the approach to the design of different Mechanical parts

Unless otherwise directed, all Units will be in ANSI

After completing this Tutorial, the designer will be able to:

• Use Constraints

• Utilize Cut-Revolve option under the Boss/Base

• Utilize Cut-Extrude option under the Boss/Base

• Use the Sweep tool

• Use the Circular Pattern

• Use Cut-Sweep tool

• Utilize the Work Plane together with Point for a sketch

• Create Parts with Loft

• Draw different Mechanical Parts

Creating different Parts

1. Start a new Part using English.ipt and use the line tool to place an outline on the graphics area with dimension text.

2. Exit the sketch and add a depth of 0.44 using the Extrude feature

3. Save the Part as Angle Base.

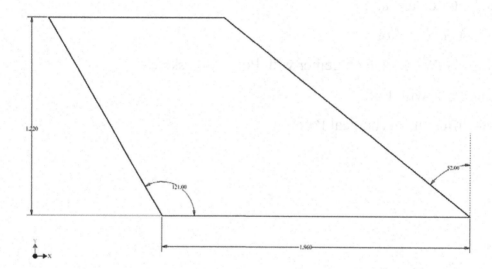

Angle Base Sketch

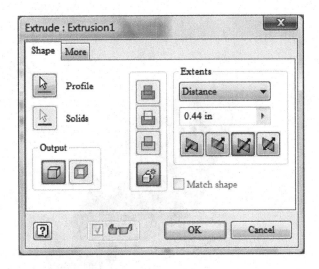

Extrude dialogue box

4. Use the Free Orbit tool on the far right-side of the screen to rotate the part to view the bottom face.

5. Add a new sketch on the bottom and use the line and arc tools to add a new outline as shown below.

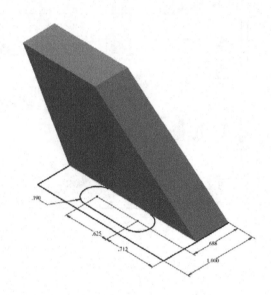

Sketch on bottom of Part

6. Select the Extrude Feature, click inside the rectangular shape to highlight it and change the distance to 0.50.

7. Click on Apply and Cancel button to exit.

8. Click on the inclined face on the right and add a new sketch.

9. Place two 0.25 inch circles on the flat face and add dimension text.

10. Extrude Cut the circles 0.50 inch deep into the part.

11. Add a New sketch on the Front flat face and place a 0.375 inch diametric circle on it.

12. Exit the sketch and Extrude cut the circle using the 'All' option.

13. Click on Apply and Cancel button to exit and save the model.

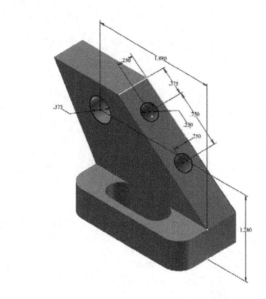

Angle Base Model

Transition Pipe

1. Start a new drawing on the *XY* Plane and create an arc of 5.0 inch radius from the Origin.

2. Use Construction lines to add a 45^0 angle and trim the arc outside the construction lines.

3. Exit the sketch and click to select Work Plane.

4. Click on the endpoint of the arc to place a plane at the end.

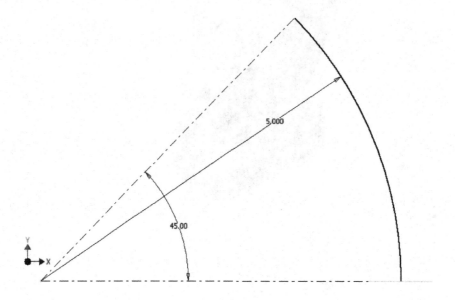

Work Plane at endpoint of Arc

5. Add a new sketch on the work plane create a 1.00 inch and a 1.500 inch concentric circles.

6. Exit the sketch and use the Sweep feature with the circles as Profile and the Arc as the Path.

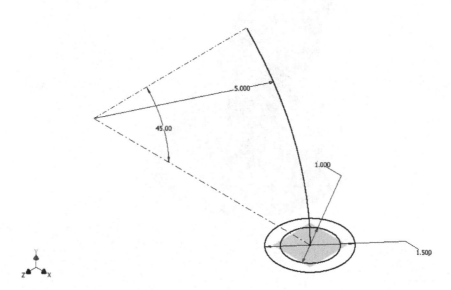

Concentric Circles on endpoint of arc

7. Click on Ok and Cancel button to exit.

8. Add a new sketch on the flat bottom and add two concentric circles of 1.00 and 3.50 inches.

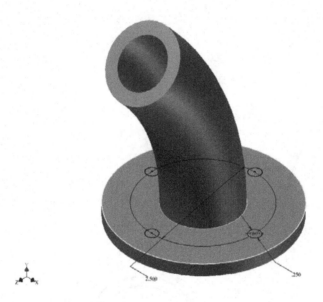

Extruded Circles

9. Exit the sketch and add a depth of 0.250 inches using the Extrude Feature.

10. Click on the top face of the part and add a new sketch.

11. Add a fillet with radius of 0.125 between the pipe and the top and bottom flanges.

12. Add a new sketch on the flat bottom and add two concentric circles of 1.00 and 3.50 inches.

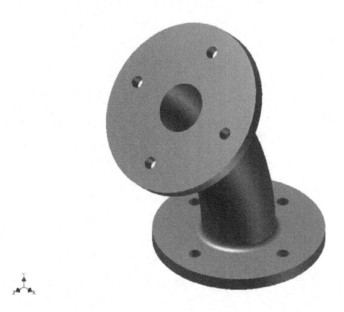

Transition Pipe

13. Exit the sketch and add a depth of 0.250 inches using the Extrude Feature.

14. Click on the flat face of the extruded circles and add a new sketch.

15. Place 4 circle 0.250 inch 90° apart on a 2.50 B.C.D. (Bolt Circle Diameter)

16. Exit the sketch and extrude the circles using *'To'* option and click on Apply button and Cancel to exit.

Angle Jig

1. Start a new Part on the **YZ** Plane and draw the sketch as shown below.

2. Add all dimension text and exit the sketch.

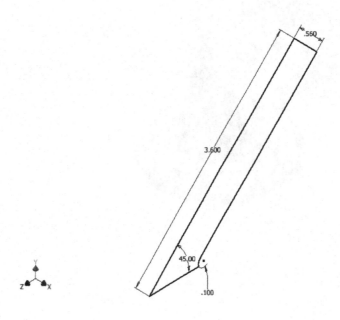

Sketch A

3. Use the Extrude Feature to add a depth of 1.40 with the Symmetric option.

4. Click on the Flat bottom and add a new sketch.

5. Place a rectangle on the bottom and add all dimension text.

6. Use the Extrude Feature with a distance of 0.750 to add a depth to the sketch.

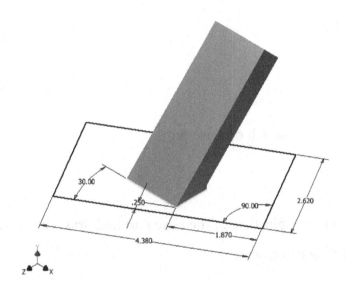

Sketch on bottom of Part

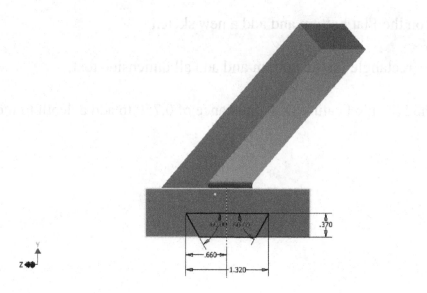

Sketch on base part

7. Add a new sketch on the right face of the base part and draw the sketch as shown below with dimension text.

8. Use the Extrude Feature with the 'All' option to add a cut at the bottom of the part.

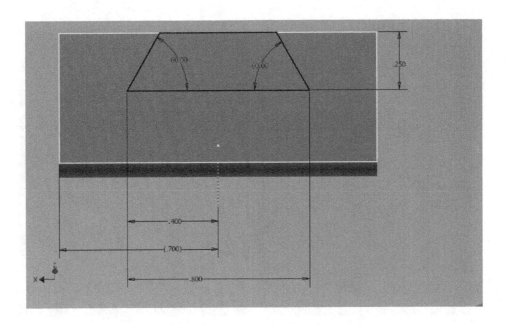

Sketch on Top part

9. Use the Extrude feature with the Cut option and add a distance of 2.40.

10. Click on OK button and the Cancel to exit the Extrude feature.

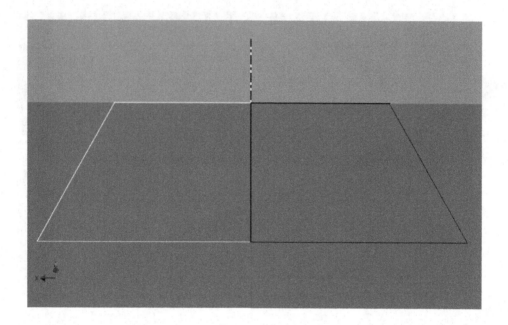

Sketch outline

11. Click on the face of the cut just completed and add a new sketch.

12. Create an outline as shown above and add a centerline.

13. Exit the sketch and use the Revolve Cut feature to remove the base part.

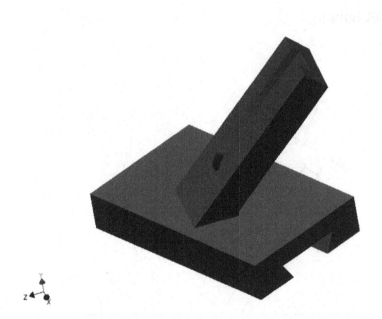

Angle Jig

Centering Jig

1. Start a new part and draw the sketch below with all dimension text.

2. Add a depth of 3.50 using the Extrude Feature with Symmetric option and click on the OK button.

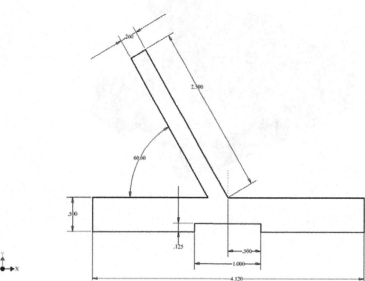

Centering Jig Sketch A

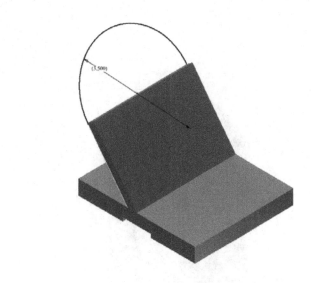

Centering Jig Sketch B

3. Add a new sketch on the flat face at the back and create a 3.50 inch diametric circle from the midpoint.

4. Exit the sketch and add a depth of 0.50 inch with the Extrude feature.

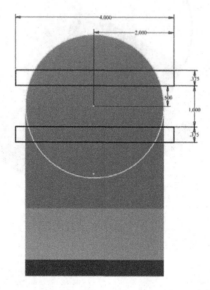

Centering Jig Sketch C

5. Place a new sketch on top of the flat circular plate and draw two rectangular sketches.

6. Add dimension text and exit the sketch.

7. Use the Extrude feature to add a cut of 0.125 on top of the circular plate and save the part.

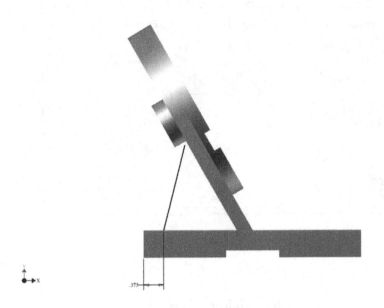

Sketch for Rib Feature

8. Add an offset plane from the front face at a distance of 0.375 and add a sketch.

9. Place an inclined line 0.375 from the edge as in the sketch above and exit the sketch.

10. Select the Rib feature from the Model tab, enter 0.38 under Thickness and click on the inclined line to create a rib.

11. Use the mirror feature to add a copy using the XY Plane as the mirror plane.

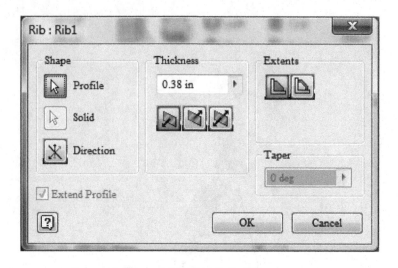

Rib dialogue box

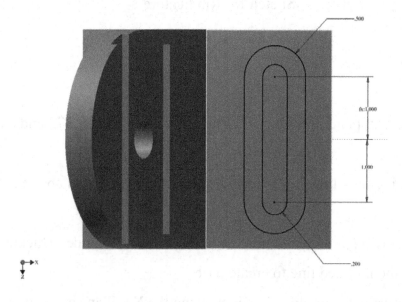

Slot Sketch on top face

12. Place a new sketch on the top face of the model and create two slots as shown in the sketch above.

13. Exit the sketch and add a depth of 0.125 using the extrude feature.

14. Use *'All'* option in the extrude feature to add a cut with the inside slot.

15. Save the Model.

Centering Jig

218

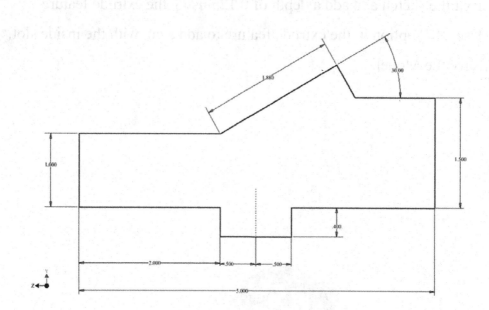

Tool Jig Sketch A

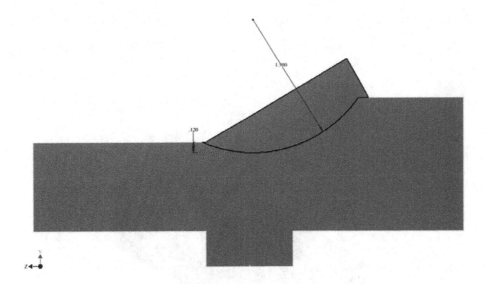

Tool Jig Sketch B

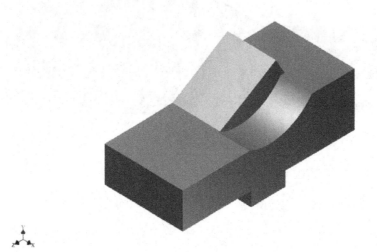

Tool Jig Sketch C

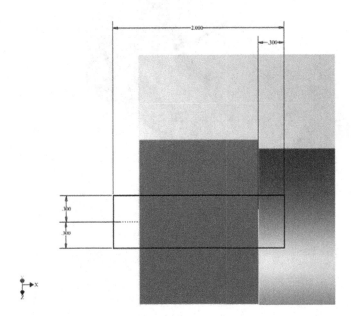

Tool Jig Sketch D

222

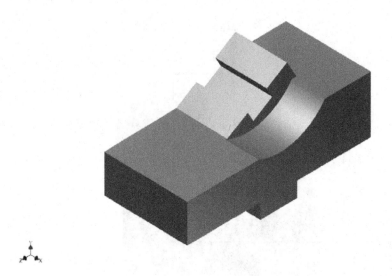

Tool Jig Sketch E

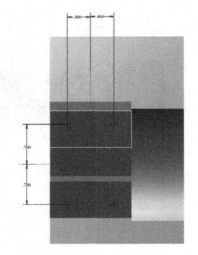

Tool Jig Sketch E

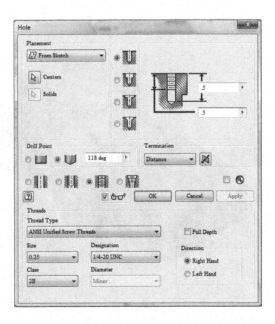

Hole dialogue box

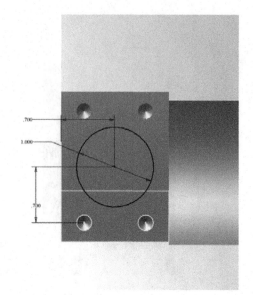

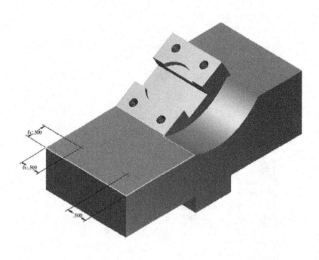

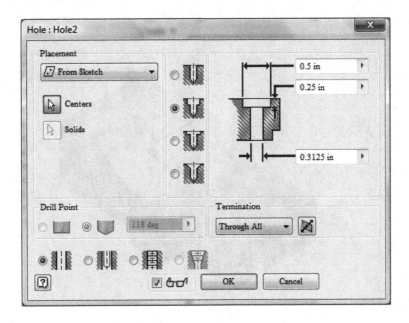

Hole dialogue box

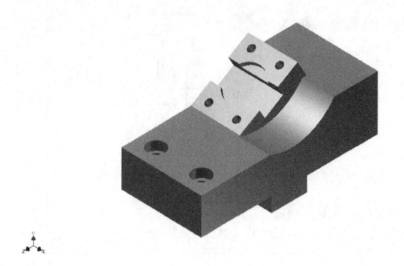

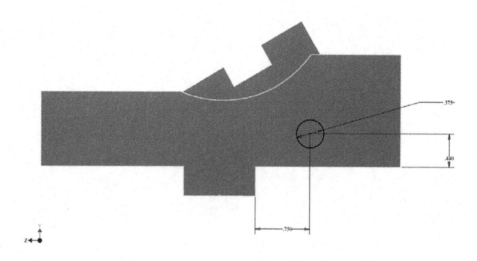

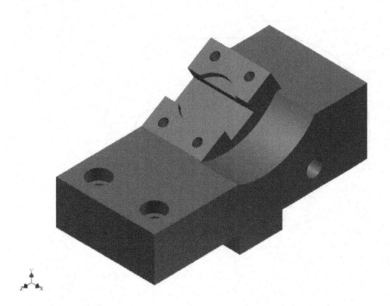

Tool Jig

Bend Device

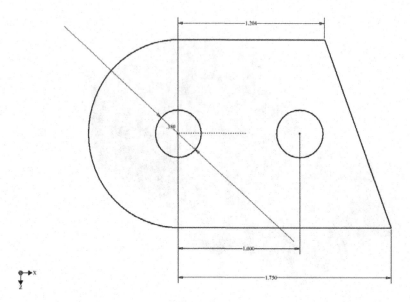

Bend Device Sketch A

1. Using the top plane create a sketch as shown and add dimensions.
2. Add a depth of 0.125 using the extrude feature and click on OK button to exit the model.

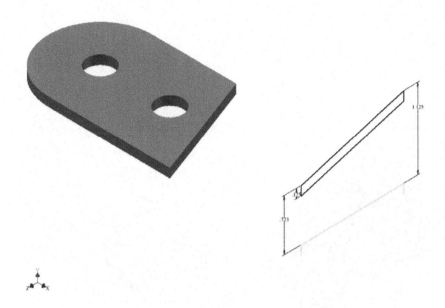

Bend Device Sketch B

3. Offset a plane as shown and add a rectangular sketch with dimensions.

4. Extrude the outline with a distance of 1 inch.

5. Using the loft feature use the two faces to join the model.

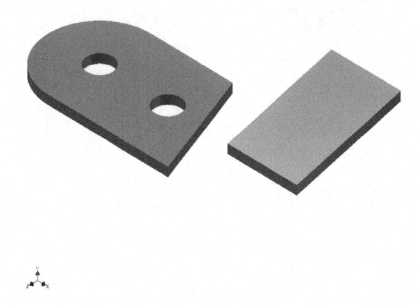

Bend Device Sketch C

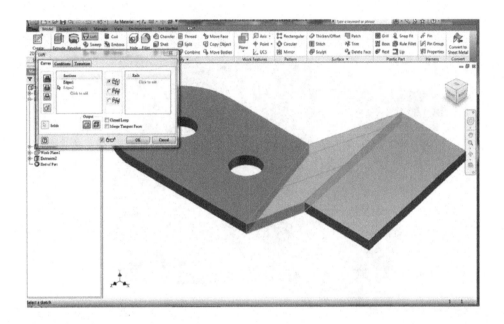

Bend Device Sketch D

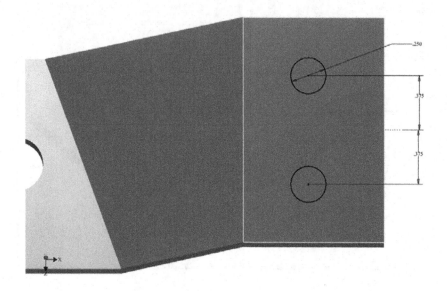

Bend Device Sketch D

6. Click on the flat face as shown and add two circles with dimensions.

7. Using the extrude-cut option add a hole using the circles.

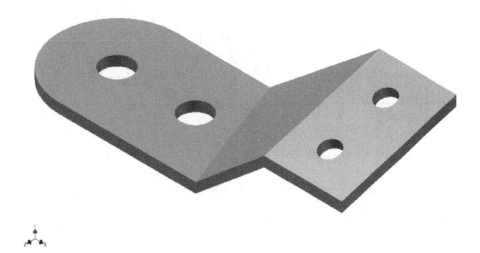

Bend Device

Controller

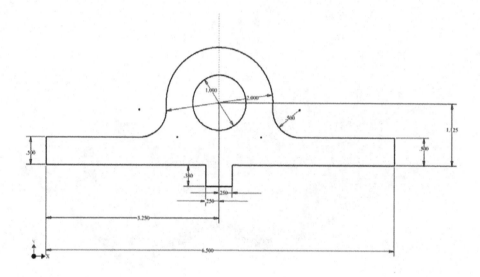

Controller Sketch A

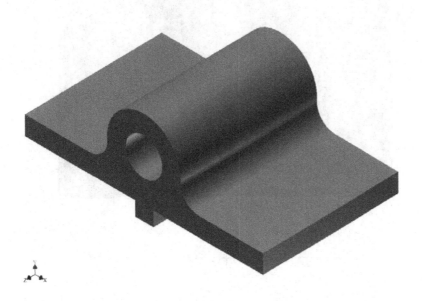

Controller Sketch B

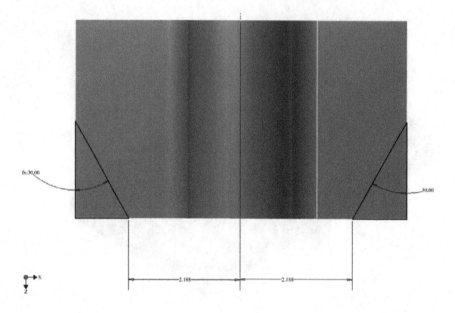

Controller Sketch C

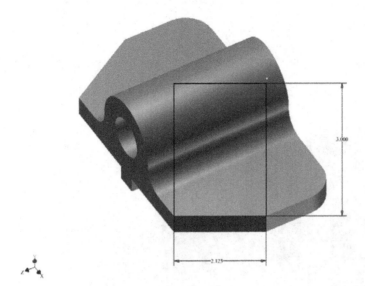

Controller Sketch D

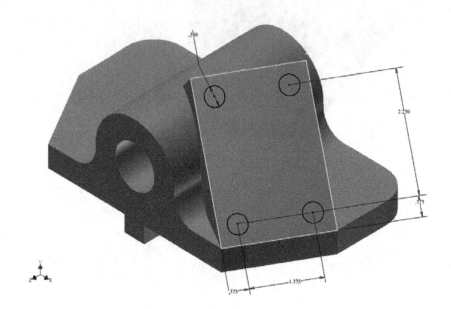

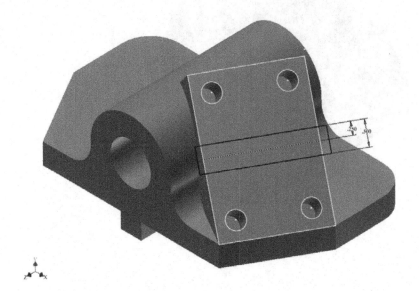

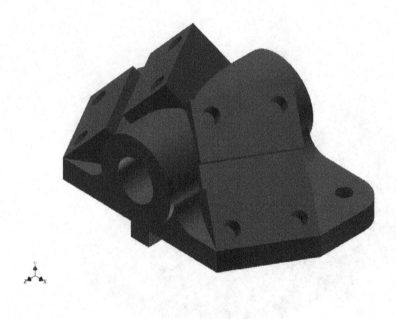

Controller Final

Fixture Base

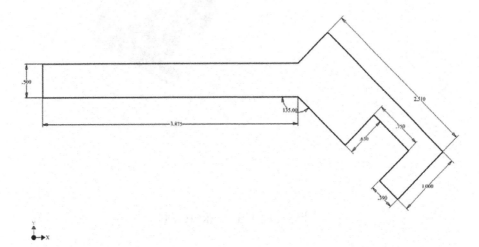

Fixture Base Sketch A

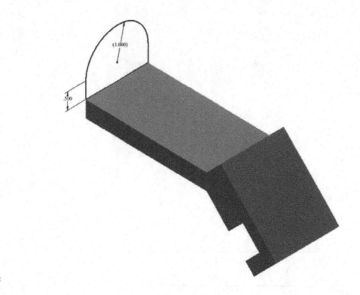

Fixture Base Sketch B

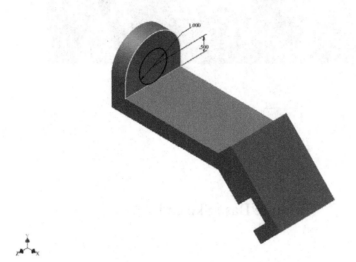

Fixture Base Sketch C

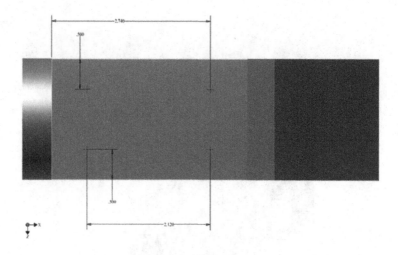

Fixture Base Sketch D

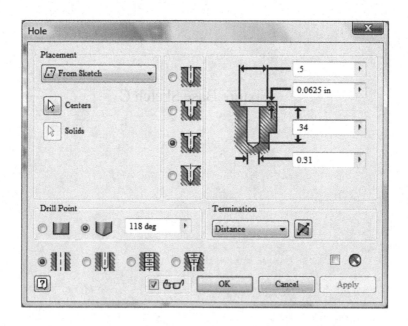

Hole Feature

Automatic Stop

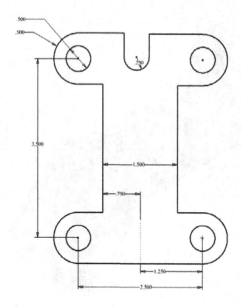

Automatic Stop Sketch A

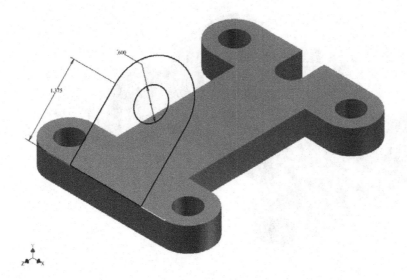

Automatic Stop Sketch B

Automatic Stop

Machine Parts

1. Start a new sketch on the right plane and add a 6-sided polygon from the origin.

2. Add a depth of 0.188 inches using the extrude feature and click on the check mark.

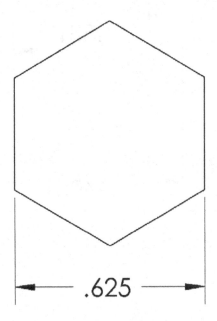

Latch Nut Sketch

3. Click on the flat side of the Latch Nut and add a new sketch.

4. Add a circle of diameter 0.531 inches to the top of the part and add a depth of 0.218 using the extrude feature.

5. Click on the XZ Plane add a new sketch.

6. Select View Face and click on XZ Plane in the Browser under Model, to orient the sketch on the Plan view.

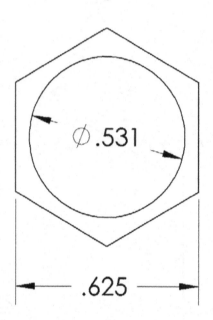

Latch Nut with 0.531 diametric circle

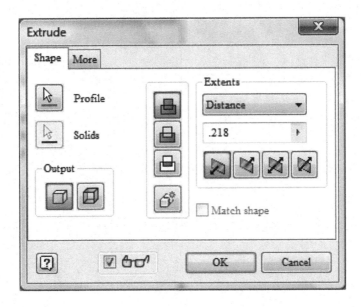

Extrude dialogue box

7. Create a sketch of the outline as depicted in Revolve Cut sketch and click on Finish Sketch check mark to exit.

8. Click on the Revolve Feature under the Model tab on the Ribbon, and select the X Axis under the Origin folder in the browser and click on OK.

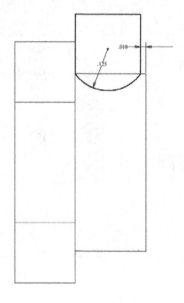

Revolve Cut Sketch

Revolve dialogue box

9. Click on the flat face create a new sketch and place a point on the origin.

10. Click on Finish Sketch to exit and click on the Hole Feature.

11. Use the following data from the Hole feature dialogue box to place a counter sink on the Latch Nut.

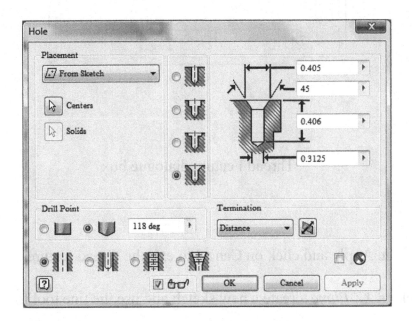

Hole Feature dialogue box

12. Click on OK to exit and save the drawing.

13. Click on the Thread icon, click inside the Latch nut to add a thread feature.

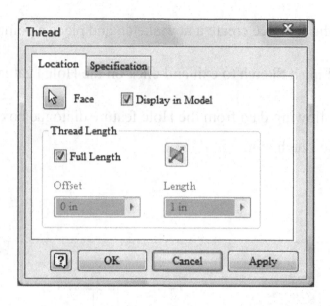

Thread Feature dialogue box

14. Click on Apply and click on Cancel to exit the thread feature.

15. Click on *XZ Plane* create a new sketch and use the line tool to add two equilateral triangles of 0.031 to each vertex as depicted in the drawing.

16. Use the *X Axis* together with the Revolve cut feature to add a cut at the ends.

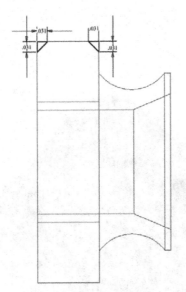

Equilateral Triangle on Latch Nut

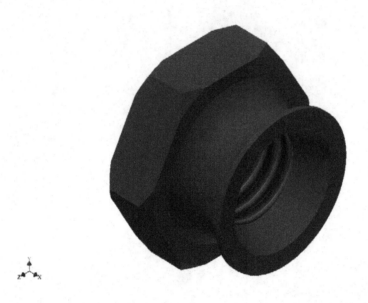

Latch Nut

Top Bracket

1. Start a new drawing and create a new sketch as the Top Bracket.

2. Use the extrude feature to add depth of *8.00 inches* to the sketch using the *Symmetric* option.

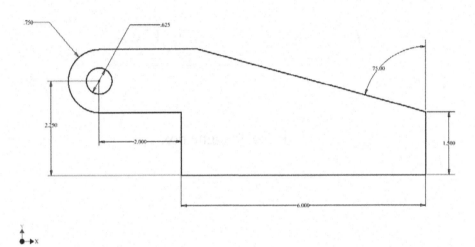

Top Bracket

3. Click on the right flat side and create a new sketch using the rectangular tool.

4. Add a 0.125 inch fillet to the bottom corners with a 0.125 inches thickness all around and exit the sketch.

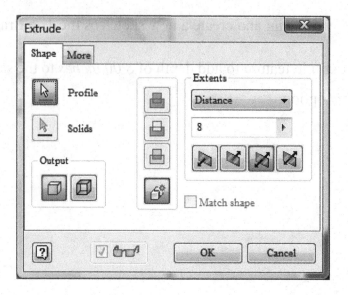

Extrude dialogue box

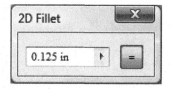

Fillet dialogue box

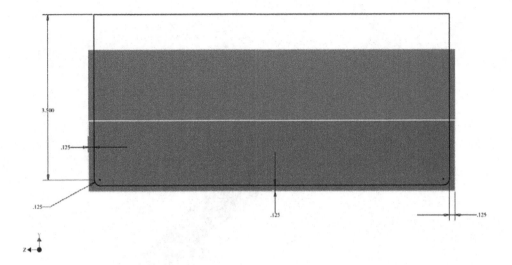

Rectangular Sketch

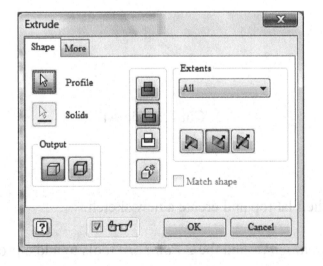

Extrude dialogue box

5. Use *"All"* under Extents in the Extrude dialogue box to add a cut on the part.

Cut Extrude All

6. Click on the Flat top and create a new sketch.

7. Use the *Rectangular* and the *3 Point arc* tools to add a profile on the plate and mirror it to the opposite side.

8. Add all dimension text and use the Cut Extrude feature to add slots to the part.

9. Click on the Finish Sketch check mark to exit and use the cut extrude to add
   a cut for the slot.

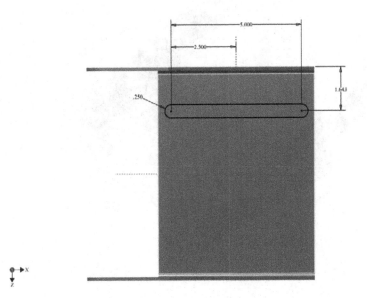

Sketch of a Slot

10. Save the Model.

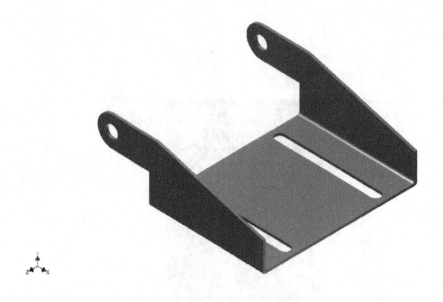

Top Bracket

Propeller

1. Start a new drawing using Standard (mm).ipt and click on OK.

2. Draw a horizontal centerline from the Origin and click on Finish Sketch.

3. Right-click on *Sketch1* in the Browser select *Redefine,* expand the arrow by the Origin folder on the browser and click on *YZ Plane*.

4. Click on the graphics area to re-orient the plane.

5. Expand the arrow below *Plane* and click to select *Angle to Plane around edge.*

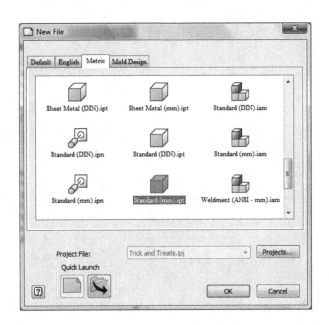

New File dialogue box

6. Move the mouse pointer to the Browser area and click to highlight the *YZ Plane.*

7. Next click on the centerline to tilt the plane, change the angle from *90 to -15* and click on the check mark.

8. Click on View Face and click on the *YZ Plane.*

9. Use the Circle and the line tools together with the dimension text to create the sketch in the Propeller Sketch.

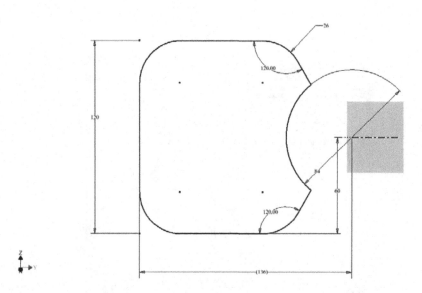

Propeller Sketch

10. Add a depth of *12 mm* with the extrude feature using the Symmetric option.

11. Expand the arrow by the Origin folder in the browser, right-click on YZ Plane and add a new Sketch.

12. Select View Face and click on the YZ plane in the browser to orient the sketch plane.

13. Place a diametric circle of 84 mm on from the origin.

14. Add a depth of 86 mm using the Symmetric option in the Extrude feature.

Extruded Circle

15. Add a new sketch on the flat face of the cylinder, add a diametric circle of 68 mm, and exit the sketch.

16. Add a depth of 24 mm using the extrude feature.

Propeller Model

17. Add a new sketch on the extruded cylinder face and place two concentric circles with diameter of 32 mm and 52 mm.

18. Use the cut extrude option with a depth of 5 mm to add a cut on top of the cylinder.

19. Place a sketch on the flat face again and add a circle of 16 mm and use the cut All option under extrude to add a hole.

20. Finally place an *8 X Ø5, 8 X 45°* with *Ø42 B.C.* on top of the cylinder and extrude cut using the *All* option.

21. Use the Circular pattern to add three more blades to the Propeller and Save the Model.

Gear Index

1. Start a new drawing using Metric – Standard.ipt and click on OK.

2. Place an Ø116 diametric circle on the origin and click on the Finish Sketch Check mark.

3. Use the Extrude feature to add a depth of 8mm and click on OK.

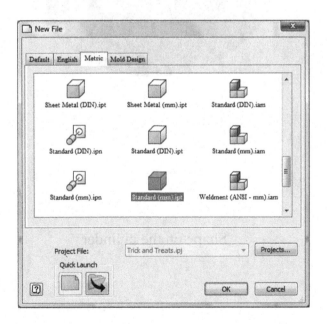

New File dialogue box

4. Click on the flat face of the extruded circle and add a new sketch.

5. Place a circle with 56mm diameter and draw the shape below with 12 mm high and a 3Point arc from the intersection of the 56 mm circle.

6. Use Extrude Cut with the *'All'* option to add a cut on the cylinder.

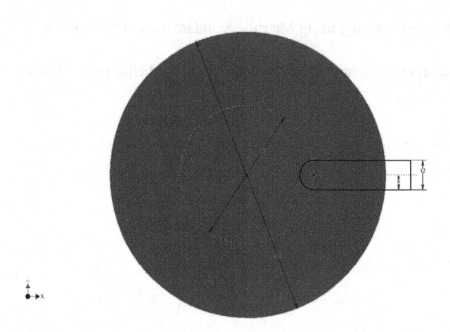

Shape on the cylinder

7. Add a circular pattern to create five cuts on the Gear Index.

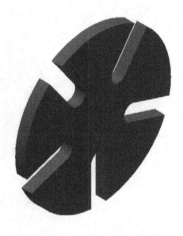

Circular Pattern

8. Click on top of the cylinder and add a new sketch.

9. Place a circle of 60 mm on top of the cylinder and add dimension text.

10. The endpoint of the 60mm circle that touches the edge of the first cut should be 8 mm (Refer to screen shot).

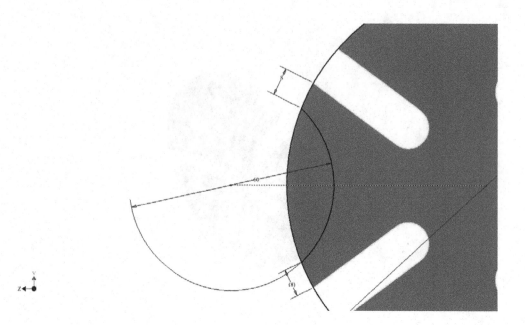

Sketch of a cut

11. Use *'All'* option in the Extrude feature to add a cut on the Gear Index.

12. Add a circular pattern of five cuts on the gear index and save the drawing.

13. Click on the flat face add a new sketch and place a Point on the center of the part.

14. Exit the sketch mode and click on the Hole icon under the Model tab.

15. Make the following entries in the hole dialogue box and click on OK.

271

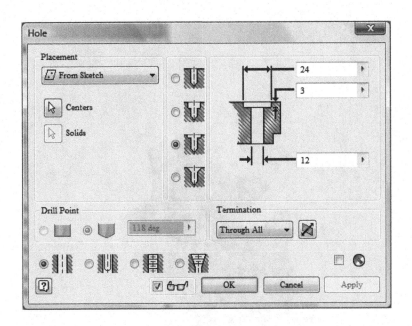

Hole dialogue box

Gear Index

Spherical Spacer

1. Draw the outline below and add all dimension text.

2. Revolve the outline click on the XY plane and add a new sketch.

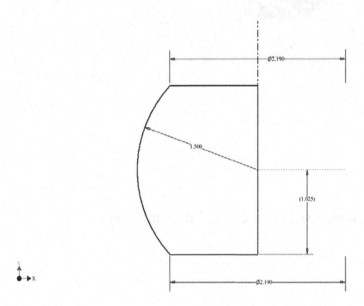

Outline

3. Place a 5.00 inch diametric circle on the orgin with two centerlines as shown in drawing below and exit the sketch.

4. Add a new sketch on the Plane just created and add dimension text of ø2.50.

274

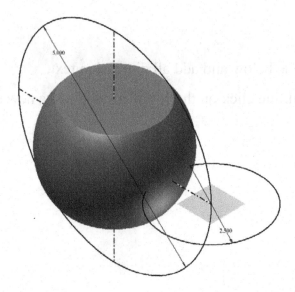

Sketch with two center lines and Plane

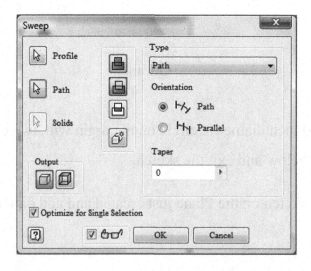

Sweep Cut dialogue box

5. Use the Sweep Cut option to add a cut on the sphere.

6. Repeat the steps on a 90 degree using the *YZ plane* and use the Sweep Cut again.

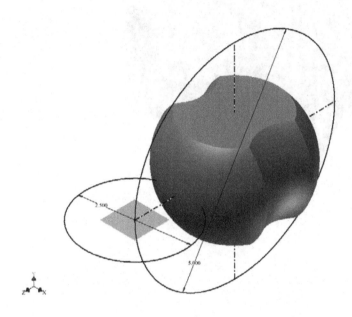

Plane on 90 degree from origin

7. Click on the Flat face and add a new sketch with a 1.350 diametric circle.

8. Extrude Cut with *'All'* option add a Chamfer of 0.0625 X 19 degree.

276

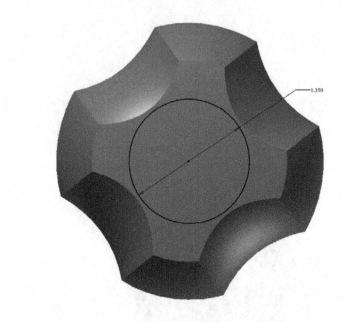

1.350

Spherical Spacer

Evaporator Cover

1. Start a new part using English.ipt on XZ plane and draw a 4.00 inch diametric circle from the Origin and click on Finish Sketch to exit.

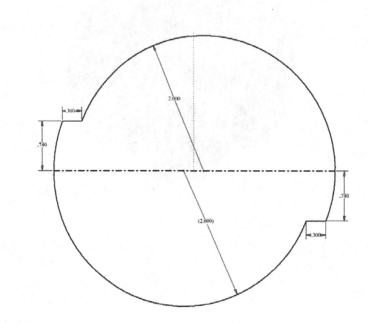

Evaporator Cover Sketch

2. Create the outline as in the sketch above with all dimension text.
3. Use the Extrude feature to add a depth of 0.49 inches, click on Ok button and Cancel to exit.

Plane on outer surface of Model

4. Click on the *XY* plane to highlight it in the browser, click on the *Work Plane* in the Work Features tab and click on the surface body of the model.

5. This action places a Plane parallel on the outer body of the model to the *XY* Plane in the center of the model.

6. Add a new sketch to the plane just created and use the *View Face* to orient it on a plan view.

7. Click on View on the Ribbon expand the arrow under *Visual Styles* and click on Wireframe.

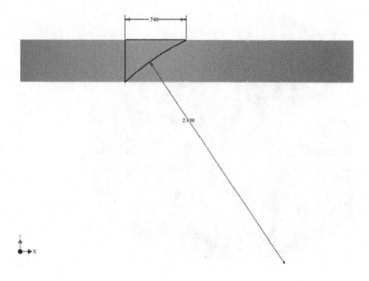

.740

2.830

Sketch with arc on Model

8. Click on the Home icon and select the Extrude feature with the Cut option.

9. Select *'To'* under Extents click on the body of the part and the OK button to complete the process.

10. Select Cancel to exit the extrude feature.

11. Repeat this process for the other side of the part and save the model.

Model with two cuts

12. Click on the top face of the model and add a new sketch.

13. Place a 0.59 inch diametric circle on a 2.52 B.C.D. and use circular pattern to create a total of 6.

14. Place another circle from the origin with a diameter of 1.10 inches.

15. Use the cut option from the extrude feature, together with *'All'* under Extents to add through holes on the part.

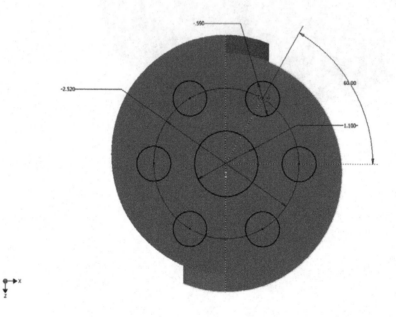

Patterned circles on top of model

16. Click on the bottom of the model and add a new sketch.

17. Add a diametric circle of 5.03 inches from the origin and extrude it 0.13.

18. Click on top of the bottom plate and add a new sketch.

19. Add circles of 0.28 in diameter as shown on the model below.

20. Extrude the four circles 0.73 inches each and save the model.

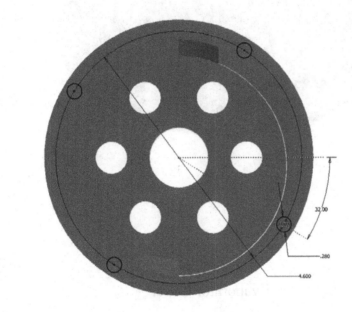

Patterned circle

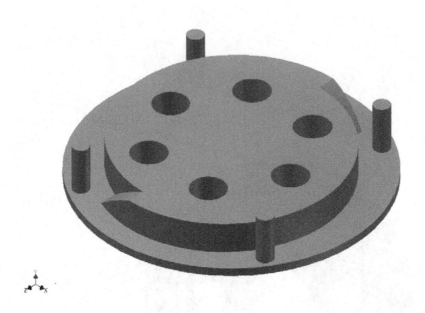

Evaporator Cover

Drawing Sheet

1. Click on New select Drawing and click on Base to insert Front, Top and Right side views.

2. Click on Save and accept the default name with a click on OK button.

3. Select the Annotate tab and click on Center pattern.

4. Click inside of the center hole, followed by a click inside the six holes one after the other.

5. Click inside the first selected hole again, right-click and Create to complete the circle for the B.C. diameter.

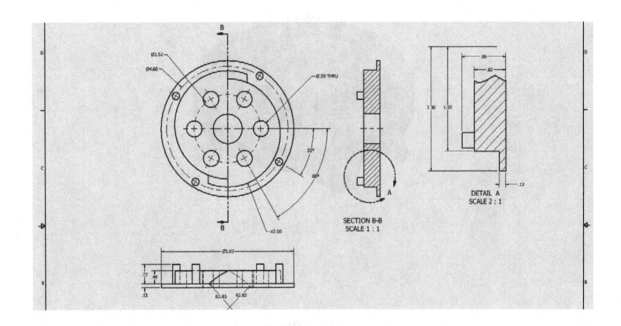

Drawing Sheet

Slice in Inventor

1. Place a part on the graphics area and click on the View tab.

2. Expand the arrow by Slice Graphics on the Appearance section and select Quarter Section.

3. A rectangular icon should be attached to the base of the mouse pointer.

4. Move to the Browser column and click on the plus sign by the Origin folder.

5. Click on the YZ Plane and type in an offset of 1 and click on the check mark.

Back Plate

6. Click on XZ Plane and click on the check mark to complete the operation.

7. Click on the arrow by Slice Graphics again and select End Section View.

Quarter Section

Half Section

1. Place a part on the graphics area and click on the View tab.
2. Expand the arrow by Slice Graphics on the Appearance section and select Half Section.

3. A rectangular icon should be attached to the base of the mouse pointer.

4. Move to the Browser column and click on the plus sign by the Origin folder.

5. Click on the YZ Plane and type in an offset of 1 and click on the check mark.

6. Click on XZ Plane and click on the check mark to complete the operation.

7. Click on the arrow by Slice Graphics again and select End Section View.

Half Section View

Three Quarter Section View

1. Place a part on the graphics area and click on the View tab.

2. Expand the arrow by Slice Graphics on the Appearance section and select Three Quarter Section View.

3. A rectangular icon should be attached to the base of the mouse pointer.

4. Move to the Browser column and click on the plus sign by the Origin folder.

5. Click on the YZ Plane and type in an offset of 1 and click on the check mark.

6. Click on XZ Plane and click on the check mark to complete the operation.

7. Click on the arrow by Slice Graphics again and select End Section View.

Three Quarter Section View

290

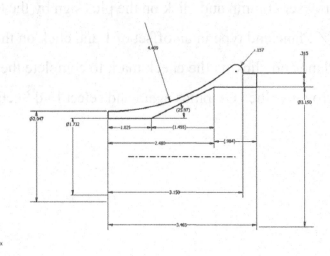

Inlet Sketch

Inlet Model

1. Start a new sketch on the Front view and create an outline with all dimensioning as shown.

2. Revolve the sketch to add volume turning it into a 3D Model.

3. Add a new sketch using the inside flat face and create a rectangular outline of 0.75 x 1.325 inches.

4. Add a depth of 0.32 inch pointing outward.

5. Using a Plane click on three different points of the boss extrude and add a new sketch.

6. Create an outline of 0.5 x 1.1 in and extrude-cut symmetrically about 1 inch.

7. Fillet the entities and save the part.

Final Model of Inlet

Creating Twisted Wire

1. Start a new document using the Top Plane and the Line Tool, create a 24 inch line from the origin.

2. Click on Finish Sketch check mark select the Work Plane and click twice on the endpoint of the line.

3. Right-click on the Work Plane in the Browser and select New Sketch.

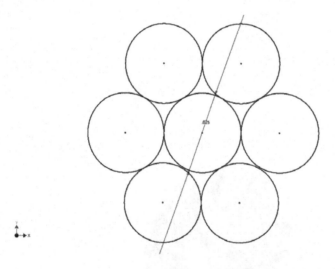

Circular Pattern

4. Place seven 0.25 inch circles starting from the endpoint of the line and exit the sketch.

5. Click on Sweep from 3D Model tab on the ribbon, select the center circle as the object and the line as Path.

6. Enter 360° * 5 in the Twist text box and click on OK button.

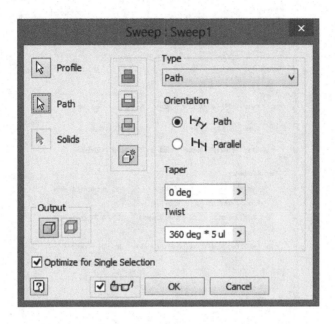

Sweep Dialogue box

7. Right-click on Sweep1 and click on the arrow by Profile and click on the next circle and click on OK button.

8. Repeat this for the rest of the circles and save the model as Twisted Bundle.

9. Right-click on Twisted Bundle in the Browser and select iProperties.

10. Click on Physical tab, expand the arrow by Material and select Steel.

11. Click on Apply then Cancel buttons to exit the dialogue box.

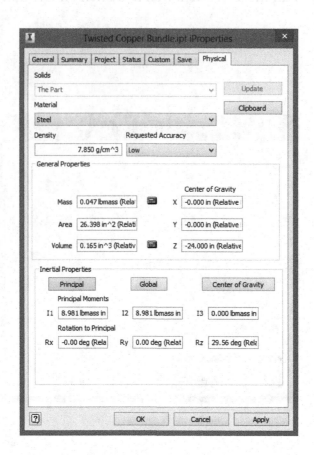

iProperties dialogue box

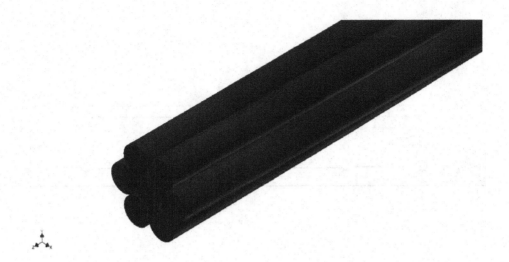

Twisted Bundle

Break

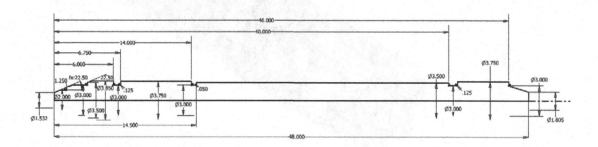

Shaft Sketch

1. Start a new part document on XY Plane and create the outline shown.

2. Revolve the outline into a 3D Model and assign Stainless Steel as material.

3. Save the model as shaft and start a new drawing using Standard.Dwg.

4. Click on Base and Insert the shaft on the drawing sheet using the Right View.

5. Right-click on Sheet1 select Edit Sheet and click on Side D.

6. Use Section icon to create a section as shown.

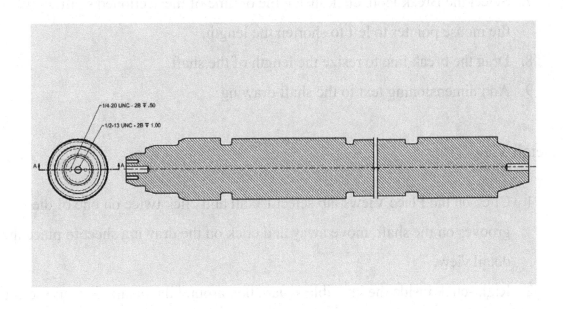

Section & Break Views

Shaft

7. Select the Break icon, click inside the outline of the sectioned shaft, move the mouse pointer to left to shorten the length.

8. Drag the break line to resize the length of the shaft.

9. Add dimensioning text to the shaft drawing.

Detail View

1. Click on the Place Views tab select Detail and click twice on one of the grooves on the shaft, move away and click on the drawing sheet to place the detail view.

2. Right-click inside the invisible square box around the detail view and select Edit View to open up Drawing view dialogue box.

3. Change the scale as needed and click on OK button to exit.

Adding Hole Callout

1. Click on Annotate tab and select Hole and Thread option.

2. Click on the edge of the ½ inch hole on the center of the Base view and click outside of the view to place detail hole callout.

3. Repeat this for the ¼ inch hole and save the drawing.

Summary

This covered topics that included:

• Using Constraints

• Utilizing Cut-Revolve option under the Boss/Base

• Utilizing Cut-Extrude option under the Boss/Base

• Using the Sweep tool

• Using the Circular Pattern

• Using Cut-Sweep tool

• Utilizing the Work Plane together with Point for a sketch

• Creating Parts with Loft

• Drawing different Mechanical Parts

Chapter VI

After completing this session the designer will be able to:

- Create iPart Factory
- Create equations
- Learn of iPart Author
- Link values to Excel worksheet
- Create Derived parts
- Learn how to break link of derived parts
- Learn about iLogic
- Create parameters
- Use the value list editor
- Create Rules
- Section views

Inventor iPart Factory

To set up an iPart one has to first create a base part with all the necessary equations and saved in a known location. The iPart Factory is then programmed using Table-Driven options to enter all the needed data to be used for a particular part. The table when finished will be linked to the family of parts to be used as and when needed. Go through these Tutorials to setup a line of parts.

1. Start Inventor and create a rectangle from the Origin, in this case a 4 x 2 inches adding all constraints.
2. Double-Click on the 2 inch dimension to open up the Edit Dimension text box.
3. Move the mouse pointer closer to the 4 inch dimension and notice how the icon changes into a symbol of a hand.
4. Click on the 4 inch dimension to place d0 in the Edit Dimension box.
5. Type *d0/2* in the edit dimension box and click on the check mark.
6. A function represented by *fx:* should be attached to the 2 inches dimension text.
7. The equation means that the base part of 4 inches will be divided by 2 every time.

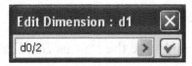

Edit Dimension

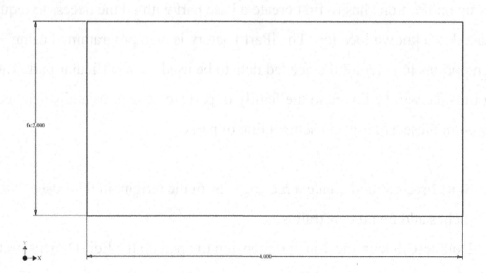

Rectangular Sketch

8. Notice that the 4 inches was the first dimension added to the part thus the d0.

9. Click on Finish Sketch check mark on the Main Menu bar to exit the sketch mode and click on Extrude.

10. In the Extrude dialogue box that pops up, make an entry in the depth text box with the following equation: d0*1.5. This means the base dimension will be multiplied 1.5 times to add depth to the part.

11. Click on OK to exit and save the Part as *BoxEquation* in a known location.

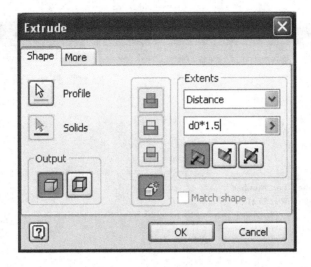

Extrude dialogue box

Box Equation

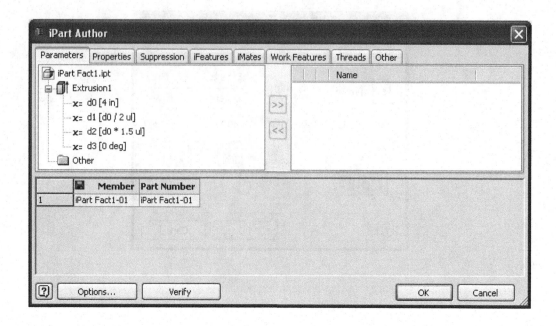

iPart Author

Setting up the iPart Factory:

1. Click on *Manage* tab from the Ribbon, click on *Author* and then *Create iPart*.

2. The iPart Author dialogue box opens up with the equations developed earlier on populating the Parameters.

3. Click on the equations one at a time and click on the top double arrow each time to make copies under Name.

4. Click on the Properties tab scroll down to Project and click to expand the plus sign to add a Part number to the Name box.

5. Right-click on the number 1 and click on Insert Row a second Row should be added to the table.

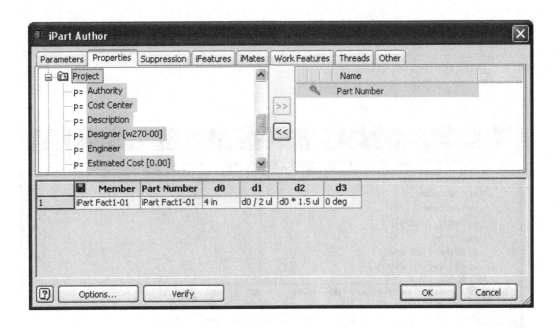

iPart Author

6. Add the Data as listed below as a new Row is added.

7. Click on OK when finished and save the drawing.

8. Notice the Table inserted under Model in the Browser has a + sign attached to it, meaning there is more to this than the eye can see.

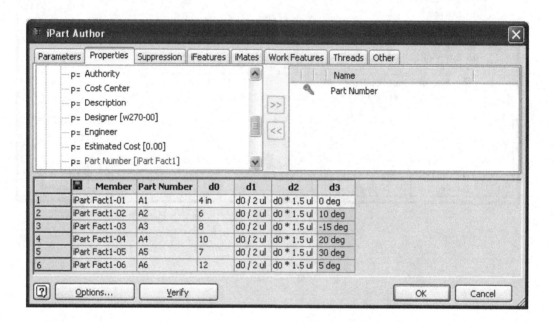

iPart data

9. Click on the plus sign to expand it and double-click on one of the Parts to see the change.

10. To add or edit the iPart setup, right-click on Table inserted into the Browser after creating the different parts and click to select, Edit via Spread Sheet.

11. A warning sign pops up informing the user of the changes to be made.

12. Click on OK to move on to the excel spread sheet.

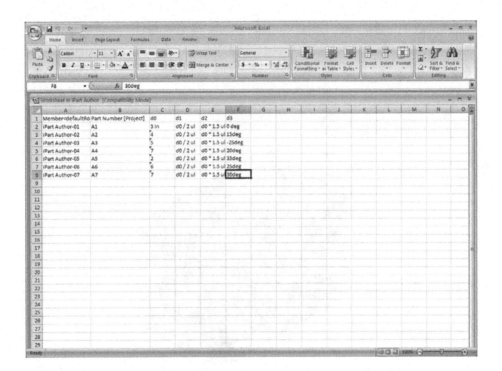

Excel Worksheet

13. Microsoft Excel® spread sheet should open up with all the functions.

14. Data set up earlier on, make the changes or additions and click on save.

15. The saved spread sheet automatically links to the Inventor model being worked on when the student exits the excel program.

Creating a Derived Part

1. Create a 7.00 X 4.50 inches sketch of a rectangle on the Top plane and add a depth of 4.50 in with the Extrude feature.

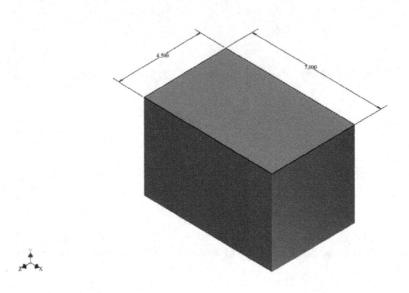

Tool Block Base Part

2. Start a new file and click on the Finish Sketch check mark to exit.

3. Click on *Insert* under the *Manage* tab on the Ribbon and select *Derive*.

4. Search for the Tool Block just saved under the Open dialogue box and click on Open to place a copy on the graphics area.

5. Derived part dialogue box also opens up on the graphics area for the user to make certain changes.

6. Let the mouse pointer rest on an icon by Derive style to reveal its function in the process, make the required changes or click on OK to accept the default setting.

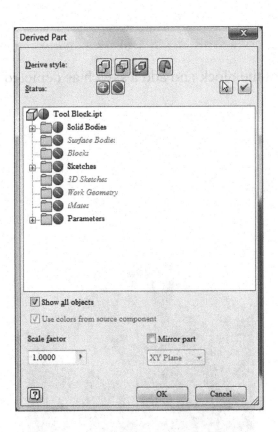

Derived Part dialogue box

7. The tool Block.ipt is now inserted in the browser under the Model.

8. Click twice on the Part3 under the Model in the browser and type *Derived Block 1a* over it and press the enter key.

9. Click on save and ok to save the new part.

Note: Changes made in the derived part do not affect the Base part, but on the other hand changes made in the Base part will reflect in the derived part when it is updated.

10. Click on top of the block and add a sketch as depicted in sketch on derived part.

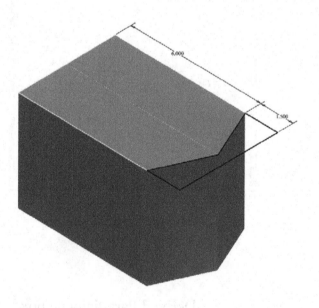

Sketch on Derived part

11. Use the cut option under the extrude feature and 'All' under Extents to remove the outlined part.

12. Place a new sketch on top of the part and add the outline and dimension text.

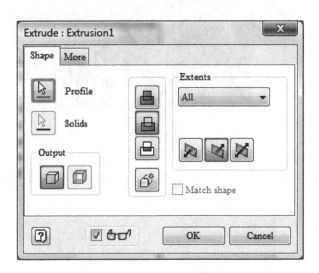

Extrude dialogue box

13. Use the cut option under the extrude feature and change the depth to 1.00 under Extents to remove the outlined part.

14. Add another sketch on top of the block and add dimension text.

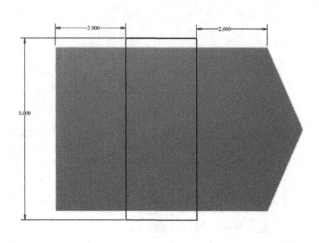

Sketch2 on derived part

15. Use the cut option under the extrude feature and change the depth to 0.50 under Extents to remove the outlined part.

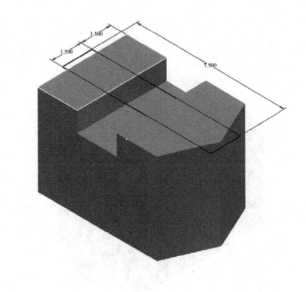

Sketch3 on derived part

16. Click inside the 0.50 groove and add a new sketch.

17. Place two 0.75 diametric circles on top of the groove and use the cut option under the extrude feature and 'All' under Extents to add holes on the block.

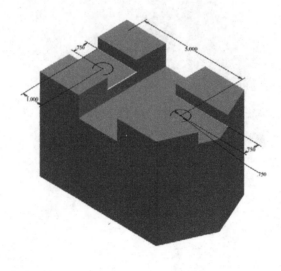

Block with two circular sketch

Tool Block

Breaking Link from Base Part

Right-click on the .ipt file under Derive Part under Model in the browser and select Break Link with Base Component. A symbol of a broken chain appears in the browser.

Any changes made in the Base part from then on will not reflect on the derived part since the link has been broken.

iLogic

1. Start a new Part and use the information on the Drawing Views to create the model as shown below.

2. Save the part as Clamp Slide, the first Hole as Top-hole and the second hole as Bottom Hole in the Browser.

3. The first cut is to be saved as *BossCut1* and the second saved as *BossCut2*

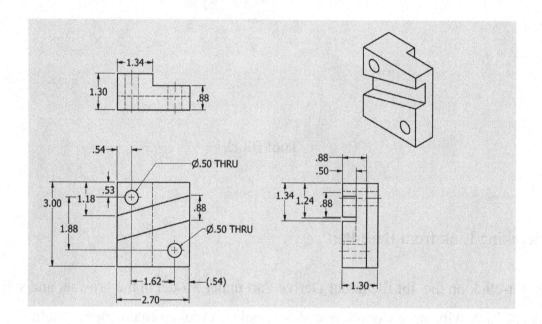

Drawing Views

4. Select Manage from the Ribbon and click on the function *fx* Parameters to open up a dialogue box.

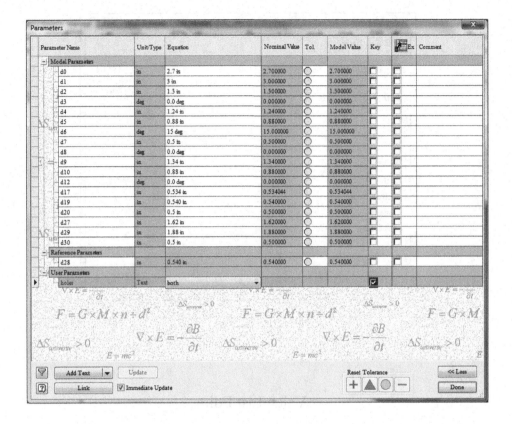

Parameters dialogue box

5. Click to expand the arrow by Add Numeric and click to select Add Text, the cursor should start blinking under the User Parameters name.

6. Type holes in the allotted cell and click in the text box under Key.

7. Right-click on Text and click on Multi Text to open up the Value List Editor.

8. Make the entries as shown below and click on *Add* to populate the *Value* section of the dialogue box.

318

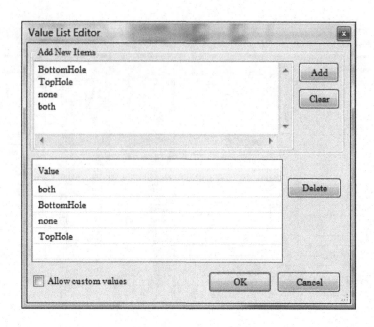

Value List Editor

9. Click on OK and click on *Done* at the bottom right corner of the Parameters dialogue box.

10. Click on Add Rule icon on top of the iLogic tab to open up Rule Name dialogue box and type *CS Program* and click on OK.

11. This action should open up the Edit Rule multi text box for programming.

12. Enter the program in the Multi box as depicted below and click on the OK button.

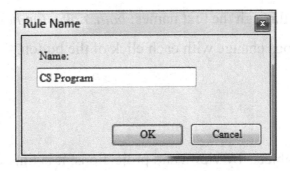

Rule Name dialogue box

13. If there are no mistakes the program should compile and automatically close the dialogue box.

Edit Rule text editor

To run the Program save the model and click on the *fx* Parameters to open it up again and cycle through the text names: *both, none, top hole and bottom hole* and see how things change with each click of the button.

Section View:

After representing objects by views and projections, it is time to cover Section Views for more details. An Invisible Cutting Plane which passes through the Part, sections the part in two halves. If the direction of sight is towards the right, then the left half will be shown as the left-side view and the other half mentally discarded.

- Sectional views help reveal interiors that cannot otherwise be clearly illustrated by hidden Lines.
- Interiors are shown just as we cut through an Orange or Pear with a sharp knife.
- These halves are known as Sectional views or Cross Sections in the Drawing views.
- When internal surfaces result in too many hidden lines, Designers and Drafters use Sectional views to improve the clarity of complex objects.
- Full Sections are obtained by passing the cutting plane fully through the Part.

For the Section Views, you will first create a drawing of a part with webs to be used for the Section.

Next you will open a new file with the Drawing Sheet and insert the Model to be used.

Follow these steps to create section views:

1. Start Inventor, click on File, New English Standard.ipt and click on OK.

2. Select Circle under the Panel Bar and draw two circles with dimensions 2 and 0.25 inch.

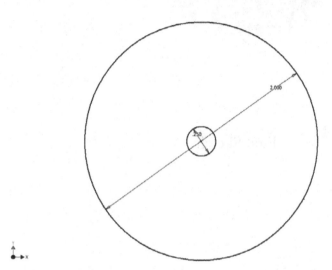

Concentric Circles

3. Click on Extrude under the 3D Model and enter a distance of 1in click inside the larger circle and click OK button.

4. Click on top of the Part and add a Sketch.

5. Use the Cut Extrude Feature, change the distance to *All* and click OK.

6. Click on Circular Pattern, and enter 5 under Placement and click on OK Save.

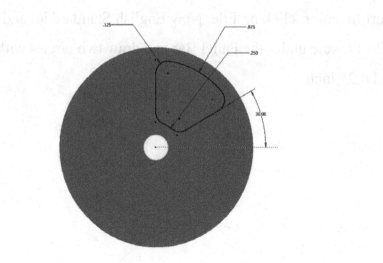

First Sketch

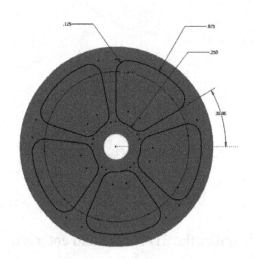

Circular Pattern

Section View:

Section Views are used to create half, aligned, offset or full section view from a Part or Model. Cutting Lines are used in defining the Geometry of a particular section and its orientation.

You are now going to use the Base part to create a Section View. Follow these steps to achieve this:

1. Click on File, New English ANSI.idw and OK A plain drawing sheet pops up
2. Click on Base View, Explorer Directories under File and select the Model
3. It Defaults to the Front view, click on the graphics area to place the first view.
4. Under Drawing View Panel, click on *Section View* and click inside the Model, the pointer turns into a cross.
5. Click on one end outside the Model and drag a straight line to the opposite end. And click again.
6. Right-click, select Continue and move the pointer away from the Base Part.
7. Click to place the section view.

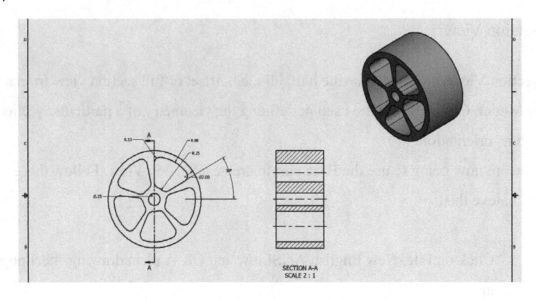

Section View

Detail View:

For a part to be properly manufactured based on the Drawing, a Detail drawing showing Multiview of a single part with dimensions and the description of the size, shape and materials used are to be represented in the Detail View.

Certain parts such as bushings, fasteners and bearings are not to be drawn as Detail view in an assembly.

These parts are normally classified as purchased items.

Detail views are used to show an enlarged view of a portion of a drawing otherwise would be too small to see or dimension. Concealed features or Parts of a drawing that are very small in the Drawing views are assigned a scale after using Detail Views to slice portions of those Parts. The Detail view is then positioned on the Drawing Sheet and dimensioned to reveal all internal parts.

Follow these steps to create Detail View:

1. Under Drawing Views Panel, select *Detail View* a dialogue box like the one shown below pops up.

2. Click in the box under Label and change the Alphabet to A or B as desired.

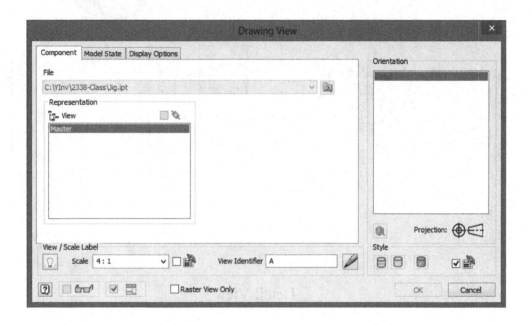

Detail View

3. Change the Scale to fit your need for an example 1:1, 4:1, or 1:2.

4. The shades under the Style could also be changed from Shaded, Hidden Line Removed to Hidden Line.

5. A circular symbol is then attached to the base of the pointer, click on the Feature and drag to place a boundary around it.

6. Move the pointer and place it in a desired location and add dimensions to the Feature.

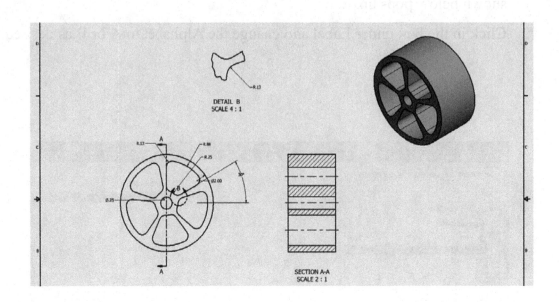

Detail View

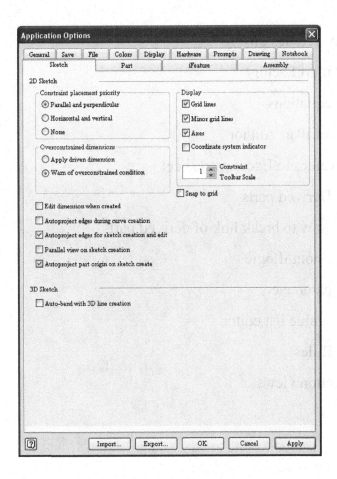

Application Options

7. For an example the designer has the option of changing the Text appearance under the General tab, but it is not recommended to change colors under Display since certain parts will be obscured if it is not done properly.

8. Click on Apply and close to exit the Application Options dialogue box.

328

Summary

The tutorials covered designs by

- Creating iPart Factory

- Creating equations

- Learning of iPart Author

- Linking values to Excel worksheet

- Creating Derived parts

- Learning how to break link of derived parts

- Learning about iLogic

- Creating parameters

- Using the value list editor

- Creating Rules

- Using Section views

Chapter VII

After completing this session the designer will be able to:

- Create a sketch to generate frame in Assembly

- Insert a Frame Generator

- Use the Miter Feature

- Edit a sketch and added more lines

- Convert model to Welding

- Apply groove welding

- Use Frame Analysis

- Create Simulation

- Add Material to parts

- Create a Skid

- Create Drawing of Frame with Balloons and B.O.M.

Frame generator

1. Open a new Assembly session click on Create on the top left of the Ribbon type the name as shown and click on OK button.

2. Expand the plus sign by Origin and click on XZ-the Top plane.

3. Click on the Top plane of the Cube on the top right corner of the screen to move to a 2D plane.

4. Create a 48 x 24 inch rectangular sketch and click on the check mark.

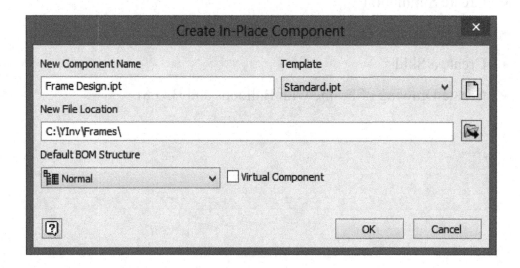

Create In-Place Component

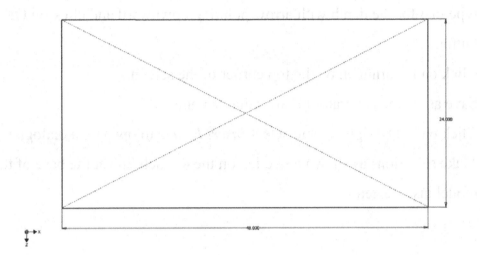

48 X 24 Sketch

Extrude dialogue box

5. Select the Extrude icon under 3D Model tab click on *Surface* under *Output* type in 4 for the depth with arrow pointing downward and click on OK button.

6. Click on Return icon on the top corner of the screen.

7. Save as Frame generator or any suitable name.

8. Click on the Design tab and select *Insert Frame* to open up a dialogue box.

9. Make selections as shown and click on the 48 inch line at the base of the model just created.

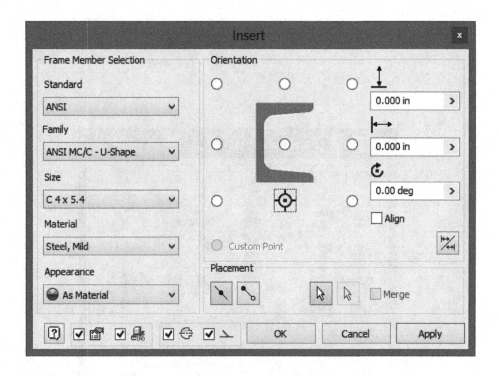

Frame Generator dialogue box

10. Select the rest of the lines in a clockwise manner and click on Apply and OK buttons when finished.

Miter

1. Click on Miter tool type 0.0625 for the weld gap and select the top of two intersecting beams and click on Apply to join it.

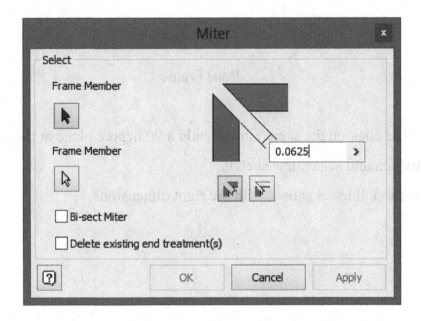

Miter

2. Do this for the rest of the corners and click on Cancel button when finished.

334

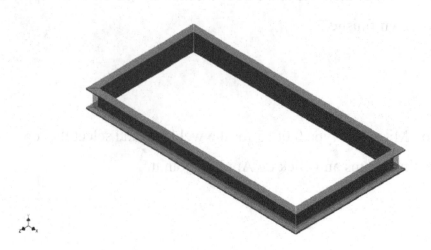

Base Frame

3. Double-click on the sketch layout, add a 90 degree plane at the edge of the extrusion and select new sketch.
4. Add more lines as shown with the right dimensions.

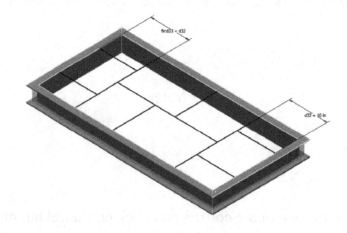

Lines Sketch

5. Click on the check mark and Return icon when finished and select Design tab and Insert Frame.

6. Using the Frame generator and the Miter tools add L2 x 2 x 1/8 to the lines.

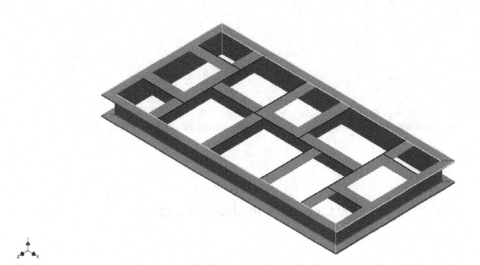

Additional Sketch Lines

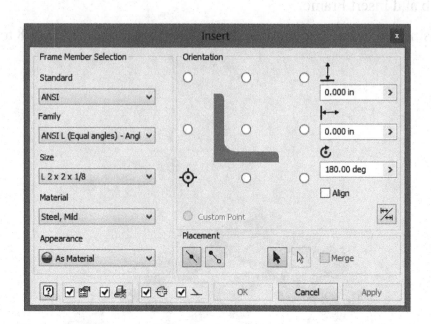

Using the Generator to change members

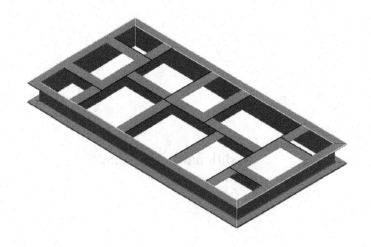

Frame

Welding

1. Click on Environment tab select *Convert to Weldment* and a warning tab should open.

2. Just click on *Yes* to accept and *OK* on *Convert to Weldment*.

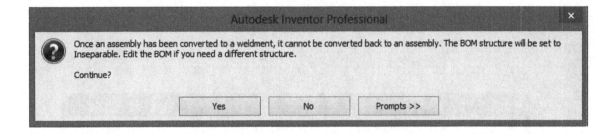

Warning tab

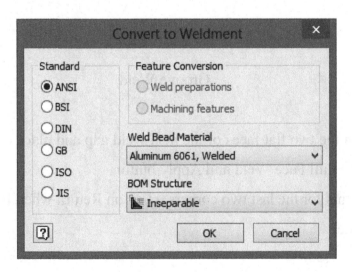

Convert to Weldment

3. Click on Welds to open up different options on the Ribbon bar.

4. Select Groove under Weld click on the flat face of one of the gaps between two frames.

5. Next click on the arrow by the number 2 and click on the opposite face of the welding gap.

6. Place a check mark in the text boxes by *Full Face Weld* and the Apply button.

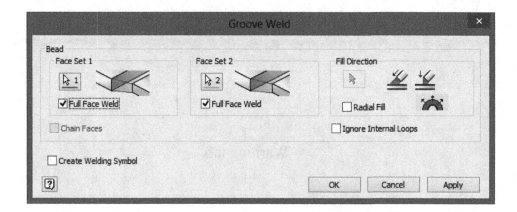

Groove Weld

7. Click on the two flat faces of the next weld gap and place check marks in text boxes by Full Face Weld and Apply button.

8. Repeat this for the last two corners, click on Return when finished and save the Model.

Frame Analysis

1. Click on *Frame Analysis* tool under Environment tab and select *Create Simulation* to use Static analysis.

Create New Simulation

2. Click on OK button to start generating the analysis and all points on the structure should have nodes with the center gravity arrow placed in the center.

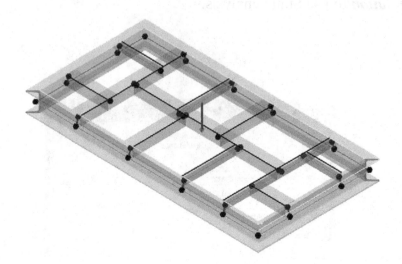

Nodes on Frame

3. Click on Fixed and click on the Nodes on the bottom of the frame.

4. Click on Continuous Load and click on the member as shown, change the Magnitude to 500 lb. and click on the check mark.

5. Repeat this for the rest of the members to obtain a total weight of 3,500 lbs. on the beam.

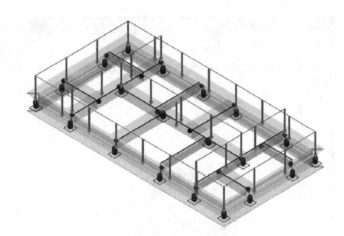

Beam Elements

Simulate

1. Click on *Simulate* icon on the Ribbon bar to run the analysis.

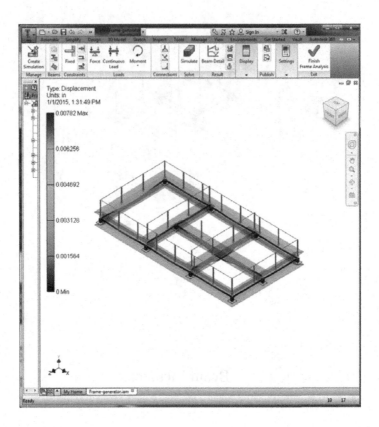

Mild Steel Results

2. Expand the arrow by Display select the arrow under smooth shading and click on Actual.

3. Click on Animate to the side of Display and click on OK button to view the reaction.

Material

1. Click on Material and place a check mark in the text box by Customize.

2. Expand the arrow under Name to enable the selection of a new material in place of the current one to make the skid stronger.

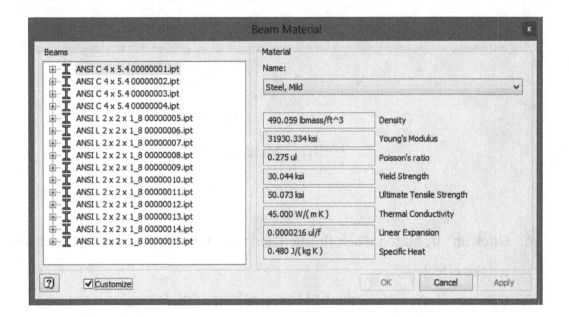

Beam Material dialogue box

3. To check whether another material will work better than mild steel, right-click on Simulation and click on Copy Simulation.

4. Right-click on materials and select Beam Materials to open up a dialogue box.

5. Place a check mark in the text box by Customize and select Aluminum 6061.

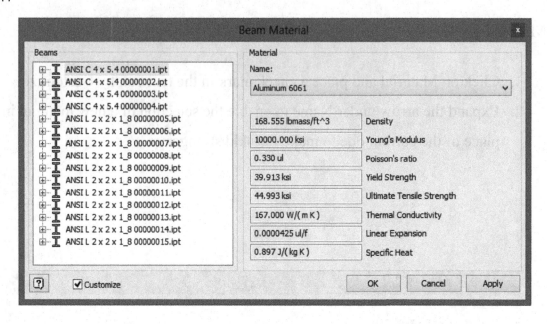

Beam Material

6. Click on OK button when finished and re-run the Simulation for the changes to take effect.

7. Compare the results of the Mild Steel to that of the Aluminum to make intelligent decisions.

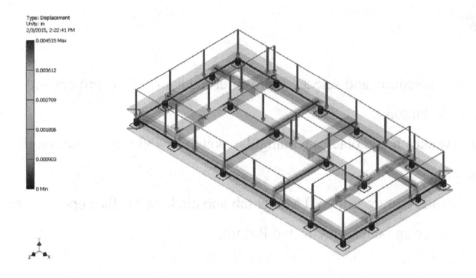

Results with Steel, Mild

Report

1. Click on Generate Report and click on OK button to run the report analysis.
2. Click on the check mark when finished and Design Frame Analysis when there is the need to edit the process again.
3. Save the Analysis.

Skid Design

1. Start a new assembly and select *Create* enter the name of the project and click on OK button.

2. Start a new sketch and place a rectangular sketch of 480 x 54 inches on the XZ plane.

3. Select Extrude feature from 3D Model tab and click on Surface option, type 54 for distance and click on OK and Return.

Extrude dialogue box

4. Right-click on the right face of the box and add a new sketch.

5. Place a vertical line 48 inches from the right edge and use Rectangular pattern to add 10 more lines.

6. Use the line tool to add cross members to the vertical lines as shown.

7. Click on Return on the top right of the screen and exit sketch.

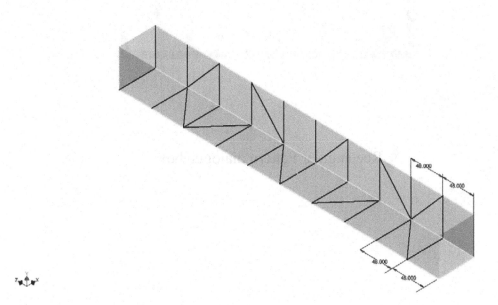

Outline Sketch

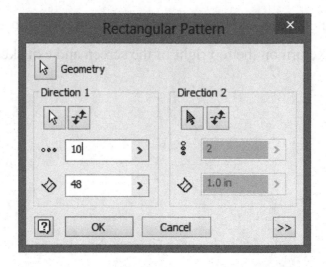

Rectangular Pattern dialogue box.

Frame

1. Click on Design tab and select Insert Frame to open up a dialogue box.

2. Select ANSI AISC (Rectangular) Tube under Family, 5x3x1/4 under Size and assign Steel, Mild as Material.

3. Click on the rectangular sketch on the base to add the structure, click on Apply then OK button twice.

4. Select ANSI AISC (Square) Tube under Family, 3x3x1/4 under Size and assign Steel, Mild as Material.

5. Click on the vertical and the inclined lines one at a time to add the structure, click on Apply then OK button twice.

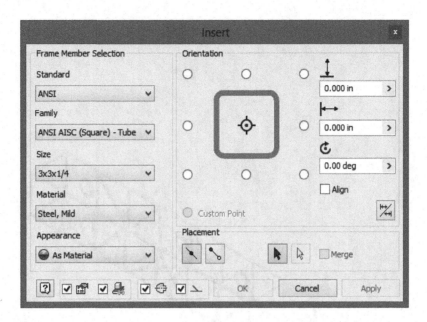

Insert dialogue box

6. Click on *'Place from Content Center'* expand the plus sign by Tube & Pipe-Fittings then Flanges.

7. Select ASME B16.5 Flange Lapped – Class 150 and place eight on the graphics area.

8. Using the Constrain option mate individual flanges as shown with the Frame assembly and save the model.

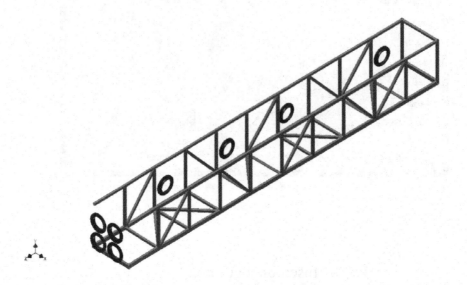

Frame and Flanges mated

Tube and Pipe.

1. Click on Environment tab on the Ribbon and select *Tube and Pipe*.

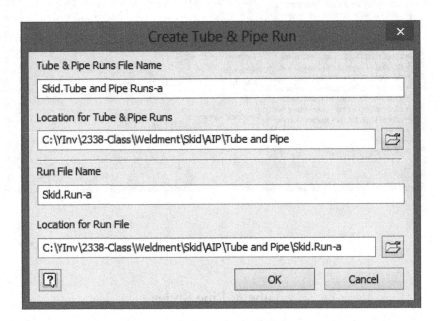

Pipe Run dialogue box

2. Type in a name for the run in the allotted text box and click on OK button.

3. Select the *Tube and Pipe Styles* under Pipe Run to open up a dialogue box.

4. Right-click on a selection click on ***Active***, move the mouse pointer to the top of the dialogue box and click on Edit-the pencil symbol.

5. Expand the arrow under Normal Diameter and select 8 inches to correspond to the Flange size.

6. Click on Save and the selected in this case ASTM A 53/A-ASME B16.5 should appear on the Ribbon.

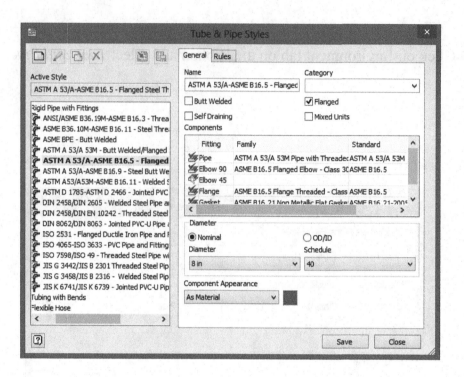

Tube & Pipe Styles

7. Click on *New Route* click on OK button to accept the default name.

8. Click on Route move the mouse pointer inside the top right flange to place an arrow.

9. Move the mouse pointer to the end of the frame and click inside the flange to add another arrow.

10. Use the green arrows for the segments to adjust the routing and click on the middle box to accept.

11. Select Route again and add lines for pairs of flanges and click on Finish Route to exit.

12. Click on *Populate Route* to add all connections.

Frame & Pipe Route

13. To re-arrange the routing right-click on Route01 and select Edit.

14. Use Move Segment icon to re-position the route lines and click on the check mark when finished.

Pipe/Frame & Tube design

1. Start a new Standard Assembly, select Create enter a name for New Component and click on OK button.

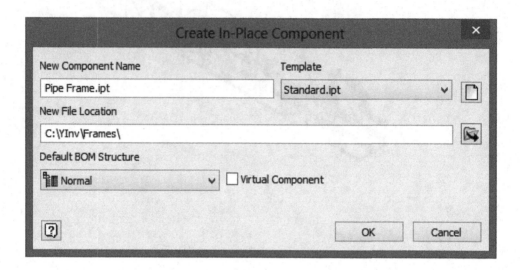

Create In-Place Component

2. Expand the plus sign by Origin and click on XZ plane.
3. Select 'Start 2D Sketch' from the Ribbon and click on XY Plane.
4. Create an 84 x 54 inch sketch and click on Finish Sketch.
5. Extrude the rectangle select surface icon and type 60 for distance and click on OK button.
6. Double-click on one of the faces add a new sketch and create lines.
7. Add more lines in different faces to complete the outline.

355

Extrude dialogue box

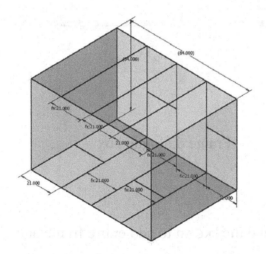

Frame Outline

8. Select Design from the Ribbon bar and select Frame generator from the design tab.

9. Use the selection as shown in the Frame dialogue box to add new frame.

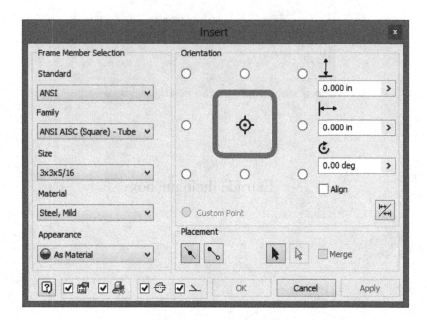

Frame dialogue box

10. Drag a window around the sketch to add entire frame and click on Apply button.

11. Press down on the Shift key to deselect lines not needed in the frame.

12. Expand the plus sign in the Browser and click on Sketch to add frame as well.

13. Click on Apply-OK and OK button again to generate the Frame.

14. Right-click on the sketches on the browser and uncheck the Visibility.

Miter

1. Click on Miter under Design, type 0.125 for the weld gap and click on two intersecting frames on the front plane, to highlight both.

2. Select Apply button to join the two and repeat this operation for the opposite frame.

3. Click on Cancel when finished.

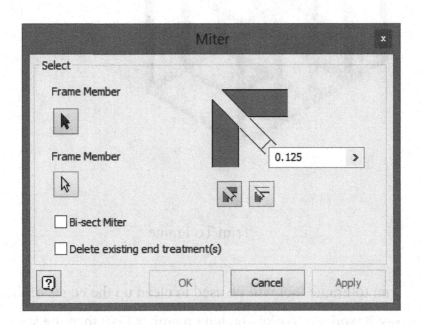

Miter dialogue box

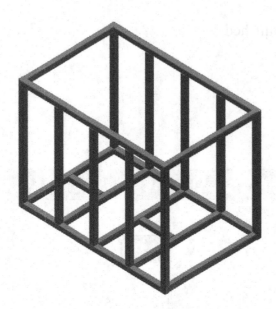

Trim To Frame

4. The Trim to Frame tool will be used to clean up the edges of the platform.

5. The way it works is to pick the long member first, then the short member to move from one to the other.

6. Click on intersecting members then the Apply button to trim to frame.

7. Use the same process for the base members of which the Channel is the long member and the square tube the short member.

8. Continue for the rest of the members and click the Cancel button when finished.

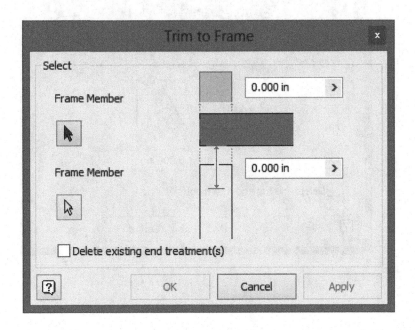

Trim To Frame

Trim Extend:-

The trim Extend feature can be used to trim multiple objects to a selected face.

1. Click on Trim/Extend feature select four legs of the frame, click on the arrow under Face and click on a flat face of connecting beam.
2. Click on the Apply button to extend the beam to the face of another beam.
3. Repeat this for the rest of the beams.

360

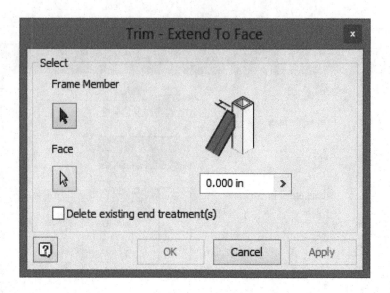

Trim – Extend To face

Drawing Documentation

1. Click on New document, select DWG file to open up a drawing sheet.
2. Click on Base and place four views on the drawing sheet.
3. Double-click the Isometric view and select shaded and OK button.
4. Click on Annotation, select general dimension icon, expand the arrow under Standard and click on Architectural ANSI format.
5. Add dimensions to the frame as shown.
6. Click on Parts List under Annotate, click inside the Isometric view and click on the drawing sheet to place the list.

Balloons

1. Click on Balloon under Annotate and click on a beam then on the drawing sheet to place a balloon.

2. Right-click and select Continue to finish the operation.

3. Hit the escape key on the keyboard, right-click on a balloon just added and select Edit Balloon Styles to open up a dialogue box.

4. Expand the arrow under *Balloon Formatting Shape* and select Split balloon.

5. Click on the item chooser at the end of ITEM, QTY to open up property chooser.

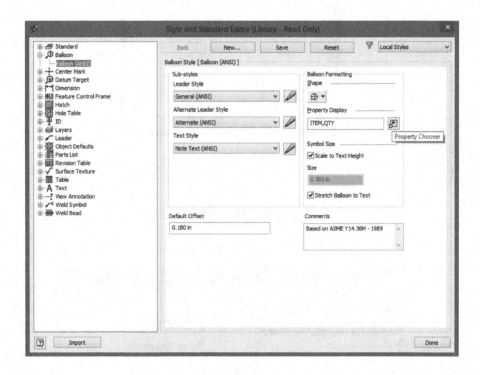

Style and Standard Editor

6. Click on New Property to open up Define New Property dialogue box.

7. Type *G_L* to represent the length of the part and click on OK button.

8. Click on Move up to place it on top of the list.

9. Click on OK and Done buttons to exit.

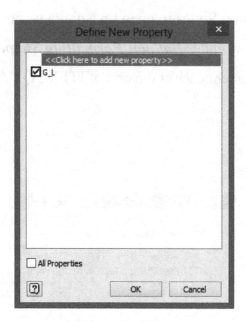

Define New Property

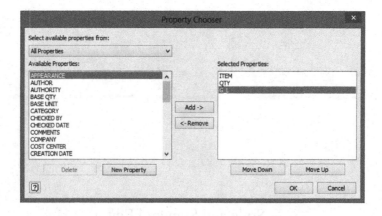

Property Chooser

Style and Standard Editor

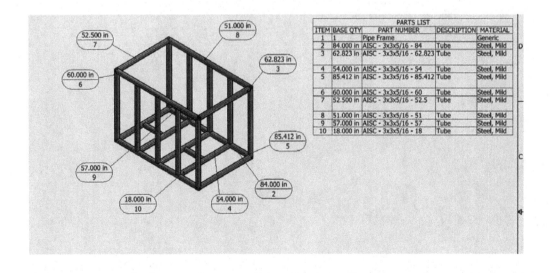

Drawing Sheet

364

Summary

- Created sketch to generate frame in Assembly

- Inserted a Frame Generator

- Used the Miter Feature

- Edited a sketch and added more lines

- Converted model to Welding

- Applied groove welding

- Used Frame Analysis

- Created Simulation

- Added Material to parts

- Created a Skid

- Used tube and pipe feature with fittings

- Created Drawing of Frame with Balloons and B.O.M.

Chapter VIII

After completing this session the designer will be able to:

- Create a Pressure Vessel

- Use iLogic Rule

- Create a Base part

- Work with Parameters

- Set up equations

- Learn to write a program

- Add material

- Use the value list Editor

- Alternate between sizes

Pressure Vessel

1. Start a new Part Document on the XZ plane and create a 54" x 36" x 1" plate.

2. Add a new sketch on the XY plane and create a 36 inch diametric circle.

3. Extrude the circle using symmetry option 46 inches.

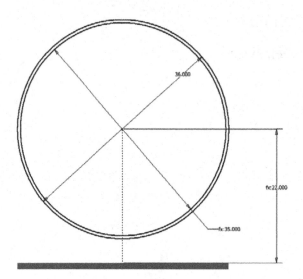

Vessel Sketch

Body of Vessel

4. Insert two flanges one on the side and one on top as shown.

5. Click on top of the base pad and add a new sketch.

6. Create the sketch as shown and click on extrude and use to Next option.

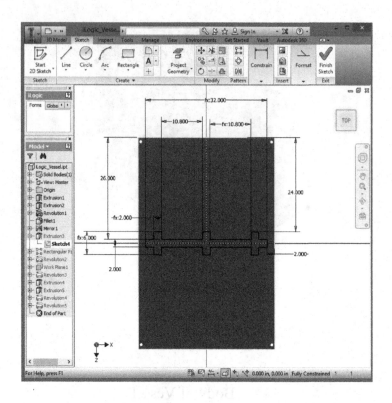

Sketch of Support

iLogic Rule

1. Click on *Manage* select the function *fx Parameters* expand the arrow by *Add Text* and select *Add Numeric*.

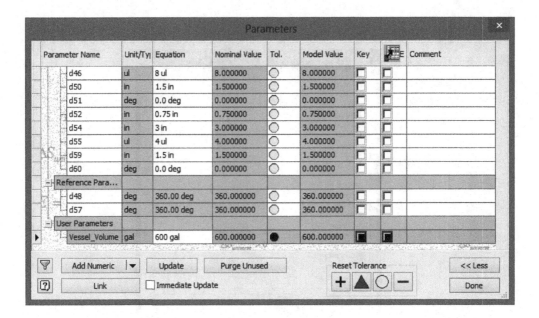

Parameters dialogue box

2. Click in the in text box expand the plus sign by *Volume* and select *Gallons*. And click on OK button.

3. Type 600 under *Equation* and hit the tab key on the keyboard.

4. Click on Done button to exit the Parameters dialogue box.

5. Select *iLogic Rule* and type Vessel Size in the text box.

6. Click on OK button to open up Edit Rule dialogue box.

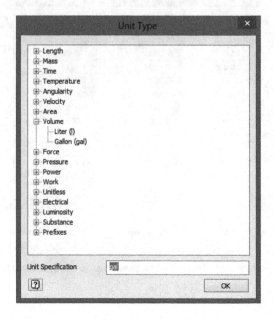

Unit Type dialogue box

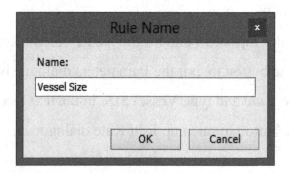

Rule Name

7. Insert an *If...Then...End ...If* from the Edit Rule, delete *My_Expression* from the statement.

8. Click on User Parameters under Model tab, right-click on *Vessel_Volume* under Parameter, select Parameters and *Capture Current State*.

9. Place the cursor between *If...Then...End ...If and End If* and click on Model Parameters.

Edit Rule

10. Press the *ctrl* on the keyboard and select all items as shown in the dialogue box to highlight it.

11. Right-click on the selection and click on *Capture Current State*.

12. Copy/Paste the data as shown and change the values in the dialogue box.

13. Click on OK button when finished.

14. Click on the function *fx* Parameters change the 600 gallons to 700 gallons, click on Done button and Update to see the changes.

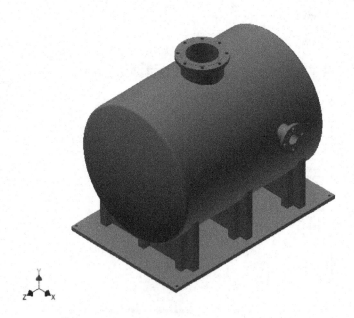

Pressure Vessel

Add Material

1. Open the Parameters dialogue box, expand the arrow by Filter and Add Text.

2. Type Vessel_Material under Parameter name, right-click on Text and select *Multi-Value List*.

3. Type three different materials and click on Add in the *Value List Editor*.

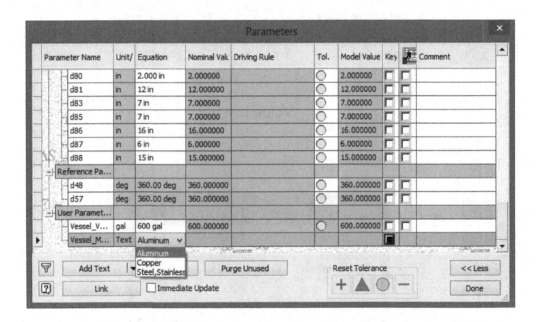

Parameters

4. Click on OK button to exit and click on Done in the Parameters dialogue box.

374

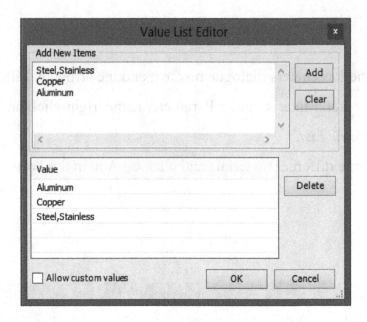

Value List

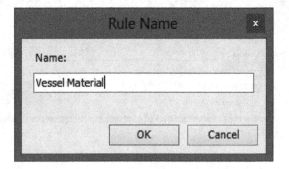

Rule Name

5. Click on Rule and create a new rule as Vessel Material.

6. Click on User Parameters, right-click on Vessel_Material and select Capture Current State to replace *My Expression*.

7. Expand the plus sign by iProperties under Snippets and double-click on Material.

Edit Rule dialogue box

8. Add an equal sign in front of the iProperties.Material and type the word Material.

9. The system will replace the correct material for a selected volume any time it encounters the word material.

10. Expand the plus sign by Documents double-click on Document Update and click on OK button to exit.

11. Open *fx* Parameters and change the tank volume to 700 gal and notice the change in color.

Wrong Size:

To avoid placing a wrong size the following code will be added to avoid any errors.

1. Create a new iLogic Rule and type Size Warning in the Name Text box and click on OK button.

2. Type the code as shown and press the Enter key to move to the next line.

3. Expand the arrow by *Message Box* and double-click on *Show*.

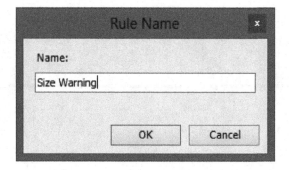

Rule Name

4. Finish the code entries and click on OK button to exit.

5. Select *fx* Parameters and change Vessel Volume to 500 gal and notice the warning sign.

Size Selection

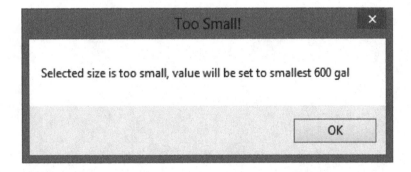

Warning Sign

6. Select the function *fx* Parameters and change Vessel Volume to 500 gal and notice the warning sign.

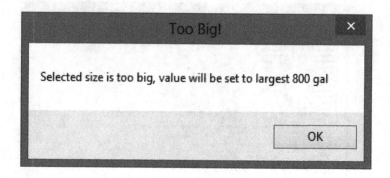

Warning Sign

7. Select the function *fx* Parameters and change Vessel Volume to 900 gal and notice the warning sign.
8. Save the model.

Calculate Internal Volume of Vessel

1. Start a new Assembly file and place the Pressure Vessel on the assembly.

2. Click on Create icon under Assemble tab on the Ribbon.

3. Type VolCalc in the text box under New Component Name.

4. Expand the arrow under Default BOM structure, select Reference and click on Ok button.

Pressure Vessel

5. Click on the Graphics area and the model should turn transparent.

6. Expand the arrow under Modify and select Copy Object.

7. Click on radio button to the side of Body select Surface icon under Create New and click on the Body of the Vessel.

8. Make sure the text box to the side of Associative is checked and click on Apply button.

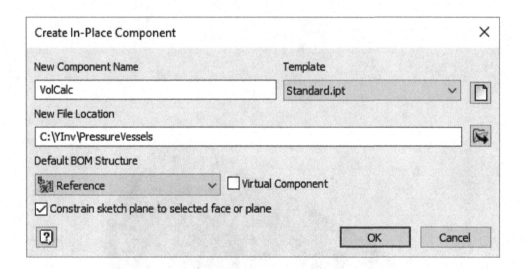

Create In-Place Component

9. Click on Cancel to exit the dialogue box and right-click on the VolCalc in the Browser and select open.

10. Click on the Home icon to view the model in its transparent form.

Copy Object

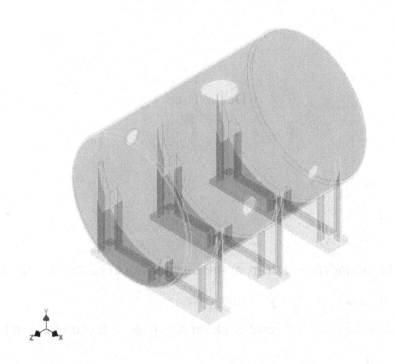

Transparent Model

Delete Face

1. Select Delete Face under the Modify tab and click on the left face of the vessel then Ok button.

2. Select Delete Face again and select the body of the Vessel and click on Ok button.

3. Select Delete Face and click on the right face of the vessel and click on Ok button.

4. Make sure all outer faces are deleted one after the other.

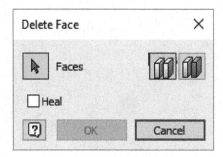

Delete Face

Boundary Patch

1. Select the Boundary Patch from the Surface tab click inside the first hole on the Vessel and then Apply button.

2. Repeat this for each hole and click on Apply button each time until all holes are covered.

3. Click on Done to exit after covering all openings.

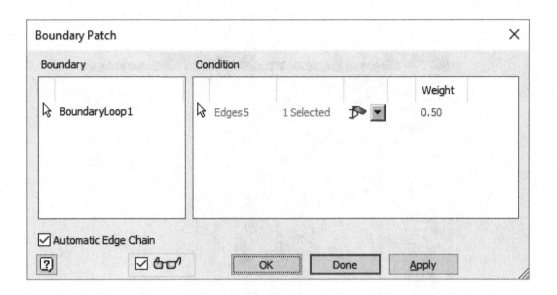

Boundary Patch

Sculpt

1. Select Sculpt from the Surface tab and click on all the Surfaces and Boundary Patch from the Browser and click on Ok button.

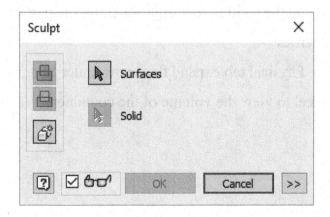

Sculpt Dialogue box

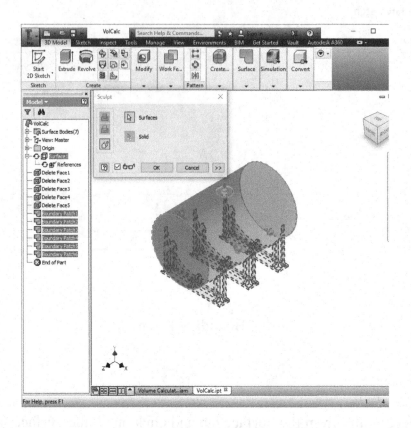

Sculpt Surfaces

2. After obtaining the solid model, right-click on the part in the Browser and select iProperties.

3. Click on the Physical tab expand the arrow under Material and select Stainless Steel to view the volume of the container.

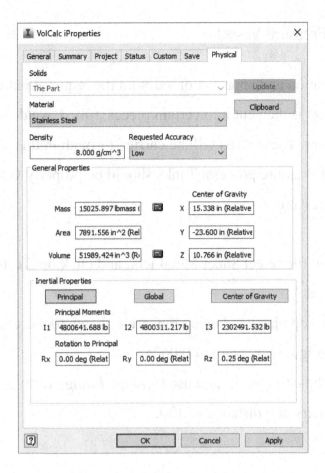

Volume Calculation iProperties

Steps to Build Pressure Vessel

After the presentation and approval of a design the required materials and sheet is selected. The sheet is then cut into certain pieces, rolled, welded at the seams and assembled together. These steps will be carried through in this section for better understanding of Pressure process. Tanks should be properly vented or it will collapse under pressure.

1. Start a new file select Sheet Metal icon and click on create to open up the design sheet.
2. Select the Top plane and using the circle sketch tool create an Ø61.00 inch from the origin with a gap of 0.0625.
3. Click on the check mark and use *Contour Flange* from the Feature tab using the Symmetry at a distance of 120.

Cylinder

4. Click on OK button to exit and save as Cylinder.

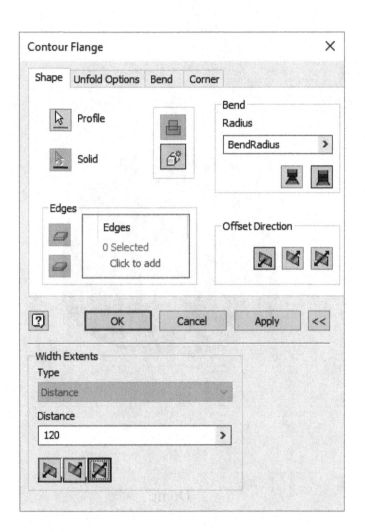

Contour Flange

5. Start a new drawing on the Top plane and create an Ø61.00 inch with a gap of 0.0625.

6. Click on the check mark and use *Contour Flange* from the Feature tab at a distance of 12 inches.

Dome

7. Select the flat top face and add another sketch.

8. Create half circle as the diameter of the cylinder and place a centerline along the center of the sketch.

9. Use the Revolve feature with an angle of 180 to add a dome on top of the 12 inch cylinder.

10. Save as Dome.

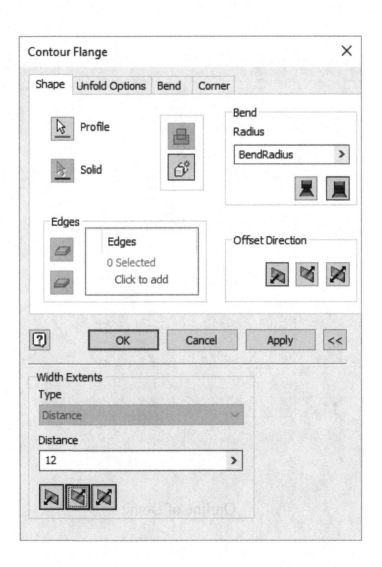

Contour Flange

390

11. Place a sketch on the XY-plane and add a rectangular sketch with a center line as shown.

12. Click on the check mark and use revolve-cut to remove material from the Dome.

13. Add another hole on the very top of the dome as shown.

14. Use Revolve-cut to add a manhole to the cylinder.

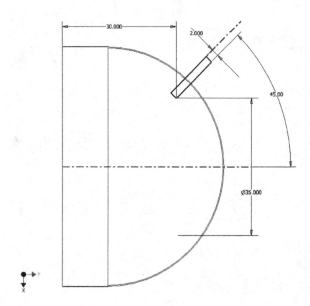

Outline of Dome

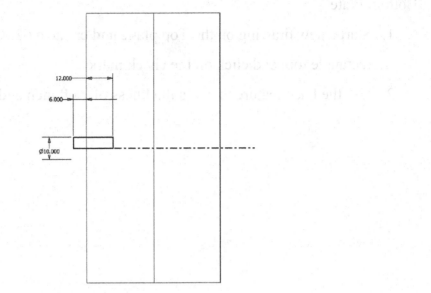

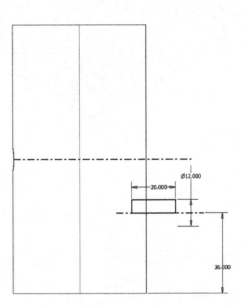

Bottom Plate

1. Start a new drawing on the Top plane and create a 62 X 62 inch square using rectangle tool and click on the check mark.

2. Use the Face feature to add a thickness of 2.00 inch and save as bottom plate.

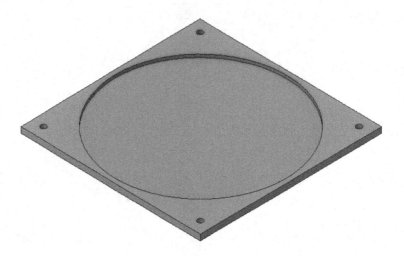

Bottom Plate

3. Assemble the bottom plate with the main assembly and click on Save again.

Assembled parts

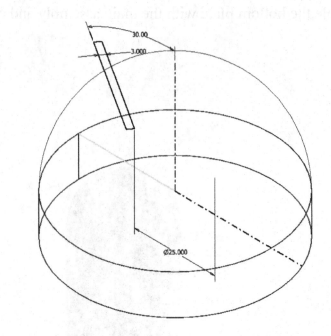

Flange Hole

4. Assemble with coupling and Flanges as shown and save the model.

Weldment

1. Click on new select Weldment.iam and click on Create.

2. Save the model as Pressure Vessel.

3. Click on *Place* under Assembly tab locate the Pressure Vessel model and click on Open button.

4. Double-click on Welds and select Fillet Weld to open up a dialogue box.

396

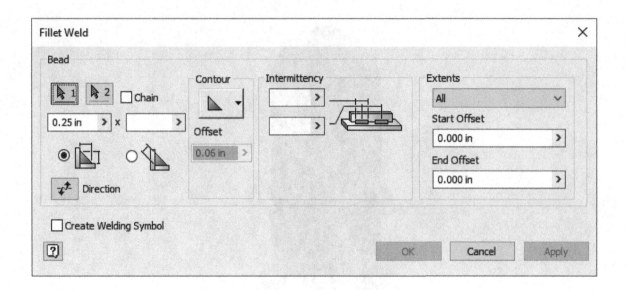

Fillet Weld dialogue box

5. Click on the body of the Dome select the number 2 and click on the body of the Flange then the Ok button to add a weld bead.
6. Repeat this for the rest of the Fittings.

Fillet Weld

Completed Fillet Weld

9. Click on Return icon on the top right corner of the Ribbon when finished.

Summary

Using the program the designer/student

- Created a Pressure Vessel
- Used iLogic Rule
- Created a Base part
- Worked with Parameters
- Set up equations
- Learned to write a program
- Added material
- Used the value list Editor
- Volume Calculations
- Learned how to use Alternate between sizes option
- Create Pressure Vessel

Chapter IX

After completing this session the student/designer will be able to:

- Create a new plastic part and add features.
- Use the Lip tool to add lips to the part.
- Create grill on the cover
- Use the Plastic Boss feature to add parts
- Start the Mold assembly and bring in the part
- Learn to re-orient the part
- Add Material
- Add Core and Cavity to the part
- Create a Workpiece setting
- Learn to use the Patching Surface tool
- Create Runoff Surface
- Utilize the Gate Location for the part
- Create Part Process Setting
- Create Part Fill Analysis and finally
- Produce Results study.

1. Start a new part on the XZ plane and create a 5 inch diametric circle from the Origin.

2. Add a depth of 6 inches, shell of 0.125 thick and save as base container.

3. Start a new part on the XZ plane and create another 5 inch diametric circle from the Origin.

4. Add a depth of 1 inches, shell of 0.125 thick and save as cover.

Base Container

Lip

1. Click on the icon under 3D Model, select the top icon known as Groove and click on the outer rim of the cylinder, then the body.

2. Select the Groove tab make the following changes and click on OK button.

3. The 0.625 entered changes the distance between the OD and ID and the vertical one the height.

4. Open the cover created earlier and add a lip by clicking on the inside rim then the inside body.

5. Select Groove tab and add 0.625 to the distance and height.

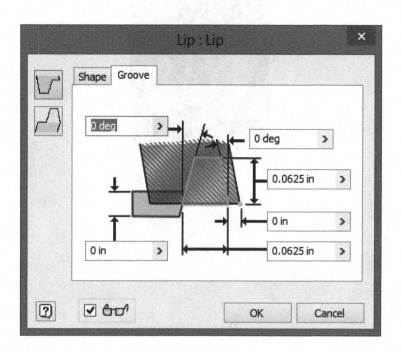

Lip dialogue box

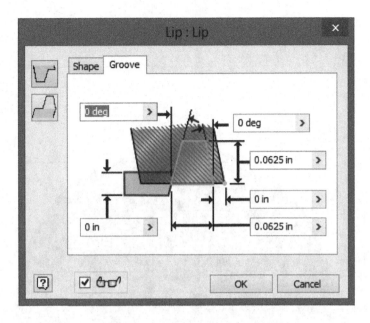

Lip dialogue box

Cover

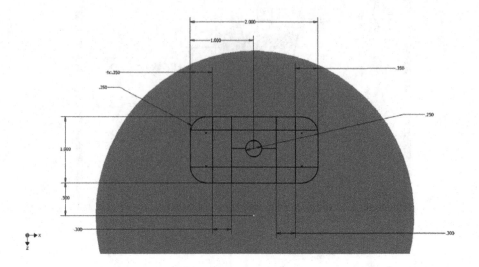

Sketch Profile

Grill

1. Click on the top face of the cover and add a new sketch as shown.

2. Click on Finish sketch and save the drawing.

3. Select grill under 3D Model by Plastic part and click on the outline.

4. Select the Island tab and click on the inner circle.

5. Select the Rib tab and click on the horizontal lines.

6. Select the Spar tab and click on the vertical lines.

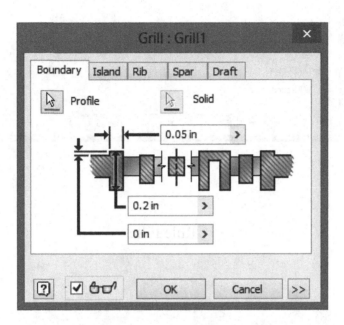

Grill dialogue box

Rule Fillet:

Create a constant fillet radius based on a list of rules that tell the feature how to discover edges.

1. Expand the arrow under Plastic Part and select Rule Fillet to open up a dialogue box.
2. Click on the Grill on the lid to highlight it and change the radius to 0.02.
3. Uncheck All Rounds and select All Edges under Rule and click on OK button.

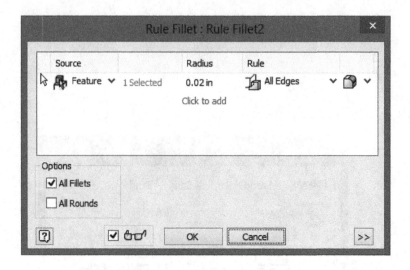

Rule Fillet

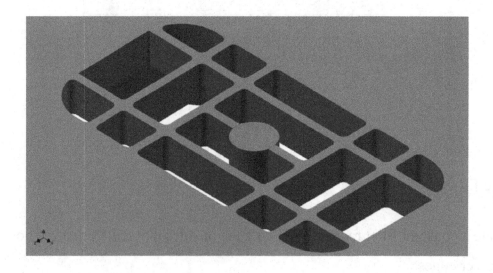

Rule Fillet on Grill

Assembly

1. Open a new Assembly file and bring in the Base Container.

2. Place the cover in the assembly and add mates.

3. Save the model.

Grill Feature

Container Model

Boss:

Creates a raised protrusion fastening, facilitating alignment and adding strength.

1. Start a new part using the XZ Plane, create a 4 inch circle from the origin and add a depth of an inch using the Extrude Feature.
2. Add 0.25 fillet to the base edge and shell the flat face with a thickness of 0.625 inch.

Pattern

3. Create a pattern on the top using 3 Point Arc Slot and extrude-cut to next.
4. Click on top face of the 0.625 thickness and add a new sketch.
5. Place 4 points 90 degree apart and exit the sketch.
6. Click on Boss from the Plastic Part tab, select Thread icon from the left of the dialogue box and OK button to exit.

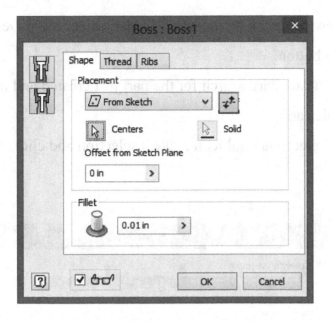

Boss dialogue box

Slot Pattern with Boss Feature

1. Start a new part click on the Mold Folder, select Mold Design.iam and click on Create button.

2. Click on Plastic Part, search for the part just created and open, click on top of the graphics area.

3. Click on Select Material icon make a selection and click on OK button.

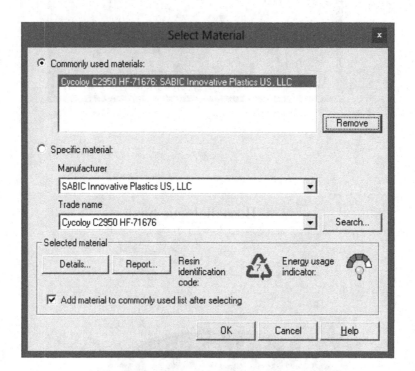

Material Dialogue box

4. Click on Part Process Settings to open up a dialogue box.

5. Click on the Suggest tab and select Start button.

6. Click on Part Fill Analysis and click on the Start button to generate the Results.

7. Click on Core/Cavity icon to open up other features.

8. Click on Gate Location click on outer rim of the part and type 0.125 for the value.

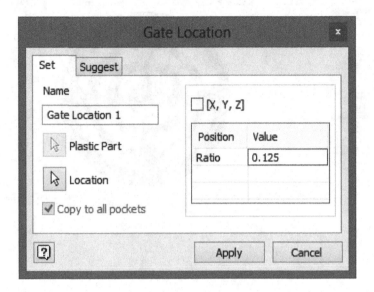

Gate Location

9. Click on Apply and Done button to exit.

10. When finished expand the plus sign by Results and double-click on *Confidence of fill*.

11. Study the graph and the values.

12. Double-click on Fill time, expand the arrow under Tools from Core/Cavity tab and select Animate Results.

13. Click on the Play button and observe how the mold get filled.

14. Double-click on *Quality prediction* and make changes to portions with coloration and run the analysis again.

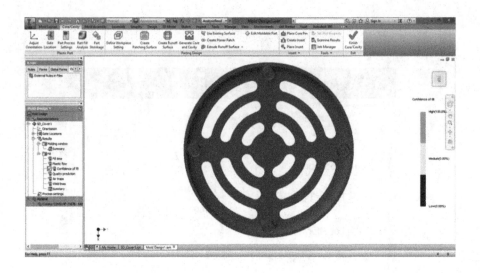

Mold Part

Create Mold Design

Plastic Mold Setup:

1. Start a new part click on the Mold Folder, select Mold Design.iam and click on Create button.

2. Click on Plastic Part, search for the part just created and open, click on top of the graphics area.

3. Select Adjust Orientation icon, double-click inside the cavity to orient the arrows perpendicular to the flat edge and click on OK button.

4. Click on Select Material select a Manufacturer and the Trade name.

5. Click o OK button when finished.

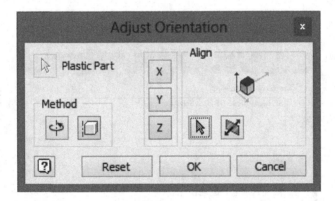

Adjust Orientation

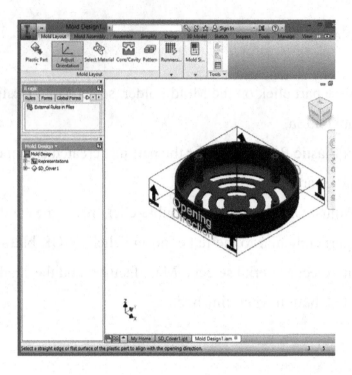

Notice Arrow Direction

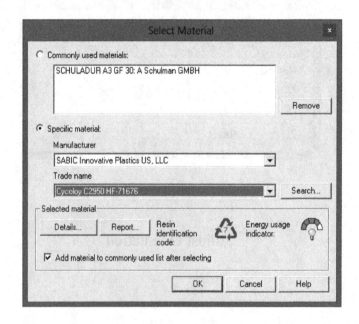

Material dialogue box

Core & Cavity

1. Click on Core/Cavity icon and click on Define WorkPiece Setting.

2. This action should place a rectangular block around the part that could also be adjusted.

3. Make the necessary changes to XYZ_Total and click on OK button.

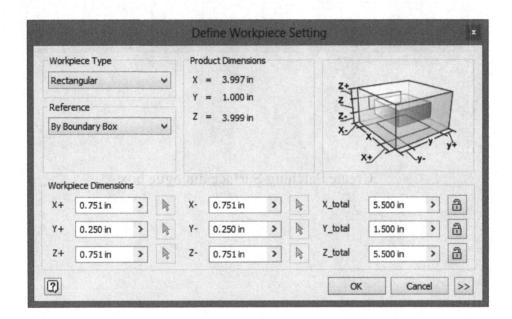

Define Workpiece Setting

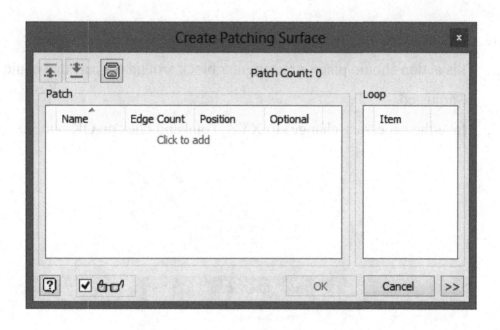

Create Patching Surface dialogue box

Patching Surfaces

1. Click on Create Patching Surface icon, select Auto Detect icon and click on OK button.

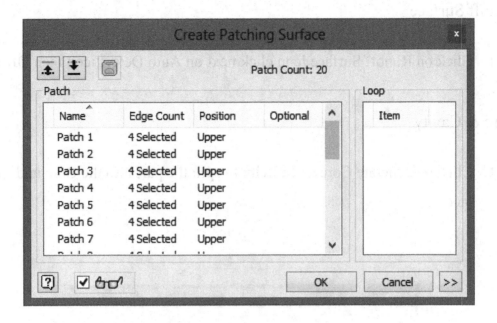

Create Patching Surface

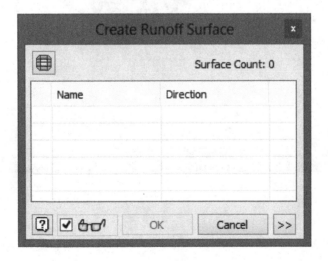

Runoff Surface

Runoff Surface

1. Click on Runoff Surface icon click next on Auto Detect icon then OK button.

Core & Cavity

1. Click on generate Core and Cavity to split the part into the Core and Cavity pieces.

Core & Cavity

Gate Location

1. Click on Gate Location icon and click on the edge of the opening end.

2. Change the Value of the Gate Location to 0.5 and click on Apply and Done button to exit.

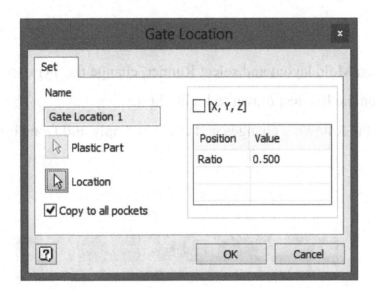

Gate Location

Manual Sketch

1. Click on Manual Sketch and click on the Front Surface of the part.

2. Click on OK button and Project Geometry on the outer rim of the part.

3. Using the line tool place a 0.25 inch line and exit the sketch.

Runner

1. Click on Mold layout and select Runner, change the Type to Semicircle and click on the line just drawn to highlight it.

2. Make the following changes and click on Apply and Done button.

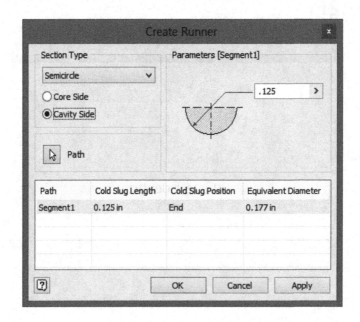

Create Runner

Gate

1. Click on Gate icon click on the gate point then the endpoint of the line.

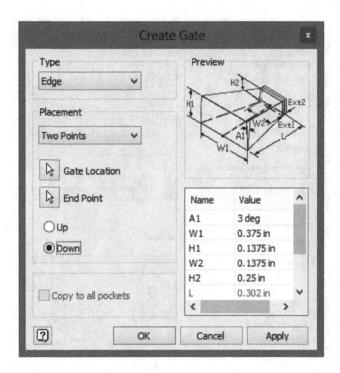

Create Gate

Mold Base

1. Click on Mold Assembly tab and select Mold Base to open up a dialogue box.
2. Accept the system selection click on the arrow by Placement Reference and click on the corner point of the part.

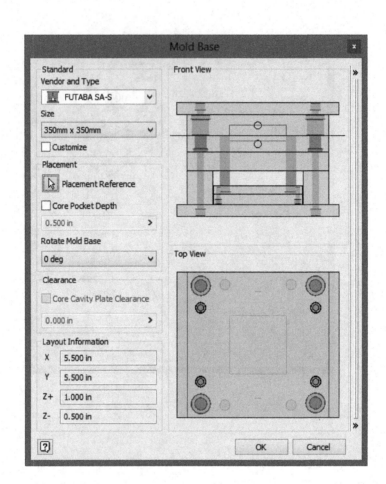

Mold Base Dialogue box

423

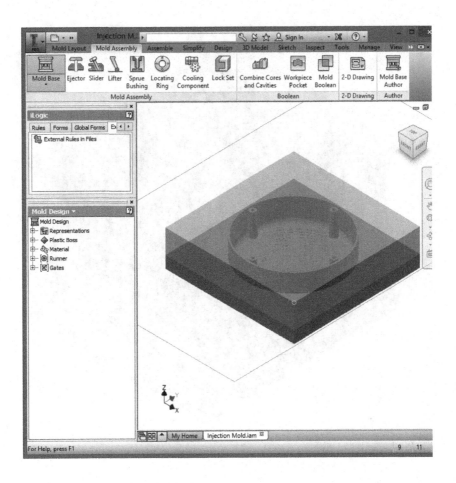

Selected Point

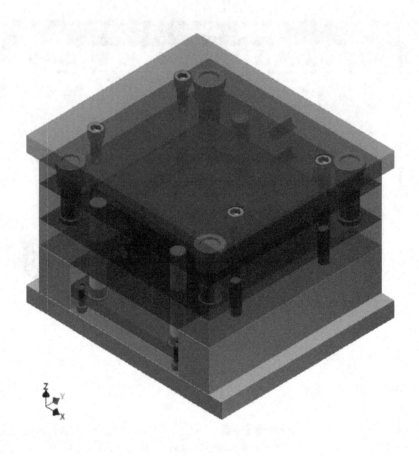

Mold Base Design

Ejector

1. Under the Mold assembly tab select the Ejector icon to bring up a dialogue box.

2. Using the Place Ejectors arrow click on 5 different spots on the part and click on Apply button.

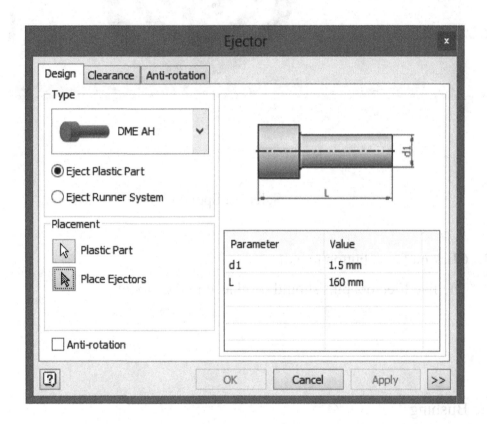

Ejector dialogue box

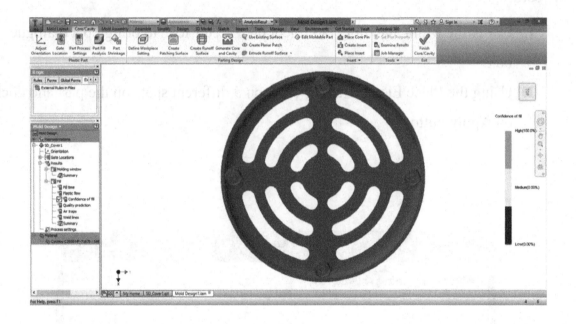

Selected Spots

3. Click on Done button to exit.

4. The five Ejectors pins should be placed in the model.

Sprue Bushing

1. Select the Sprue Bushing icon to open up a dialogue box.

2. Click on the arrow and click on top of the part.

3. Click on OK button to exit.

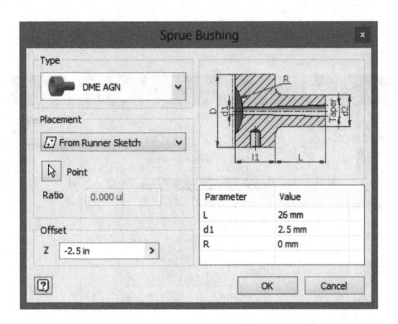

Sprue Bushing

Locating Ring

1. Click on Locating ring make the following changes and click on OK button.

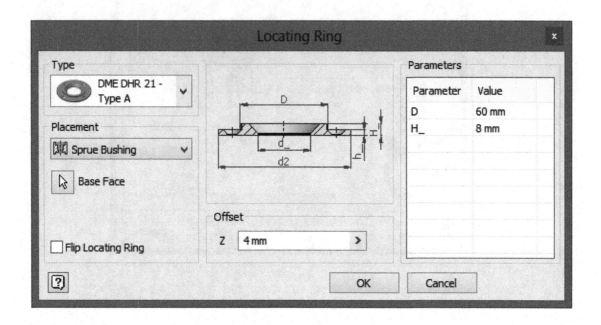

Locating Ring

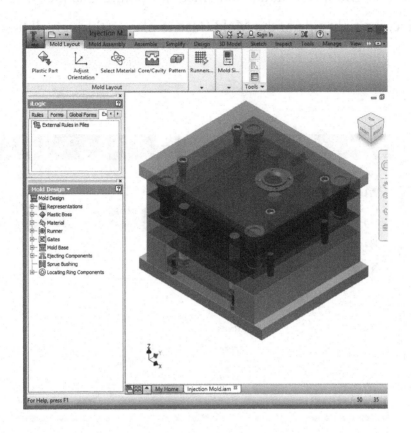

Locating Ring on top of Mold Base

Cooling Channel

1. Select the Mold Layout tab and click on Cooling Channel.

2. Select the right side of the Mold Base to place a through all tube.

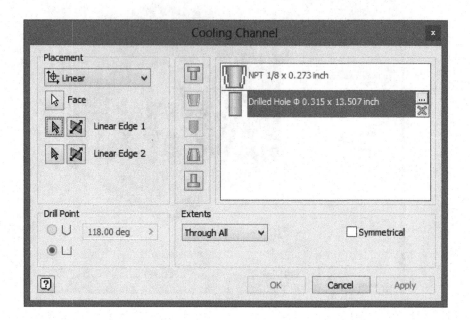

Cooling Channel dialogue box

3. Click on the face of the right side of the Base mold, click the vertical and the horizontal edges and make changes to the distances.

4. Click on Apply button to place the channel and click on the adjacent side to add two more channels one after the other.

5. Remember to edit the distances and click on Apply button each time.

6. Select Done button when finished.

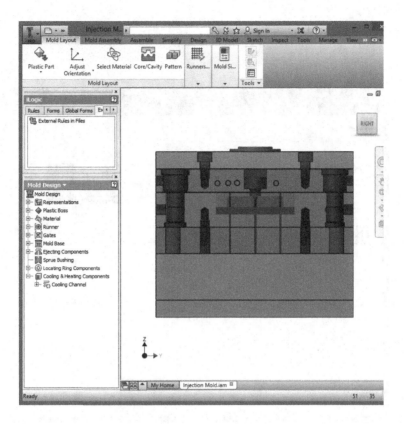

Model with four cooling channels

Cooling Component

1. Click on Cooling Component to open up a dialogue box.
2. Select the arrow by cylindrical Edge and click on each of the eight cooling channel, to place fittings at the ends.
3. Click on Apply button each time and click on the Done button when finished.

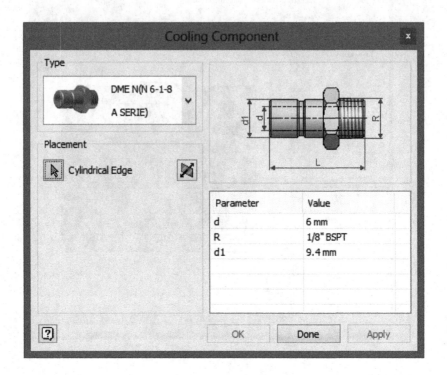

Cooling Component

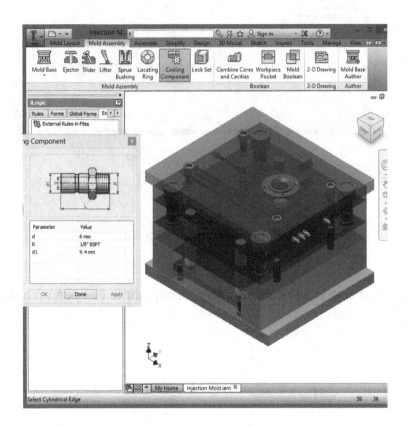

Fittings at ends of cooling channel tubes

2D Drawing

1. From the Mold Assembly tab select the 2-D Drawing icon.
2. Click on Filter symbol and make a selection with views needed to be displayed.

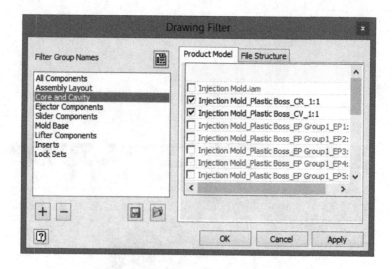

Drawing Filter

3. Click on the icon adjacent to Filter Group name to open up a drawing settings.

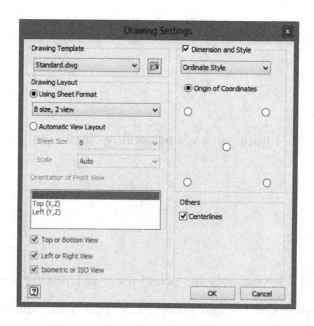

Drawing Settings

4. Place a check mark in the text box by Select All under 2-D Drawing dialogue box and click on Apply button.

5. The system will automatically generate all drawings including B.O.M.

6. Move to individual drawing sheet and resize drawings and add omitted dimensions.

7. Save the drawing sheet.

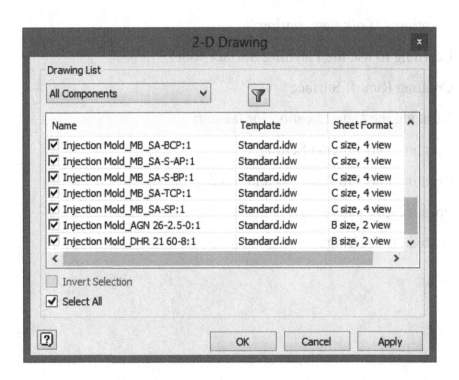

2-D Drawing

Summary

The student/designer went through a process of:

- Creating a new plastic part and adding features.
- Using the Lip tool to add lips to the part.
- Creating grill on the cover
- Using the Plastic Boss feature to add parts
- Starting the Mold assembly and bringing in the part
- Learning to re-orient the part
- Adding Material
- Adding Core and Cavity to the part
- Creating a Workpiece setting
- Learning to use the Patching Surface tool
- Creating Runoff Surface
- Utilizing the Gate Location for the part
- Creating Part Process Setting
- Creating Part Fill Analysis and finally
- Producing Results study.
- Added 2D drawings

Chapter X

After completing this session the student/designer will be able to:

- Convert 2D sketches into 3D Models
- Assemble the parts and adding material
- Use one of the parts in starting stress analysis
- Create new simulation
- Add Pin Constraint
- Learn of Radial; Axial and tangential constraints
- Utilize the mesh setup tool
- Use Bearing Constraint
- Learn about Convergence settings
- Setup the Safety Factor
- Study the Von Mises; 1st Principal and 3rd Principal stresses
- Create Configuration and the Parametric tables

1. Start a new part on YZ Plane and create the sketch shown.

2. Add a thickness of 0.125 inches using extrude boss and save as Arm.

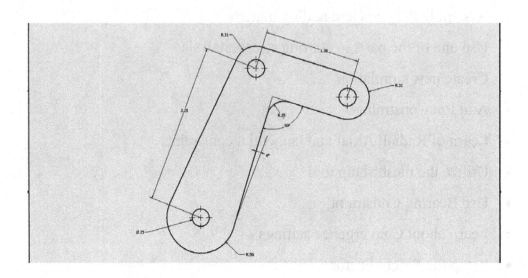

Sketch Outline

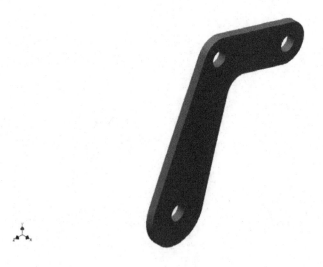

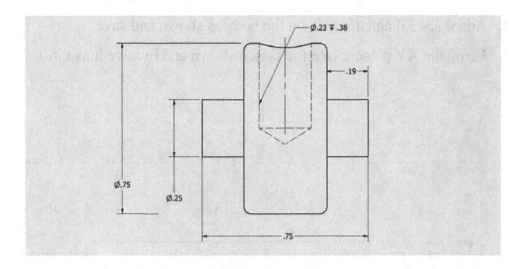

Hinge A

3. Using the XY plane create half of the sketch shown horizontally and turn it into a 3D model using the Revolve feature.

Revolved Hinge

4. Add 0.2343 diametric hole on the body as shown and save.

5. Using the XY plane create the sketch shown and revolve it as Pin 1.

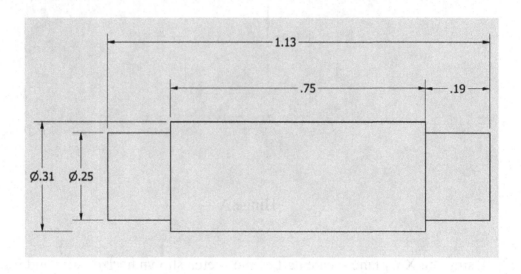

Pin 1 Sketch

Pin 1

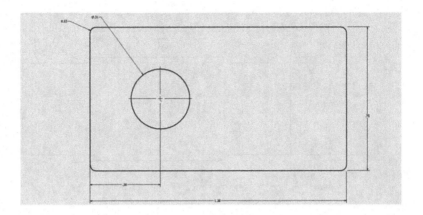

Grip Sketch

6. Using the YZ plane create the sketch shown and add a depth of 0.250 using the Extrude feature.

Grip Model

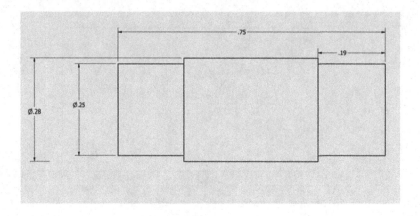

Pin 2 Sketch

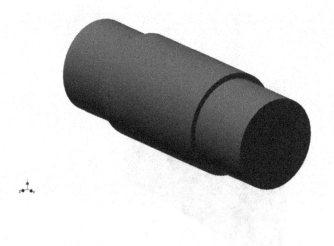

Pin 2

7. Using the XY plane create half of the sketch shown and revolve it as Pin 3.

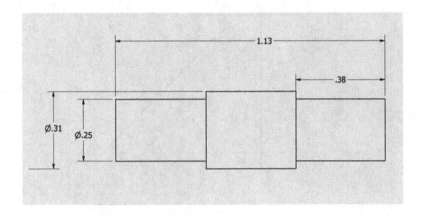

Pin 3

Pin 3

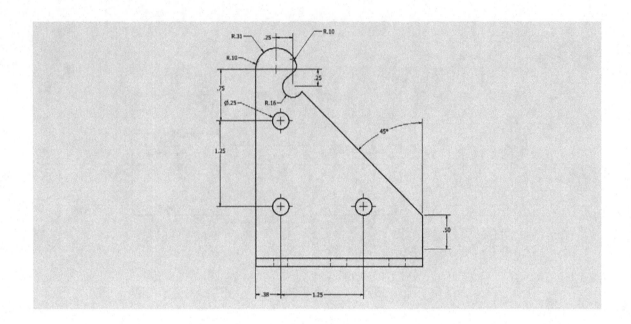

Support Sketch

8. Use the outline to create the Support with 0.125 thickness.

Right Support

Left Support

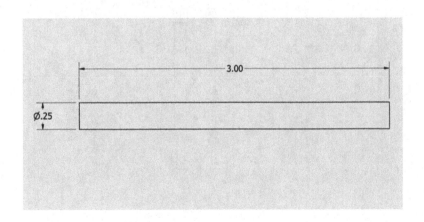

Handle Sketch

Handle

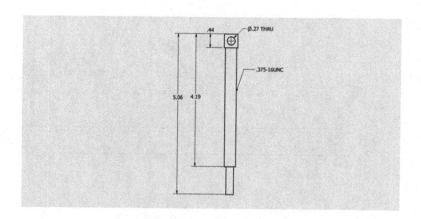

Shaft Sketch

9. Create the sketch shown and revolve to form the shaft.

Shaft

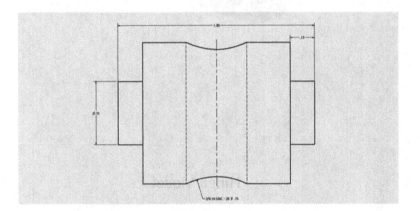

Hinge Sketch

10. Draw half of the sketch shown and revolve to form the Hinge.

448

Hinge Model

Assemble of Parts

1. Open a new Assembly and bring in the Support as the base model.

2. Bring the rest of the parts one at a time and add constraints as shown in the final assembly.

Hold-Down Clamp

3. Insert the Pins then the arm lining it with the pins as shown.

4. Complete the assembly as shown and save the model.

Stress Analysis

1. Right-click on the Arm from the assembly and select open to place it in a separate window.
2. Click on the Environment tab and select *Stress Analysis* icon.
3. Expand the arrow under Manage icon and click on *Create New Simulation* to open up a dialogue box.

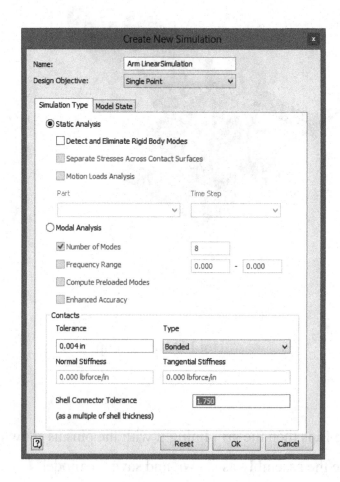

New Simulation dialogue box

4. Type in a new name for the simulation and click on OK button.

5. The Stress Analysis features should open up under the Browser.

6. Right-click on Material and select Assign Material.

7. Expand the arrow under Override Material and select the required material, in this case Steel.

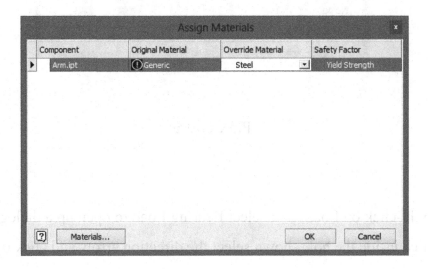

Material dialogue box

8. Click on OK button to exit.

9. Right-click on Constraints and select *Pin Constraint*.

10. The *pin* constraints the Radial, Axial and Tangential.

11. Uncheck the Fixed Tangential constraint, click inside the two end holes and click on Apply button each time.

12. Excluding the Tangential constraint, allows the hole to rotate about the axis.

13. Click on Cancel when finished.

Pin Constraint

14. Right-click on Loads and select Bearing Load to open up a dialogue box.

15. Click inside the hole shown select the direction arrow and click on the flat edge of the part to change direction of the arrow.

16. Type in a load by Magnitude of 150 lb. and click on Apply and Cancel buttons.

17. High concentration of stress in the hole itself should be exhibited using the bearing load.

18. The Contact primarily is used in an Assembly and would be overlooked in this analysis.

19. Right-click on Mesh and select Mesh View to mesh the part..

20. Click on Simulate icon when the mesh is done and click on Run.

Bearing Constraint

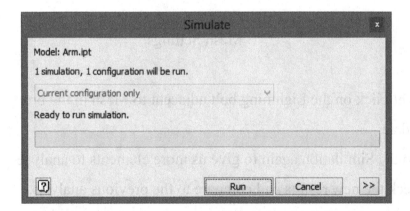

Simulation dialogue box

Mesh Settings

1. Expand the arrow under Mesh and select Mesh Settings to open up a dialogue box.

2. Change the Average Element Size to 0.050 and click on OK button.

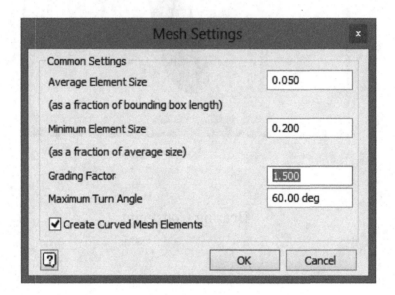

Mesh Settings

3. Right-click on the Lightning bolt adjacent to Mesh in the browser and select Update.

4. Run the Simulation again to give us more elements to analyze.

5. Check the new results and compare to the previous analysis.

6. Next expand the arrow under Mesh tab and select Local, which allows certain areas to be manually selected.

7. Click inside the red spots inside and outside the hole and change the size to 0.025.

8. Right-click on Lightning by Mesh and select Update.

9. Right-click on the Graphics area and select Simulation and click on Run button.

10. The local produces a highly accurate results.

Local Mesh and Simulation

Convergence Settings:

1. Right-click on the Arm Linear Simulation icon under the Browser and create a copy.

2. Rename it as Convergence Settings, expand the plus sign by Mesh and the Local Mesh Control folder and delete the Local Mesh.

3. Right-click on Mesh and select Mesh View, expand the arrow under Mesh on the Ribbon and select Convergence Settings.

4. Make changes to the values as shown and click on OK button and Yes.

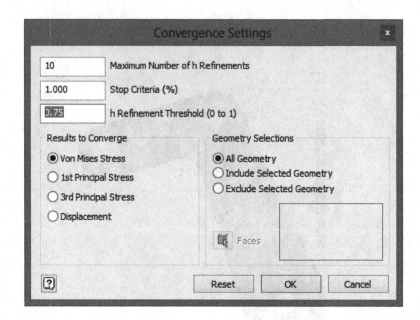

Convergence Settings

5. Run the Simulation again and click on convergence settings result plot.

6. Looking at the graph one will observe that, the study was run several times and more elements were added in the process.

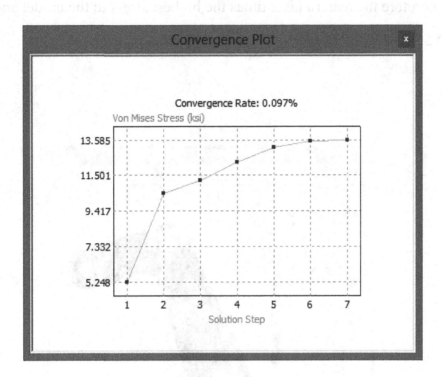

Convergence Plot

7. Expand the arrow under the Display tab on the Ribbon and select Maximum Value, to show the highest concentration of stress on the part.

Safety Factor

1. This is used to determine whether or not the material will fail, and the safety factor plot determines the right material choice.
2. Double-click on Safety Factor under Results under the browser and notice the value in the legend.

458

3. The minimum safety factor in the legend is 2.21 meaning the yield strength of the material being used is 2.21 in the model.

4. Therefore the material is 2 times the highest stress in the model and the part is good and will not fail.

Safety Factor

Von Mises Stress

1. This type of stress works well with ductile material and it is always positive.

2. Expand the plus sign under Results in the browser and double-click on Von Mises Stress, to view the stresses in the holes.

1st Principal Stress

1. This type demonstrates the stress under tension and uses brittle material for better results.
2. Stresses produced in the 1st Principal are also positive.
3. Double-click on 1st Principal Stress to color change and stresses.

3rd Principal Stress

1. This type demonstrates the stress under compression.
2. It is normally used in assembly of parts to enable contact pressure
3. Stresses produced in the 3rd Principal have negative values.
4. Double-click on 3rd Principal Stress to color change and stresses.

Configuration

1. Expand the arrow under Manage and select Parametric Table to open up at the bottom of the screen.
2. Right-click on the new copy and select Edit Simulation Properties.
3. Expand the arrow adjacent to Design Objective and select Parametric Dimension and click on OK button.
4. Right-click on the part in the browser and select Show Parameters.

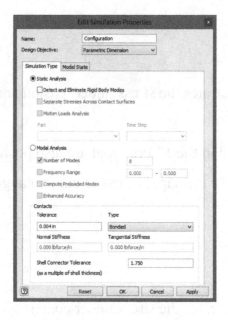

Edit Simulation Properties

		Parameter Name	Unit	Equation	Nominal Value
▶	⊟ Model Parameters				
	☑	Hole	in	0.25 in	0.250
	☑	Small_Rad	in	0.3125 in	0.313
	☐	Fillet	in	0.25 in	0.250
	☐	Offset_Angle	deg	4 deg	4.00
	☑	d5	in	Small_Rad	0.313
	☐	Hol_To_Hole	in	2.25 in	2.250
	☐	Top_Hole_Dist	in	1.375 in	1.375
	☐	Angel	deg	90 deg	90.00
	☑	Large_Rad	in	0.5 in	0.500
	☑	Thickness	in	0.125 in	0.125
	☐	d12	deg	0.0 deg	0.00
		sa_0	lbforce	150 lbforce	150.000

Select Parameters

5. Place check marks in the required dimensioning and click on OK button to populate the Parametric Table.

6. Add different dimensions for the thickness of the part by typing values next to the 0.25.

Parametric Table

5. Next right-click on the table and click on Generate All Configuration.

6. Right-click in the text box under constraint name and select Add Design Constraint.

7. Click on Mass and then the OK button.

8. Repeat for the Von Mises Stress and the Safety Factor.

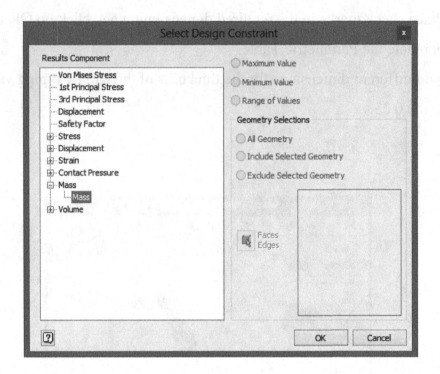

Select Design Constraint

7. Expand the arrow under Constraint Type and select Upper Limit.

8. Type the number 300 in the next text box under Limit, select Von Mises Stress and set to upper limit 150.

9. Make the Safety Upper Limit as 2.

10. Right-click on the graphics area select Simulate and click on Run button.

11. After selecting the required configuration to use, right-click on the Parametric Table and select Promote Configuration to Model.

Summary

In this tutorial, the student/designer worked on various features including:

- Converting 2D sketches into 3D Models
- Assembling the parts and adding material
- Using one of the parts in starting stress analysis
- Creating new simulation
- Adding Pin Constraint
- Learning of Radial; Axial and tangential constraints
- Utilizing the mesh setup tool
- Using Bearing Constraint
- Learning about Convergence settings
- The Safety Factor
- Von Mises; 1st Principal and 3rd Principal stresses
- Configuration and the Parametric tables

Chapter XI

The following tutorials will cover different but very necessary topics.

- Electrical Wiring
- Cable and Harness
- Adaptive Spring
- Using Work Planes
- Creating Bearing
- Creating a Shaft
- Creating Worm Gear
- Designing Spur Gear
- Designing Bevel Gear
- Creating Involute Spline
- Furniture Design
- Presentation

Electrical Wiring

1. Create a box-like tray on the XZ plane and save it as Cable Tray.
2. Design a 9Pin Female Connector pin and save it in a folder.

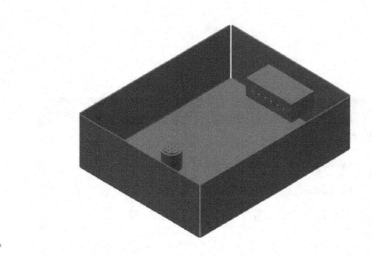

Cable Tray

3. Design a 6 Pin Male Connector and save it.
4. Using the Text option under sketch tools, engrave the side of the 9 Pin Connector with numbers 1 through 9.
5. Engrave the side of the 6 Pin Connector with numbers 1 through 6.
6. Start a new assembly and place the Cable Tray on the graphics area.
7. Bring in the 9 Pin Female Connector and mate it inside the tray.
8. Place the 6 Pin Male Connector and mate it inside the cable tray.

Cable and Harness

1. Double-click on the 9 Pin Connector to enter the Edit mode.

2. Click on the Harness Properties icon under Model to display the connector pin properties.

3. Enter the letter **"U1"** in the text box by RefDes (reference designator) and click on OK.

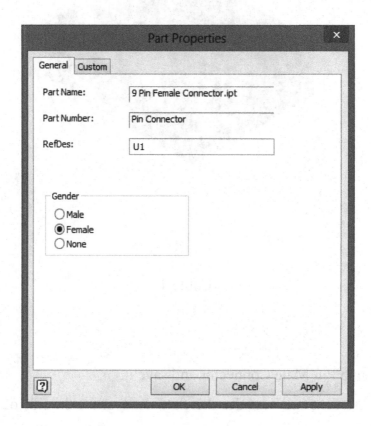

Part Properties

4. Click on Pin icon and click on the circumference of the first hole a point should be place in the center of the hole.

5. Place Pin text box opens up with the number 1 registered in the text box, click on the check mark.

6. Repeat this action for the rest of the holes and click on Return when finished.

7. Double-click on the 6 Pin Connector to enter into edit mode.

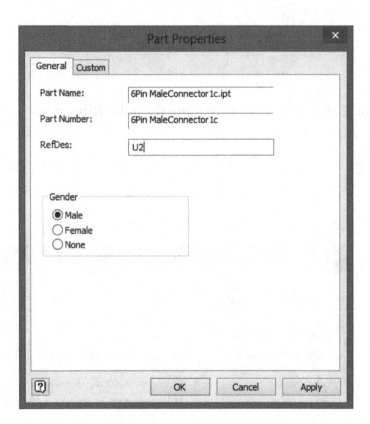

Part Properties

8. Click on the Harness Properties icon under Model to display the connector pin properties.

9. Enter the letter **"U2"** in the text box by RefDes (reference designator) and click on OK.

10. Click on Cable and Harness module from the Ribbon bar and click on OK button.

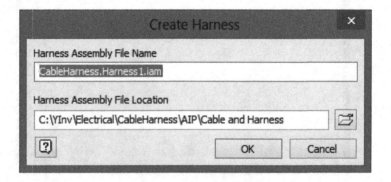

Cable and Harness

11. From the Create Wire dialogue box, select Alpha by Category and 3047-BLK by Name text box.

12. Click on the arrow by Pin 1 and click on number 1 Female Connector then number 1 Male Connector and Apply button.

13. Repeat this for the rest of the five pins from the female to the male and exit.

Create Wire

Create Segment

1. Click on *Create Segment* move to the Female Connector and click on Pin 1.
2. Click on the sides of the Tray to add connecting points and Apply when finished.
3. Select Automatic Route, place a check mark as shown and click on Apply.
4. All wires should be routed through the tube segments.

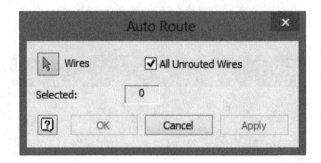

Auto Route

5. Double-click on 6 Pin Male Connector to move to the edit mode, click on Manage tab expand the arrow by Component in Author section and select Connector.
6. Click on the Flat face of the Male Connector to place a pointing arrow away from the face and click on OK button and Return.
7. The wires should be properly arranged.

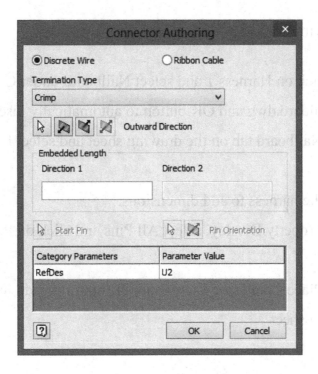

Connecting Authoring

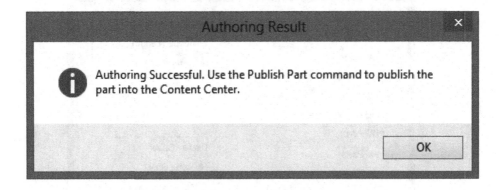

Authoring Results

Nailboard Drawing

1. Double-click on Harness 1 and select Nailboard under Cable and Harness.

2. Select Standard.dwg and OK button to automatically insert the Harness.

3. Click on Nailboard tab on the drawing sheet and select Harness Dimension tool.

4. Click on the harness to add dimensions.

5. Click on Property Display, select All Pins and click on Pin Name and OK button.

6. Click on Place Connector Views and OK button to add images of connectors on drawing sheet.

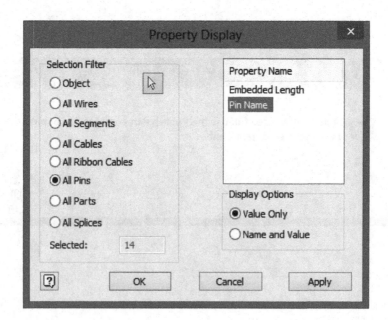

Property Display

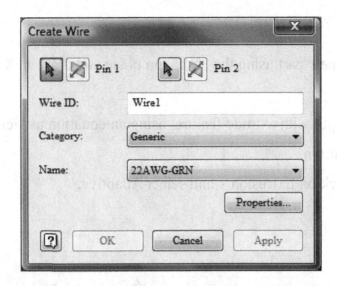

Create Wire dialogue box

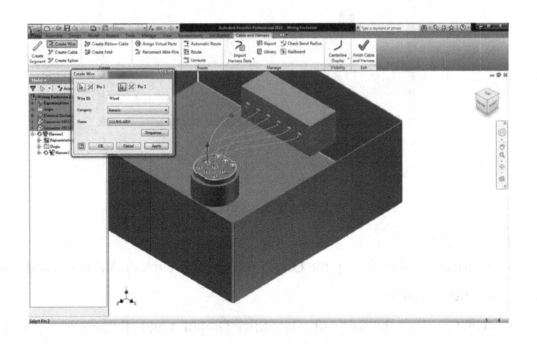

Wiring

Adaptive Spring

1. Create a new part using the "XZ" top plane and draw an 8 inch diametric circle.

2. Add a depth with extrude feature, using an equation as Height = 8 and click on OK button.

3. Right-click on Extrusion 1 and select Adaptive.

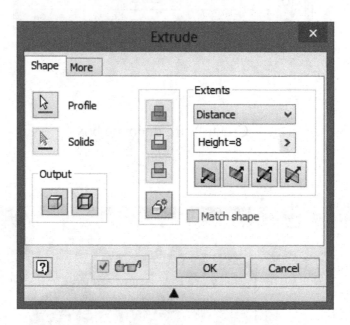

Extrude dialogue box

4. Expand the plus sign by the Origin folder right-click on YZ plane and click on New Sketch.

5. Right-click on the part and select Slice Graphics and click on Project Cut Edges.

6. Place a center line on the origin, create a 0.5 inch circle on the base and make it tangent to the vertical edge.

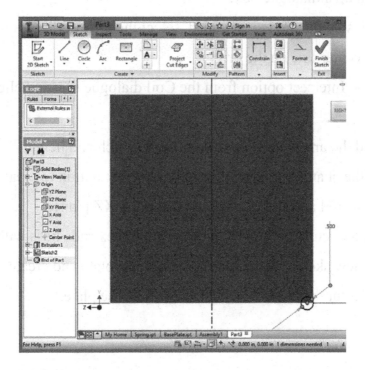

Circle Sketch

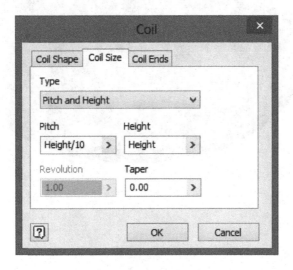

Coil dialogue box

7. Click on the check mark, expand the arrow under sweep icon and select Coil to open up a dialogue box.

8. Click inside the circle just added, select the arrow adjacent to Axis and click on the center line on the origin.

9. Click on Intersect option from the Coil dialogue box and click on Coil Size tab.

10. Expand the arrow under Type and select Pitch and height.

11. Make the changes as shown and click on OK button to create the coil.

12. Save the coil and start a new part using the XZ plane.

13. Create a circular part of 10 in diameter and extrude boss with 0.5 inches.

14. Add a new sketch on the top of the circular plate and create an 8 inch circle.

15. Extrude-cut the circle 0.25 and save it as base plate.

Base Plate

16. Start a new assembly and place two base plates on the graphics area.

17. Mate the two plates with an offset distance of 15.

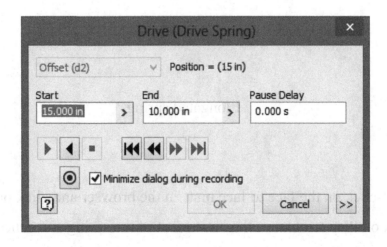

Drive dialogue box

18. Right-click on the face to face mate in the browser and click on Drive.

19. Click on Play to observe the movement and cancel to exit.

20. Place the spring in the assembly, right-click on the spring icon in the Browser and select Adaptive.

21. Mate with the bottom plate first then the top plate and Apply button.

22. The spring should stretch to accommodate the distance between the plates.

Elongated spring

23. Right-click on the face to face mate in the browser and click on Drive.

24. Click on Play to observe the movement of the spring and cancel to exit.

25. Save the assembly.

Using Work Planes

1. Start a new part using the YZ plane and create the outline shown.

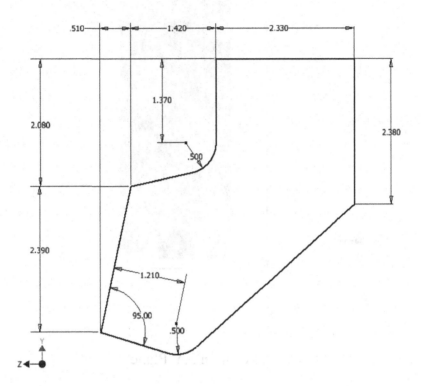

Bar Hinge Sketch

2. Add depth of 2.11 using Extrude feature and symmetric.

3. Right-click on XY plane in the browser and add a new sketch.

4. Create the outline as shown and add all dimensioning.

5. Exit the sketch and click on Extrude Cut and select symmetric option and All under Extents.

6. Click on OK button and save the model.

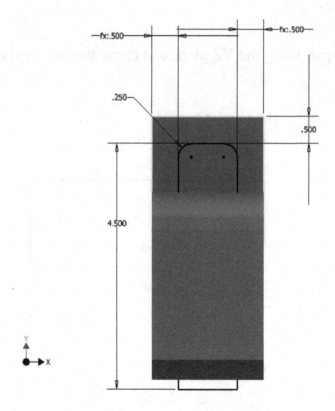

Sketch on XY Plane

Extrude dialogue box

7. Click on the top face of the part add a new sketch and create a 0.375 circle as shown with dimensions.

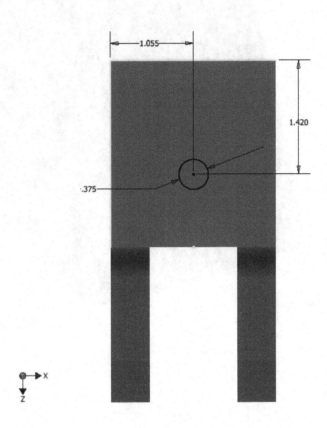

Circle on top face

8. Extrude-cut the circle using 'All' under Extents click on Ok button and save.
9. Right-click on YZ plane add a new sketch and create 0.50 circle as shown.
10. Extrude-cut the circle using 'All' option under Extents with symmetric, click on Ok button and save.

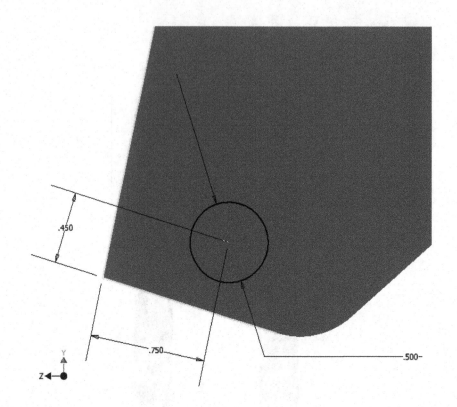

0.5 inch circle

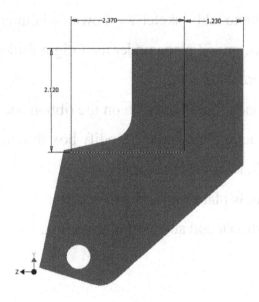

Horizontal Construction Line on Model

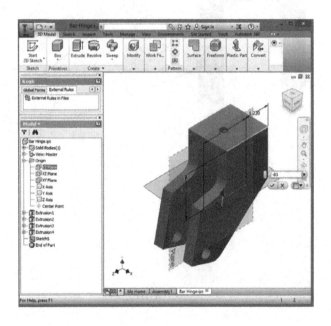

Work Plane

484

11. Click on the right face and add a new sketch.

12. Use construction line to add a sketch as shown and dimension.

13. Exit the sketch, click on YZ plane under the Origin folder in the browser, to highlight it on the graphics area.

14. Expand the arrow under the Plane icon on the ribbon and select Plane.

15. Click on the construction line and the modify box should read 90°.

16. Type in -83° and click on the check mark.

17. Right-click on the new plane and add a new sketch.

18. Create the outline shown and add all dimensioning.

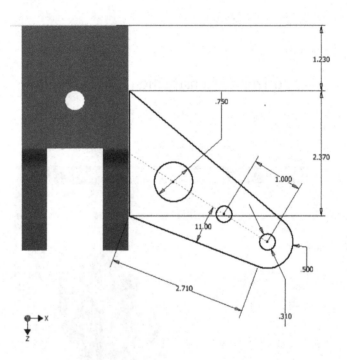

Outline

19. Using Extrude boss, click inside the outline just outside one of the circles and add a depth of 0.125, using Direction 2.

20. Offset a plane 0.435 below the first plane and mirror the part just created using the new plane as the Mirror Plane.

21. Final model is displayed below.

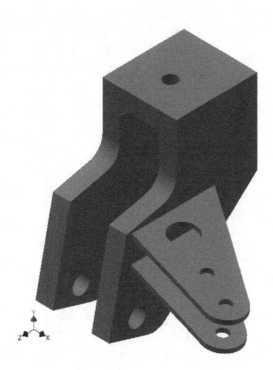

Bar Hinge

Bearing

1. Start a new part using XY plane and create the sketch with all dimensions.

2. Using the revolve feature click inside the two outlines one after the other, use the centerline as axis and click on OK button.

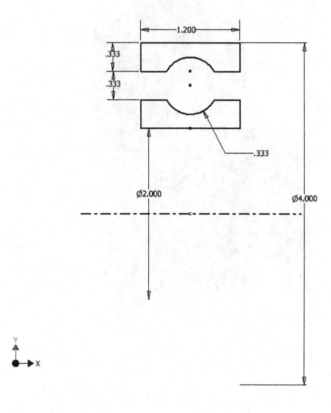

Bearing Sketch

Ball Bearing Sketch

3. Create the sketch as shown and use the revolve feature to turn it into a ball.

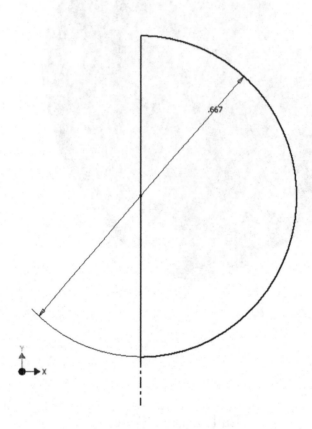

.667

Ball Bearing Sketch

4. Save the ball, open a new assembly file and place the bearing on the graphics area.

Ball Model

5. Place the ball to the side of the bearing and use Tangential Constraint to mate the ball inside the bearing.

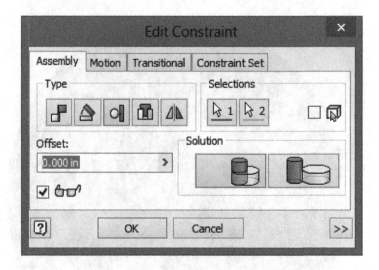

Tangential Constraint

Ball Bearing Model

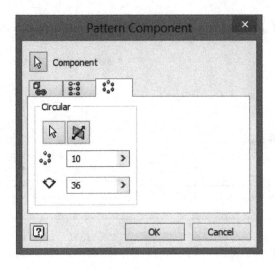

Pattern Component

6. Click and drag a ball and it should start a moving inside the bearing.

7. Save the assembly.

Shaft

1. Using the XY plane create the sketch shown and revolve to form a shaft.

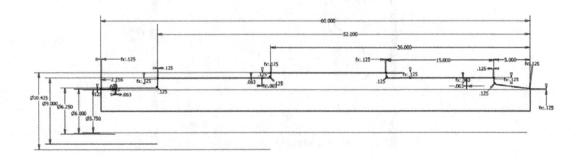

Shaft Outline

2. Add fillet radius of 0.125 and chamfer of 0.125 x 45° and save the model.

Model of a Shaft

There is a built-in program in the assembly that generates a shaft with data entries. The next steps will guide the student/designer to create a shaft using the shaft generator in Design Features.

1. Start a new assembly file and click on the Design tab and select Shaft symbol.
2. The Design Accelerator should open up, click on the OK button to save the model. And click on the graphics area.
3. From the Shaft Component Generator that opens up, enter the required data and click on the OK button.

494

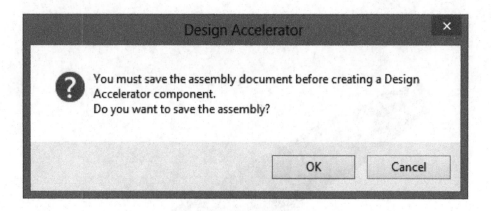

Design Accelerator

Shaft Component Generator

4. When a row in the Shaft Component Generator is highlighted the section of the shaft related is also highlighted.

5. Click on Section Properties which is the three dots at the end of the row, to open up a dialogue box to edit the data.

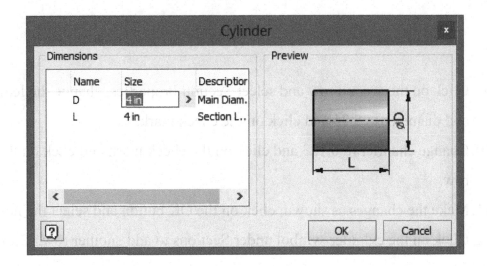

Dialogue box

6. Change the length to 4 inches and diameter to 4 inches and click on OK button.

7. Expand the arrow by the triangular symbol and click on chamfer symbol.

8. Change the distance value to 0.125 and click on the check mark.

9. Click on the second row and select Section Properties, change the length to 8 and diameter to 5.25 and click on the check mark.

10. Change chamfer to 0.125 and click on the check mark and click on the next row.

11. Make the changes as shown, click on the OK button and select the next row.

12. Click on the cylinder symbol under Sections to add another row.

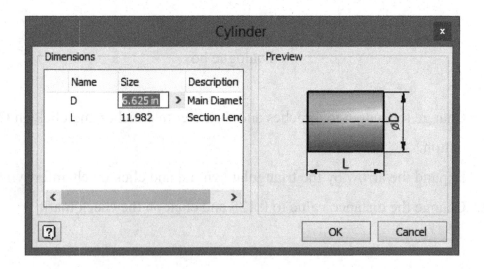

Cylinder

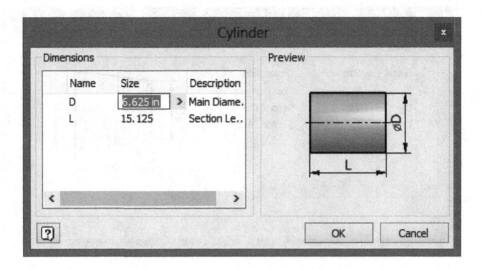

Cylinder

13. Click on Section Properties and make the changes shown and click on the
check mark.

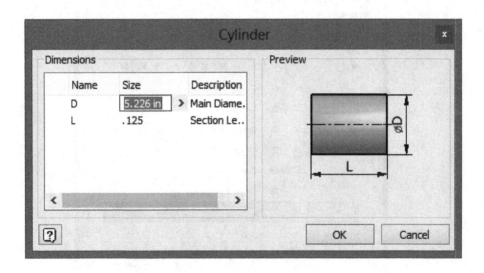

Cylinder

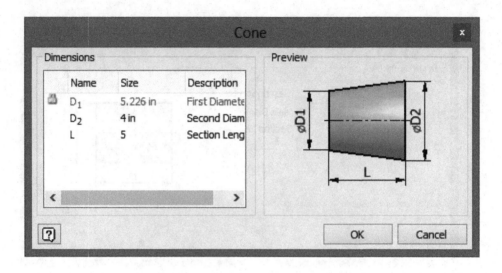

Cone dialogue box

Shaft Component Generator

Model of Shaft

Worm Gears:-

Worm gears are used in various machines to reduce speed and increase power. Uses include the ones found in clocks, double bass string instrument, rolling mills, convey belts and rotary tables.

This session will guide the student/designer in creating a worm as well as a gear.

1. Start a new part in the XY plane, create the sketch shown and revolve it to form the base model.

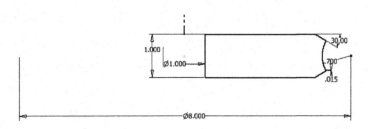

Worm Gear Sketch

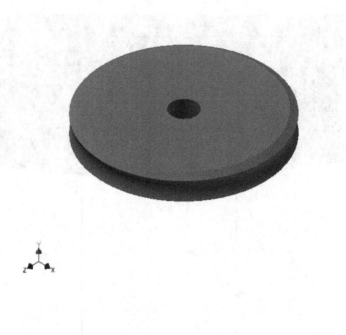

Revolved Sketch

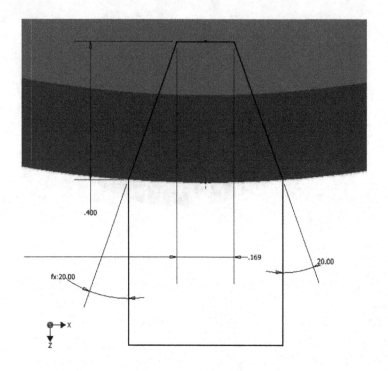

Tooth Sketch

2. Click on the top face of the model and create the tooth sketch as shown.

3. Use the Cut Extrude feature to add a cut with the tooth sketch.

4. Use the Circular Pattern to add 40 teeth to the model.

Worm Gear

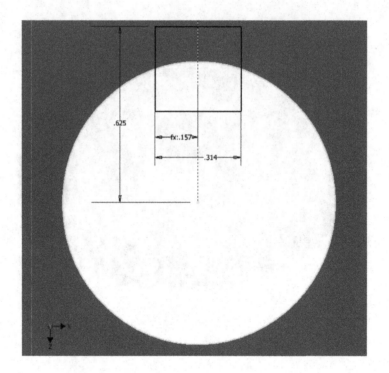

Key Sketch

5. Create the outline shown and use Extrude-cut to remove excess part to form the Key hole.

Model with keyhole

Worm Design

1. Start a new Part on XY plane and create the sketch shown.

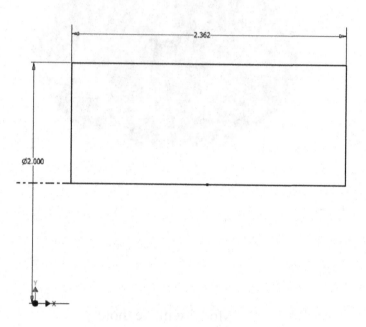

Worm Sketch

2. Use the Revolve feature to turn the sketch into a cylindrical part.

3. Expand the plus sign by Origin folder in the browser and select XY plane.

4. Start a new sketch create the sketch shown and use revolve feature to turn it into a worm.

5. Expand the arrow under Planes, select Axis and click on the body of the cylinder.

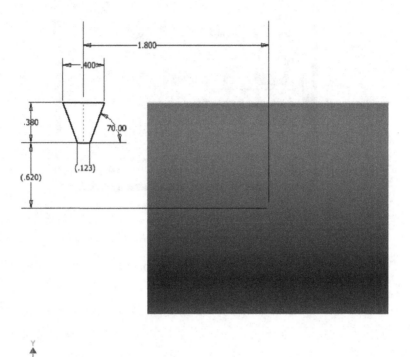

Tooth Sketch

6. Expand the arrow under sweep and select the Coil feature.

7. Click on the Axis in the center of the cylinder and select the Cut option.

8. Click on the Coil Size tab, make the changes in the Coil dialogue box and click on OK button.

508

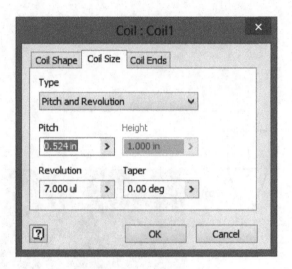

Coil dialogue box

Worm Model

Simulation

1. Start a new assembly file and place the worm on the graphics area and uncheck grounded.

2. Place the Worm Gear on in the assembly and mate it with the worm tangentially.

3. Right-click on the assembly in the browser and select Collapse All.

4. Right-click on the Worm Gear and select check Enabled.

5. Expand the plus sign by Origin folder in the browser and click on X Axis.

6. Add a Constraint with the X Axis of the worm with that of the origin X Axis and click on OK button.

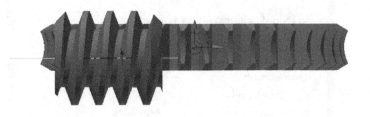

Aligned Worm and Gear

7. Apply another Constraint with the Center Point of the assembly and the Center Point of the worm.

8. Add a Mate Constraint between the XZ Plane of the Worm Gear and XZ Plane of the Assembly.

9. Add a Directed Angle Constraint to the XZ plane of the Origin and XZ Plane of the Worm.

10. Change to Modeling view from Assembly view in the browser expand the plus sign by Relationships in the Browser and right-click on Angle and click on Drive.

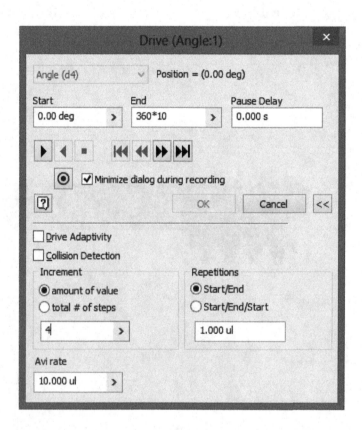

Drive Angle dialogue box

11. Enter 360*10 in the text box under End, expand the double arrow at the bottom right of the dialogue box and make the changes as shown.

12. Click on the Play button and watch how the Worm Gear functions.

13. Save the Model and exit.

Version II

Inventor has a built-in Worm Gear generator accessed through the Assembly files. After collecting all necessary data required to build a worm gear, select a new assembly file and use Design to create a model. The following steps will guide the student/designer as to how to create a worm gear assembly.

1. Start a new assembly file, click on the Design tab on the Ribbon, expand the arrow under Spur Gear and select Worm Gear.

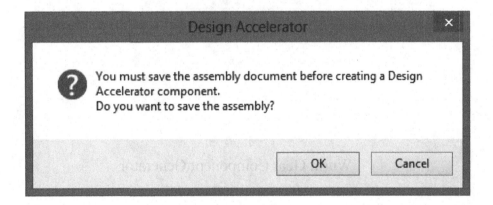

Design Accelerator

2. The Design Accelerator opens up requesting the user to first save the project, click on OK button and save as Worm Gear.

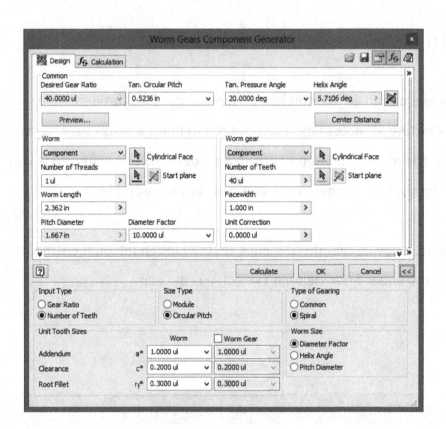

Worm Gear Component Generator

3. Expand the double-arrow to the bottom right of the dialogue box and study all data entries.

4. Click on the Calculation tab and go through the Default settings.

5. Click 2 times on the OK button when finished to accept the given data and click on the graphics area to place copies of a Worm and Gear.

6. Go through the Simulation process as outlined at the beginning of this session and save the model again.

Worm & Gear

Spur Gear: -

Designed to transmit motion and power between parallel shafts, the two meshing gears rotate in opposite direction to create the required results. Uses include but not limited to different kinds of parts and machines, that include clock windup, conveyers as well as washing machine. Other uses include that of the gear box in automobiles, steel mills as well as power plants.

Materials such as steel, aluminum, plastic and brass are usually used in the manufacture of Spur Gears. Refer to an Engineering book to read on advantages and the disadvantages of using spur gear.

1. Start a new assembly file, select the Design tab and click on Spur Gear.

2. Click on the OK tab on the Design Accelerator to open up the Save As folders.

3. Type in a name and click on save to open up Spur Gear Component Generator.

Design Accelerator

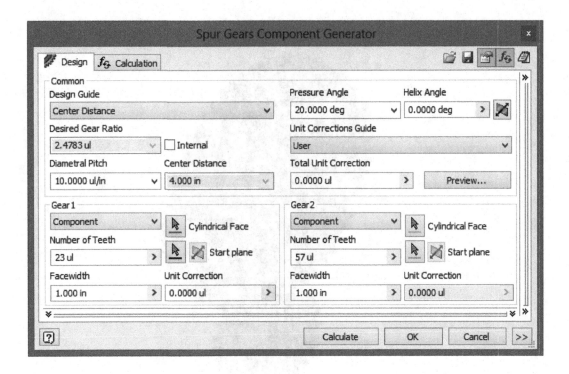

Spur Gear Component Generator

4. Click on OK button twice, to accept the Default settings and click on the graphics area to place the spur gear assembly.

5. Save the model.

Spur Gears

Designing Spur Gear

1. Start a new Part drawing in the XY plane and create Ø2.50 inch diametrical circle.

2. Add depth of 1 inch using Extrude boss and save the part.

3. Add a new sketch on the XY plane and create the tooth outline shown on the part.

4. Use Extrude-Cut to remove the space between the tooth.

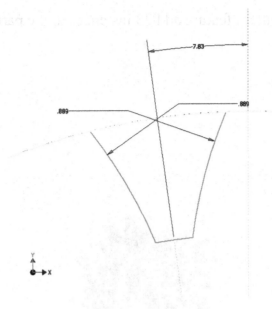

Tooth Profile

5. Using Circular Pattern feature add 23 instances to the part to form the gear.

Spur Gear A

6. Add a new sketch on XY plane and create hole with a keyway as shown.
7. Use Extrude-Cut to remove the inside part to form the Hub with keyway.

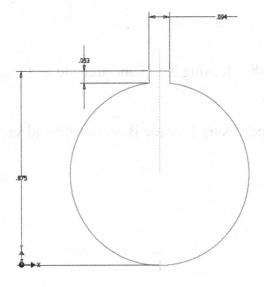

Spur Gear Hub Sketch

Spur Gear with Hub

Spur Gear B

1. Start a new part sketch using XY plane and add an Ø5.29 circular sketch on the graphics area.

2. Add depth of 1 inch using Extrude Boss feature and save the part.

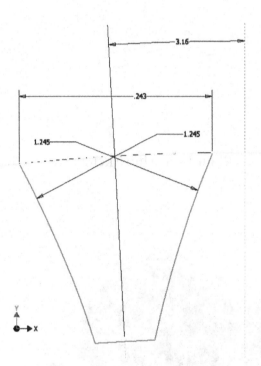

Tooth Sketch

3. Add 57 instances with the tooth using the circular pattern feature.

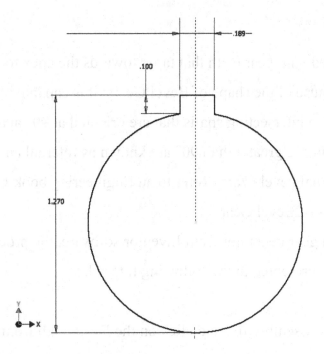

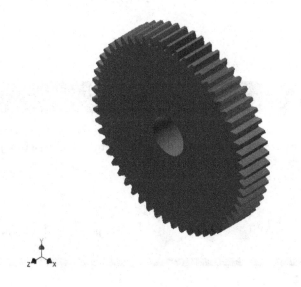

Spur Gear with Hub

Bevel Gear: -

These are designed with gear teeth that taper towards the apex to form a conical-shaped gear. Because of the shape of Bevel Gears, it is capable of transmitting power between two intersecting shafts that are oriented at 90° apart. Customized gears with pitch angles greater than 90° are known as Internal and that less than 90° classified as external bevel gears. Refer to an Engineering book for the advantages and disadvantages of Bevel Gear.

Using the built-in gear generator from Inventor software, the process of designing a bevel gear will be presented in the following tutorial.

1. Start a new assembly file and click on the Design tab from the Ribbon.
2. Expand the arrow under Spur Gear and select Bevel and click on OK button to open up Save As folders.
3. Type a new name for the Bevel Gear and click on Save to open up the Bevel Gears Component Generator dialogue box.

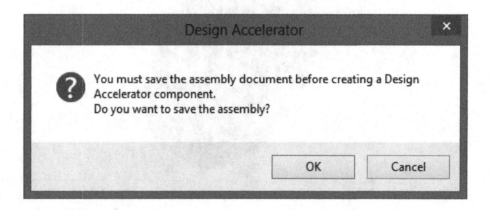

Design Accelerator

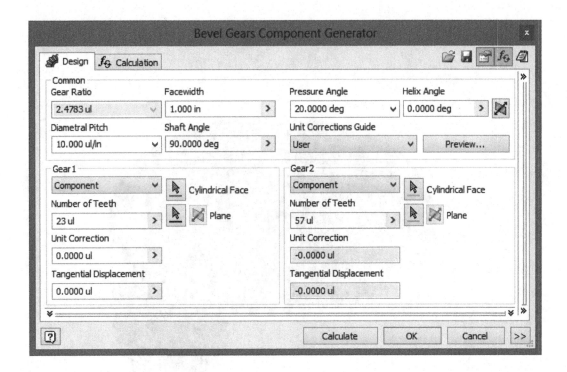

Bevel Gears Component Generator dialogue box.

4. Study all data in the dialogue box and click on OK button twice to generate the gear.

5. Click on the graphics area to place an assembled Bevel Gear using the default settings.

6. Save the assembly.

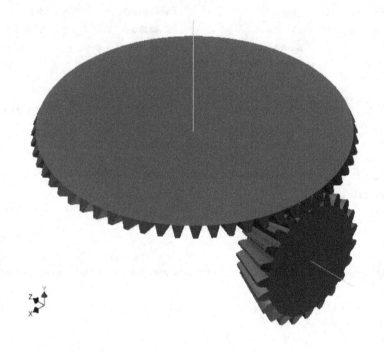

Bevel Gear assembly

Designing from Scratch

1. Start a new part on the XY plane and create the outline shown with all dimensions.
2. Use the revolve feature to turn it into a solid model and save the part.

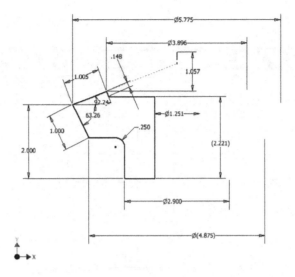

Bevel Gear Sketch

Revolved Part

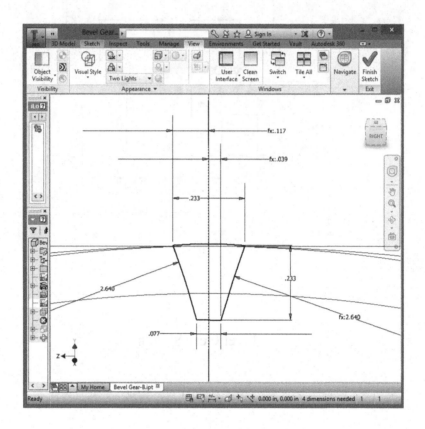

3. Use *Tangent to Surface through Point* option to add a plane on the outer body.

4. Add a new sketch to the plane and create the outline shown with all dimensions.

5. Offset the plane at a distance of 1 inch and add a new sketch.

6. Create the outline shown below and exit the sketch.

7. Use Loft-Cut to create a tooth and the circular pattern to add 57 copies to the model.

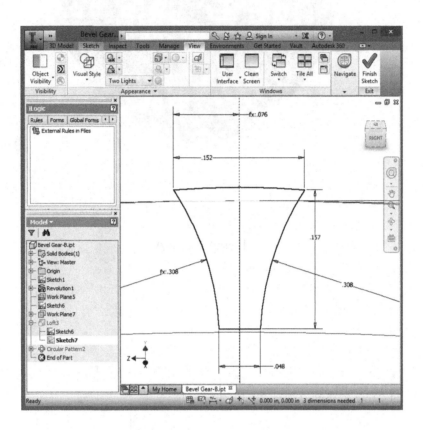

Tooth Profile

528

Bevel Gear-A

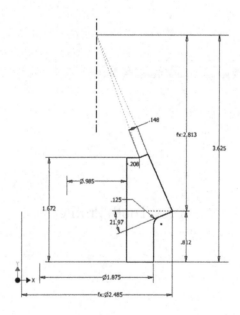

Bevel Gear Sketch

Revolved Part

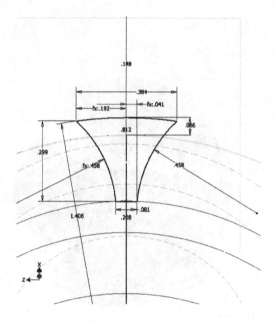

Tooth Profile-A

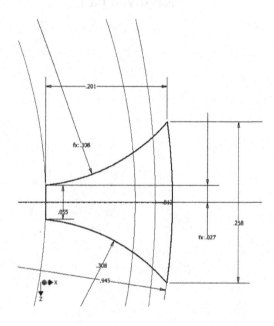

Tooth Profile-B

Bevel Gear

Gears-in-Mesh

Involute Spline

Inventor software has a built-in program to generate an involute spline with data entries and will advise the student to refer to an engineering book for detail drawing of an involute spline.

In this tutorial the student/designer will be guided through steps to take for creating an Involute Spline.

The first step is to create a shaft using the outline shown. The shaft could be drawn in two separate ways.

Using half of the sketch with the revolve feature to add a volume or knowing the diameter and the length of each cylinder in the shaft and using the shaft generator.

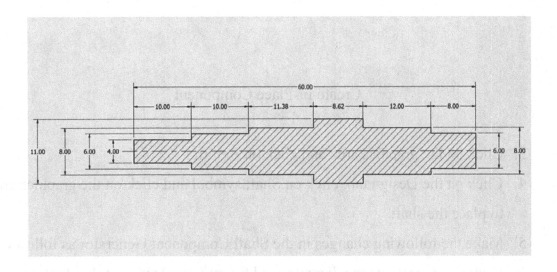

Shaft Sketch

1. Start a new assembly file and save it as Involute Spline.

2. Click on Create under Assembly tab type Shaft in the name text and click on OK button.

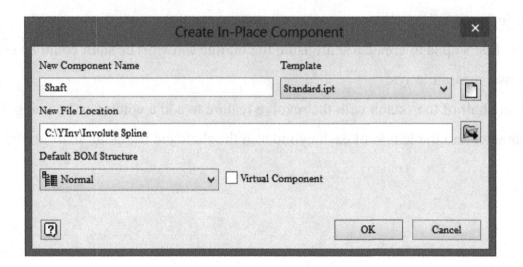

Create In-Place Component

3. Click on the graphics area and click on Return.

4. Click on the Design tab, click on Shaft symbol and click on the graphics area to place the shaft.

5. Make the following changes in the Shaft Component Generator as follows.

6. Each row represents the diameter and the cylinder length of the shaft moving from left to the right.

7. Referring to the Shaft sketch the first diameter is 4 inches and the length is 10 inches.

8. Double-click on 2 x 4 change D to 4, L to 10 and click on OK button.

Shaft Component Generator

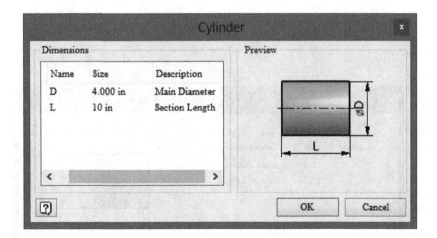

Cylinder dialogue box

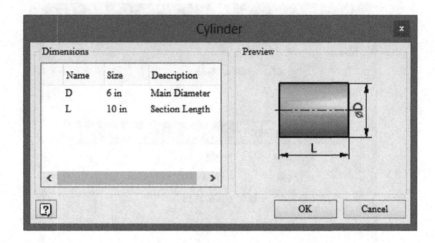

9. Double-click on 2 x 4 change D to 6, L to 10 and click on OK button.

10. Click on the cone-shape symbol on the third row, expand the arrow and select Cylinder and click on Yes for the change.

11. Double-click on the cylinder data change D to 8 and L to 11.38 click OK button.

12. Double-click on the next row make the changes shown and click OK button.

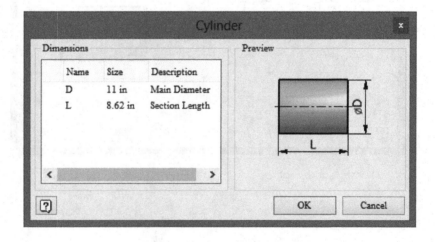

13. Click on the Cylinder symbol under Sections to insert a new cylinder.

14. Double-click on the highlighted value and make the following changes as shown, click OK button to create the cylinder.

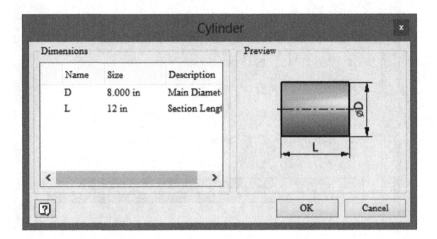

15. Insert the last cylinder, double-click on Data and make the following changes as shown below.

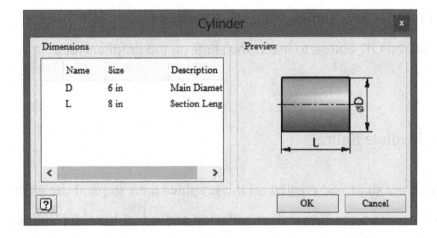

Cylinder dialogue box

Shaft Component Generator

16. This is the final entries of the shaft generator.

17. Click on OK button to insert the shaft on the graphics area.

Creating Involute Spline

1. With the shaft just created on the graphics area, expand the arrow by Parallel Splines from the Power Transmission and select Involute Spline.

2. Click on the body of the 4 inch cylinder for Reference 1 and the edge of the cylinder for Reference 2.

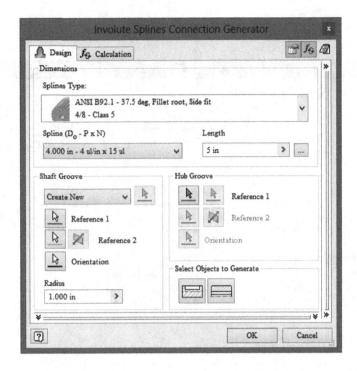

Involute Spline Template

3. Click on Calculation tab, change Hub Outside diameter to 4 and click on Calculate button.

4. Click on the Design tab change the length to 5 inches or the required length of the groove.

5. Expand the arrow under Spline (D_o – P x N) and select value shown.

6. Under *Select Objects to Generate*, click on the first groove symbol and click on OK button twice to generate the involute spline.

7. Save the part.

540

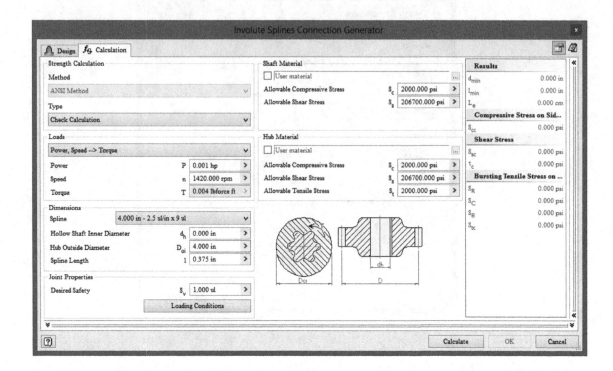

Involute Spline Connection Generator

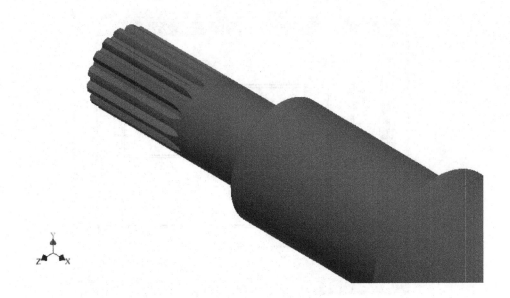

Involute Spline

Furniture Design

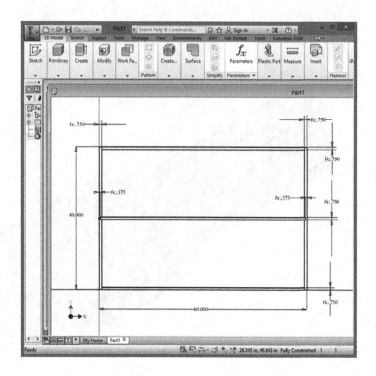

Cabinet Sketch

1. Start a new part document on the XY plane and create the Sketch shown.
2. Click on rectangle sketch tool and place a copy from the origin.
3. Click on Dimension select the base line and type "Length = 60" and click on the check mark.
4. Click on the vertical line and type "Height = 40" and click on the check mark.
5. Offset the line add dimension and type "Thickness = 0.75" and click on the check mark.
6. Place a rectangular sketch in the middle of the sketch and add dimension to it.

7. Exit the sketch and click on Extrude to add a depth to the left rectangle.

8. Type the word DEPTH = 15 in the distance text box and click on OK button.

Extrude dialogue box

9. Expand the plus sign by Extrusion 1 in the browser, right-click on Sketch 1 and select Share Sketch.

10. Click on Extrude select New Solid icon, highlight the bottom rectangle and click on OK button.

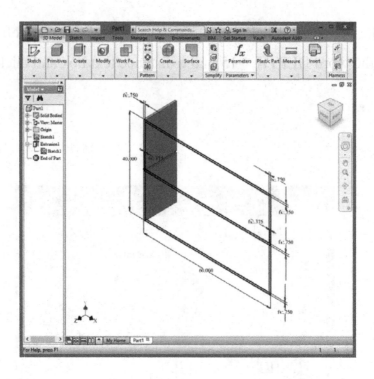

Left Panel

Extrude dialogue box

11. Repeat the Extrusion and select the right panel and OK button.

12. Complete the rest of the Extrusion with same process and save the model.

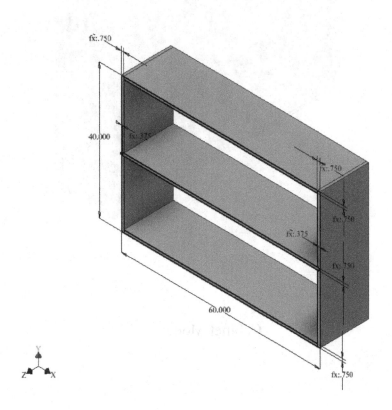

Frame of Cabinet

13. Add a new sketch on the back of the model and place a rectangular sketch clicking two diagonal corners.

14. Add a depth of 0.5 inches using extrude feature and save the model.

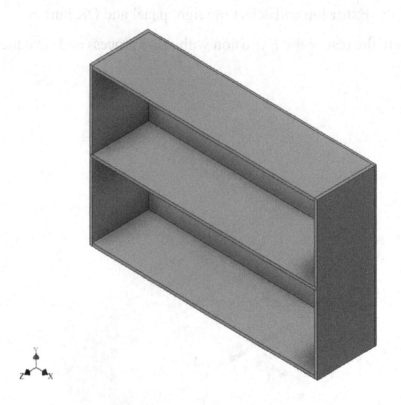

Cabinet Model

Assigning Names to panels

Assigning proper names to parts in the cabinet will help differentiate one from the other.

1. Expand the plus sign by Solid Bodies in the browser on the left column and right-click on Solid 1 and select Properties.
2. Override Solid 1 by typing L-Panel and clicking on OK button.
3. Repeat this for the rest of the Solid Bodies: - Bottom Panel; R-Panel; Top Panel; Divider and Back Panel.

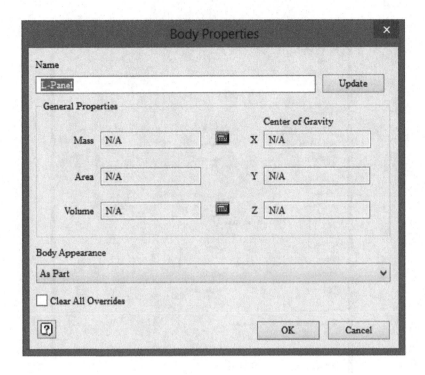

Body Properties

Document Settings

The document settings is used to assign the type of wood to be used with a Prefix.

1. Select the Tools tab from the ribbon and click on Document Settings.
2. Click on Modeling tab and Options under 'Make Components Dialog' and place a check mark in text box by Prefix.
3. Type **Birch-** in the text box under Prefix and click on OK button.
4. Note that any preferred wood could be used instead of birch.

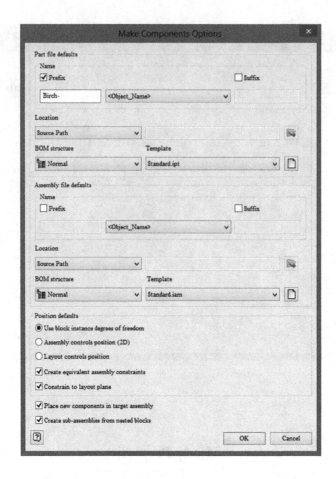

Make Components Options dialogue box

Make Components

Using Make Components will link the Model to an assembly file to add constraints.

1. Click on Manage tab on the ribbon and select Make Components to open up the selection box.

2. Click on the parts under the Solid Bodies in the browser one at a time to populate the multi-text box.

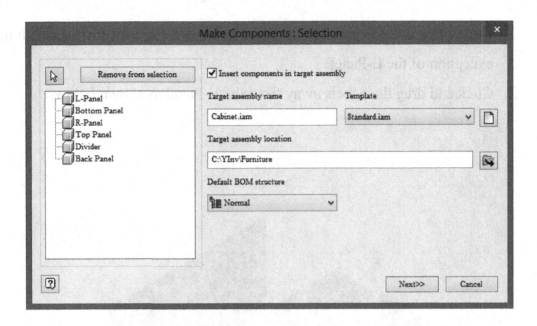

Make Components: Selection

3. Click on the Next button when finished to open up Make Components: Bodies dialogue box.

4. Note that the prefix for all the bodies read Birch.

5. Click on OK button to open up an assembly model and click on Home icon to orient it in an Isometric view.

Re-Assembly

The model just loaded into the assembly file is grounded meaning none of the parts could be moved. To re-assemble it properly:

1. Right-click on each part and un-check grounded from the browser with the exception of the L-Panel.

2. Click and drag the panels away from the L-Panel as shown below.

Re-arranged panels

3. Using the Constrain feature add mates between each panel starting with the Bottom to the L-Panel.

4. Save the model when finished.

Assigning Material

1. Click on Tools tab in the ribbon and select Material to open up the Material browser.

2. Scroll down to Wood select Birch and click on the panels' one at a time.

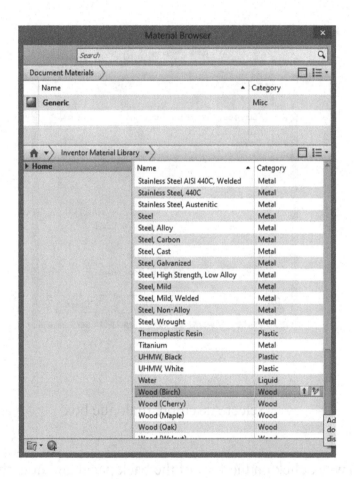

Material browser

3. Click on the Add icon to the side to change it to Birch.

4. Save the model.

Presentation

Presentation shows how the parts are assembled and the connected to one another.

1. Start a new file select on Presentation.ipn and click on Create.
2. Select Create View and OK button to insert a copy of the assembly model on the graphics area.

Select Assembly dialogue box

3. Select Tweak click on the face of the back panel and drag the panel away from the model.
4. Repeat this for the rest of the panels and save the presentation.

Drawing Sheet

1. With the presentation still on the graphics area click on New, select Ansi (in).idw and click on Create to open up a drawing sheet.

2. Click on Base icon, select Top Iso and click on the Graphics area.

3. Select Base icon again and bring in a copy of the assembly model and place it on the graphics area.

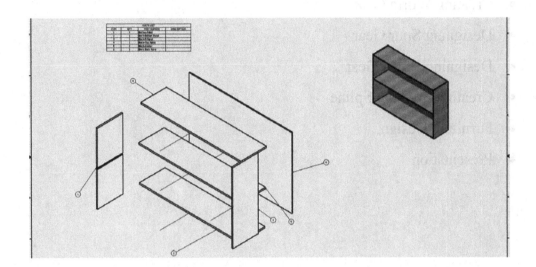

Drawing Sheet

554

Summary

This chapter covered different topics that included:

- Electrical Wiring
- Cable and Harness
- Adaptive Spring
- Using Work Planes
- Creating Bearing
- Creating a Shaft
- Creating Worm Gear
- Designing Spur Gear
- Designing Bevel Gear
- Creating Involute Spline
- Furniture Design
- Presentation

Chapter XII

After completing this tutorial the student will be able to:

- Start a new file and select a Freeform shape
- Change parameters and enter new Data.
- Create different shapes with the selected item
- Use the Match Edge option
- Learn to use Mirror
- Utilize the Split tool
- Shell a form
- Use Fillet for parts on the form
- Edit Form
- Use the Plane form
- Use the Merge Edge tool
- Use thicken on planes
- Combine Shapes.

Freeform

Freeform is used to create complex shapes that will be difficult to accomplish when using parametric modeling commands. Consumer products like hair driers, toy boxes, bowls, gadgets and equally similar shapes. The only snag is once the object is placed on the graphics area there is no option to change it. Place a box on the graphics area with certain data could not be changed. This is 2016 version hopefully, subsequent releases through the years will see a new approach to using the freeForm tools. The Edit Form tool is used to alter parts of the form.

The freeform contains six primitives with a Box; Plane; Cylinder; Sphere; Torus and Quadball. Each one could be used by looking at the end results of the project. Combine two or three to form a complex figure. For an example on creating a landscape one will use the Plane to form the hills and valleys. It will be ideal to use the cylinder to create a barrel-shaped object. There is also the Editing tools that will be covered in this tutorials. In the table below are listed most of the Editing tools for the FreeForm.

FreeForm Editing Tools

Face	Convert	Align Form	Delete
Insert Edge	Insert Point	Subdivide	Merge Edges
Unweld Edges	Crease Edges	Uncrease	Bridge
Thickness	Match Edge	Symmetry	Mirror
Clear Symmetry	Add Distance	Make Uniform	Toggle Smooth
Toggle Translucent	Select Through		

Match Edge

1. Start a new part in English.ipt and click on Create.

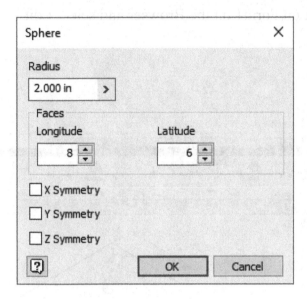

Sphere Dialogue box

2. Expand the arrow under FreeForm and select Sphere.

3. Change the entries as shown and click on XZ then the origin to place a form on the graphics area.

4. Click on Ok button to exit and click on the check mark.

5. Select the XZ plane from the Browser, click on Plane from the Work Features and drag the plane above the model at a distance of 2.50 and click on the check mark.

6. Right-click on the new plane on the Browser and select New Sketch.

7. Use the Centerpoint rectangle to add a 6 x 6 inch rectangle and click on Finish check mark.

8. Move to the Browser drag the Form1 below Sketch1 and orient the model in isometric view.

9. Right-click on Form1 on the Browser and select Edit Freeform.

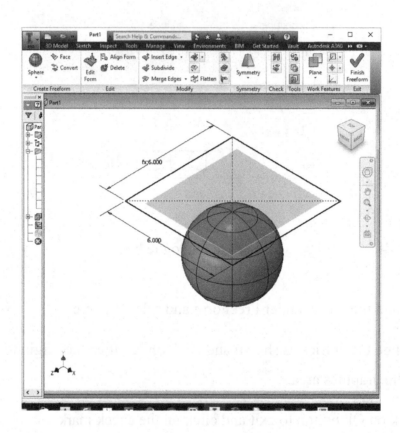

Sphere with Rectangular Sketch

10. Select Match Edge from the Modify tab, hold down on *ctrl* key on the keyboard and click on the top ring on the sphere.

11. Select the Target arrow from the Match Edge dialogue box, hold down on ctrl from the keyboard and select the lines of the rectangle one at a time.

12. Click on Ok button to complete the operation.

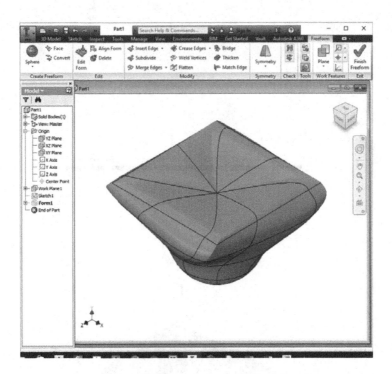

Custom Bowl

13. Click on the check mark select the XY plane and add a new sketch as shown.

14. Select Extrude from the 3D features and use Cut and All with Symmetric to remove the part shown.

15. Leave the model as a piece of furniture or use Shell feature about 0.0025 thick and add a texture to it to form a bowl.

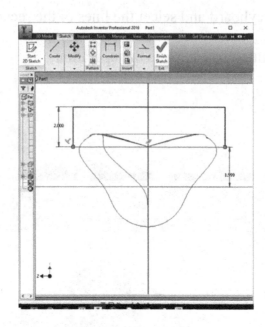

Jug

1. Start a new part select Plane from FreeForm, click on XZ then the origin using the data in the cylinder dialogue box.

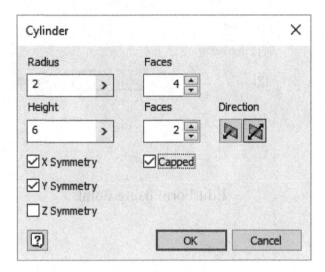

Cylinder dialogue box

2. Select Both Direction and click on Ok button to place a cylinder on the graphics area.

3. Select Edit Form and use the Point option to drag the end as shown.

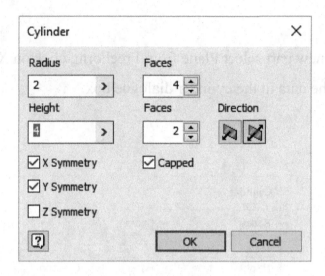

Edit Form using Point

Edit Form

Edit Form

1. Select Edit Form click on Point to add points on the form and orient the model on Right view.

2. Click on the Point on the top left to place an arrow and drag it on Z direction to the left at a distance of 3.00 units and click on Ok button.

3. Orient the view to the Front, select Edit Form and select Point.

4. Drag it on Z direction to the right at a distance of 1.500 units and click on Ok button.

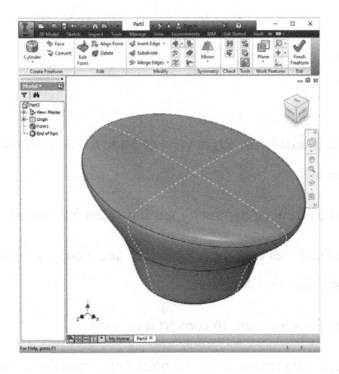

Custom Shape using points

Torus

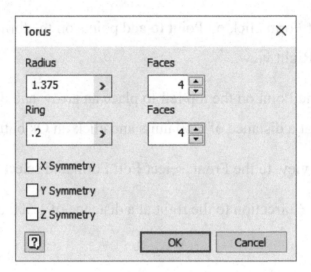

Torus dialogue box

Mirror

1. Orient the model to the Right view and add Torus with the data shown using the XY plane.

2. Expand the arrow on Symmetry tab and select Mirror tool.

3. Click on the Torus then the YZ plane to add a copy to opposite side of the model and click on Ok button.

4. Click on the check mark to convert it to solid.

5. Click on XZ plane and offset it 1.6625 units from the center of the model and click on check mark.

Split

1. Add a new sketch to the Work Plane1 and select Split under the Modify tab.

2. Click on Trim Solid icon on the Split dialogue box and select Side to remove with the arrow pointing upwards and click on Apply.

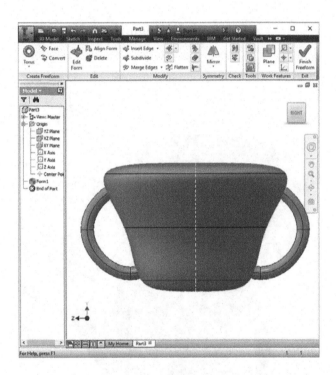

Mirror Model

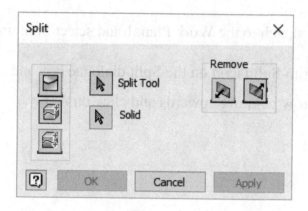

Split Dialogue box

Using Combine

1. Select Combine from the Modify tab, hold down on ctrl from the keyboard and click on both handles as the Base.

2. Select Toolbody and click on the body of the model then Apply.

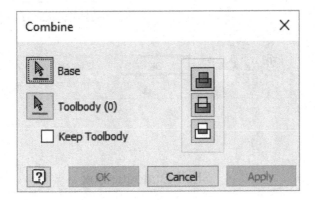

Combine dialogue box

Shell

1. Orient the model to an isometric view, select Shell from the Modify tab and click on the flat top of the model.

2. Click on the check mark to accept the default value of 0.1 to add shell to the model.

568

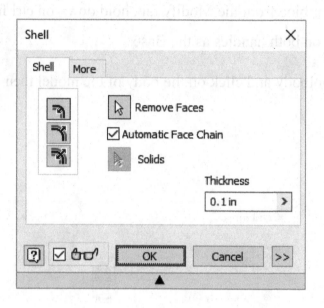

Shell Dialogue box

Fillet

1. Add Fillet between the body and the connect ends of the handles using the default settings and save the model.

Final Model

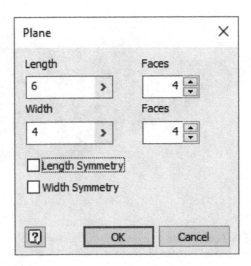

Plane dialogue box

1. Start a new Part using the Standard.ipt and click on Create button.

2. Move to the freeForm tab on the Ribbon expand the arrow for the freeform and select Plane.

3. Select the XZ Plane and click on the Origin to add a plane.

4. Click on Edit Form select Point under Filter, and click on an intersection of two lines to place an arrow on top.

5. Click on the arrow and drag it upward to create a hilly-shape.

6. Click on another point drag it down to form a valley.

7. Continue to shape the model to achieve a shape closer to the one shown and click on Ok button.

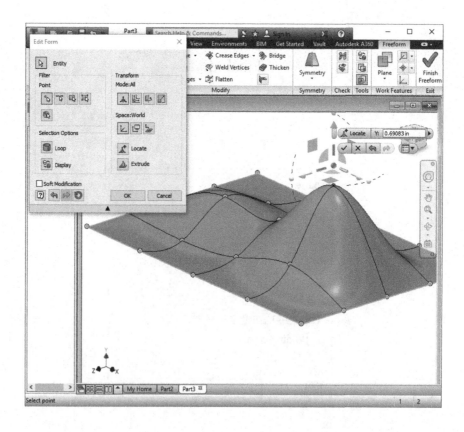

Edit Form-Plane

Swimming Pool

1. Start a new file using English.ipt and click on Create.

2. Click on 3D Model expand the arrow under Create Freeform and select on Plane.

3. Select the XZ plane and click on the origin to add the Plane.

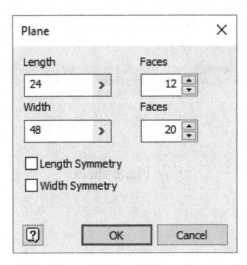

Plane dialogue box

4. Click on Ok button to exit the plane dialogue box.

5. Select the Edit Form icon hold down on the ctrl key on the keyboard and click on the squares shown (8 x 6).

6. Click on the Y-arrow pointing upwards, drag it down a distance of -4 units and click on Ok button.

7. Select the Edit Form icon again hold down on ctrl key on the keyboard and click on the squares shown (8 x 8).

8. Click on the Y-arrow pointing upwards, drag it down a distance of -12 units and click on Ok button.

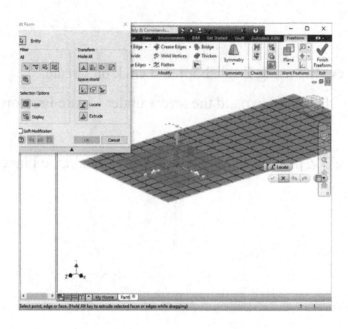

Plane sheet

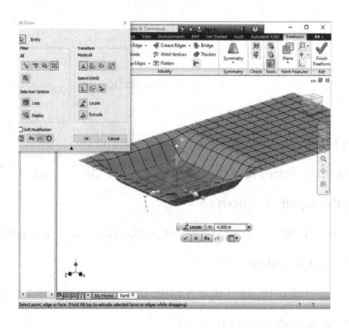

3 Units Deep

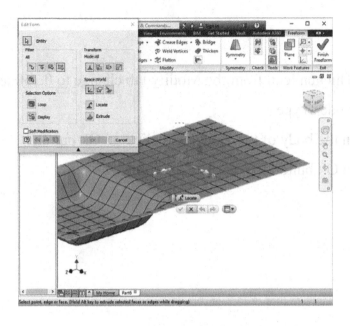

3-Units Deep

12 Units Deep

Thicken

1. Select Thicken icon from the Modify tab change to 0.250 and click on sharp option under Type.

2. Click on the body of the model and click on Ok button.

3. Click on Ok button to complete the form.

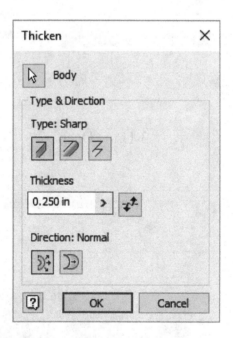

Thicken dialogue box

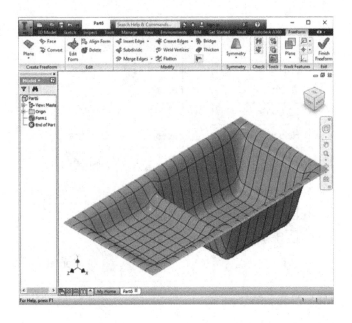

Freeform

Finished Form Model

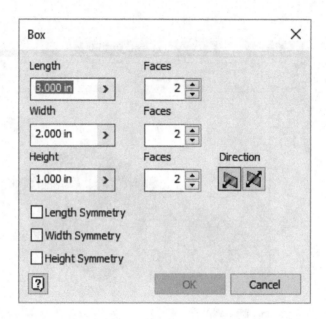

Box Dialogue

1. Start a new part and select Box.

2. In the dialogue box the student has a choice of selecting different parameters to suit what is being designed.

3. Change the length, width as well as the height together with the number of faces to work with.

4. To demonstrate the function of the parameters, change the length to 6, width to 4 and height to 2 inches.

5. To divide the faces change the Face adjacent to length to 6, the next one to 4 and the last to 3.

6. Click on Ok button to exit.

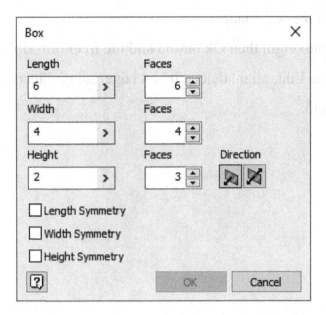

Parameters

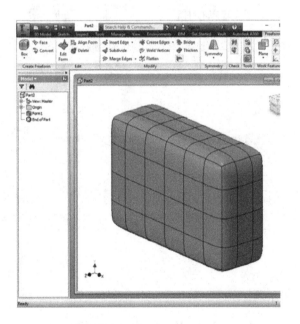

Using Box

7. After selecting the required data click on one of the planes to work on in this case select the XY-Plane.

8. Click on the origin then Ok button and the freeForm ribbon opens up.

9. There is the Edit, align, delete, insert edge, subdivide and many more tools to choose from.

Edit Form

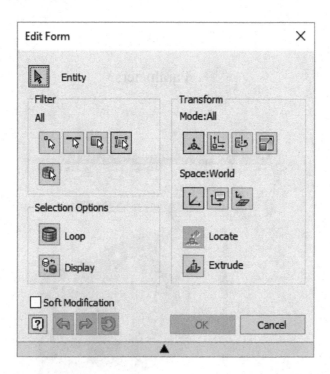

Edit Form dialogue box

10. Select Edit Form to open up a dialogue box to select any of the many controls.

11. There is the Point, Edge, Face and All under Filter.

12. Click on each tool and check out how it changes.

13. As the names depict the Point will select points on the box, the edge select edges and Face will select individual faces.

14. Press down on the ctrl on the key board to select multiple faces at a time.

15. For now select All and click on the front face of the box to place a gizmo symbol with XYZ coordinates.

16. Click on the Z arrow coming out of the box and move the mouse in and out to form a required shape.

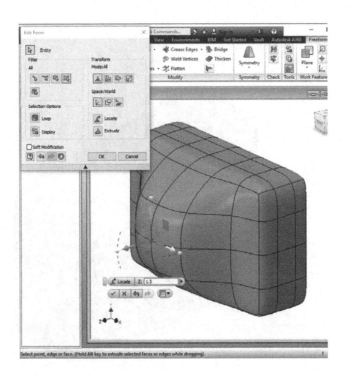

Pull on Z at 1.5 inches

17. The entry by the Z Locate can also be typed in once the face is pulled or pushed in.
18. This is a pliable material being used and it could be molded to form any required shape needed.
19. Click on the check mark when finished creating the form.
20. Select the Edit Form again rotate the box to the back and click on Scale from the dialogue box.
21. Click on top of the box and drag to scale it down or up.
22. Click on the check mark on the Ribbon when finished to convert the free form object into solid.
23. The solid part could now be used in any other 3D modelling and add a shell and slice it in half or add planes to create another part.

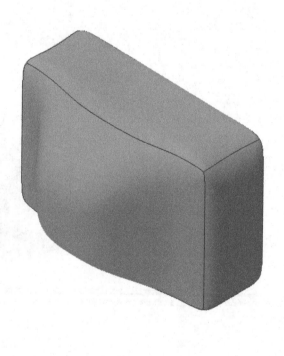

Freeform Model

Plane

This session will cover the uses of Plane in Freeform feature.

1. Start a new drawing and create the outline shown using the Spline tool.

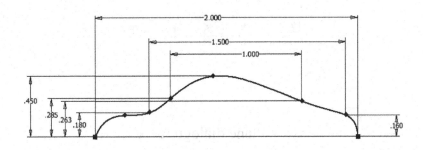

Spline Outline

2. Click on the Home icon on the top right corner of the screen and select Plane from the freeform tools.

3. Click on XY-Plane and click on the origin to add a plane at the base of the spline outline.

4. Click on Ok button and select Edit Form from the list and change the values as shown.

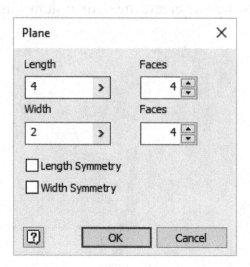

Plane dialogue box

5. Click on Ok button and select Edit Form and use the edge option to drag the edges as shown on both sides.

Merge Edges

1. Click on Merge Edges select the middle line on the plane for Set1, click on Set2 and select the spline outline.

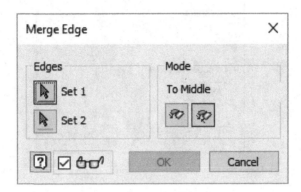

Merge Edges

Thicken

1. Select thicken icon adjust the thickness value as shown and click on Ok button.

2. This action turns the free form into a solid.

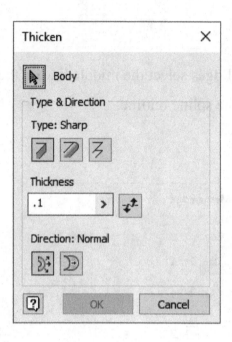

Thicken dialogue box

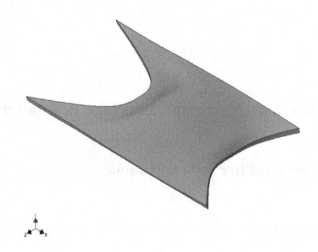

End Product

Combining Shapes

1. Start a new part and expand the arrow under the Freeform to select Box.
2. The box dialogue box should appear on the graphics area with different options to choose from.
3. Select the XY-Plane and click on the origin to place a box primitive on the graphics area.
4. Change the length to 20 and the Face 6 units.
5. Leave the rest of the entries as shown in the data entries box and click on Ok button to place a primitive box on the graphics area.
6. Form1 should also appear in the Browser.

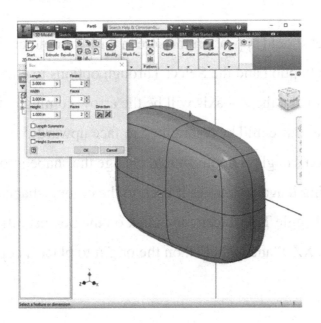

Primitive Box

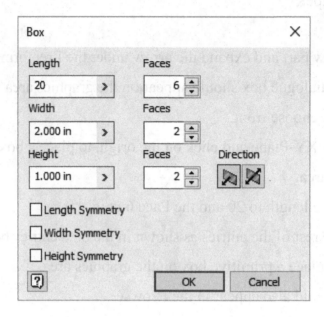

Data Entries

7. The model should appear on the screen with Smooth enabled and there is the translucent option and the Select Through options to choose from.

8. Notice also that the Z – axis will be the arrow coming out of the box towards the left and this could be re-oriented to face upwards.

9. Clicking on Toggle Smooth should change the shape into a rectangular box and clicking it again changes it back to the oblong shape.

10. Click on Toggle Translucent and click on the box primitive again.

11. Select the XZ-Plane and click on the origin to place a copy on the graphics area.

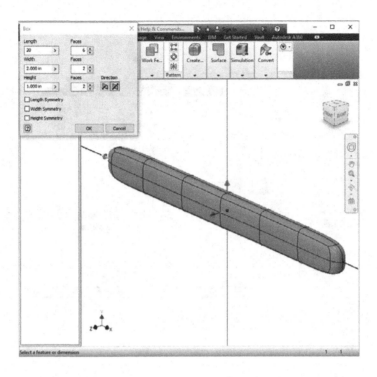

First Form

12. Toggle to Translucent and Select the box again click on XZ-Plane, click on the Origin and select Both Directions option from the Box dialogue.

13. Ok button to accept the default settings.

Edit Form

1. Select Edit Form icon, drag a window around the box just added and click on Translate under Transform.

2. Hold down on the ctrl key on the keyboard to select all faces then use the arrows to move it as shown in figure and click on OK button.

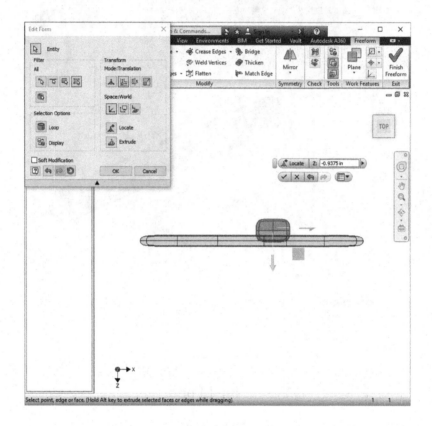

Edit Form

3. Orient the view to Top and use the Edit form to drag the arrows upward and to the right as shown.

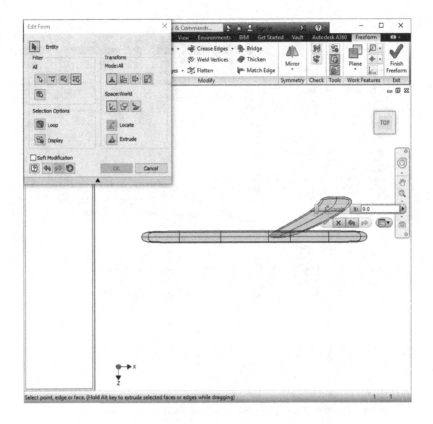

Edit Form

4. Use the Edge option from the Edit Form dialogue box and stretch the wing to the right to sharpen the end.

5. Click on Ok button to exit.

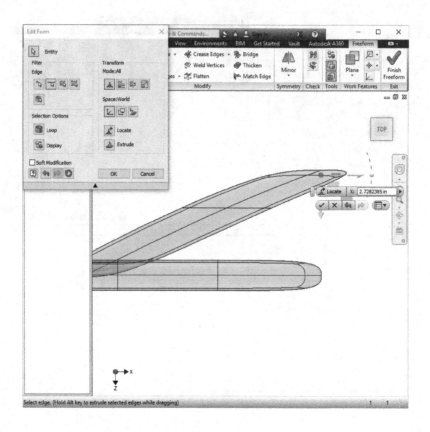

The Wing

6. Expand the arrow under Symmetry and select Mirror icon.

7. Click on the body of the wing to highlight it, click on the mirror Plane.

8. Move to the browser and click on the plus sign by Origin and select XY plane then Ok button.

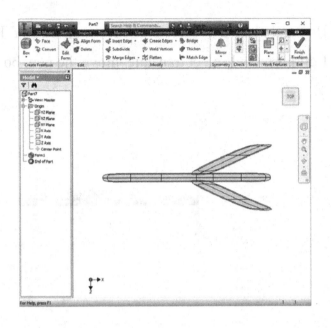

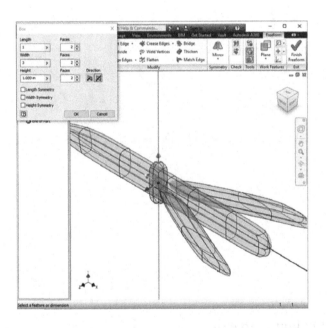

9. Click on Box and place a new form as shown on the XY-Plane.

10. Click on Edit Form and select translate, move the new box to the end of the main body.

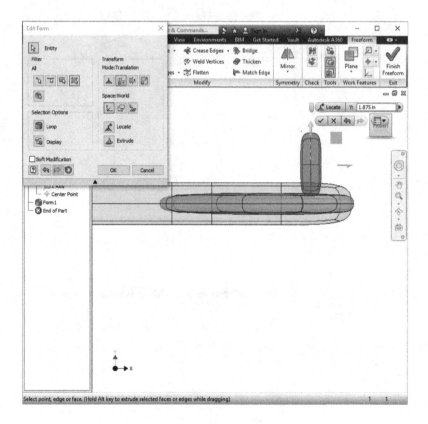

11. Click on Ok button to exit.

12. Use the Rotate option in the Edit dialogue box to tilt the object about 30°.

13. Use Point to elongate the ends to create a streamline and click on Ok button.

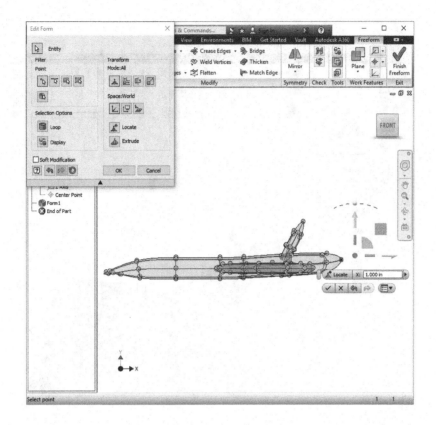

Using Points from Edit Form

14. Exit and save the model.
15. Select the Edit Form and use the all option to stretch the middle of the body and mirror it to the other side using the XY-Plane to for a shape shown.

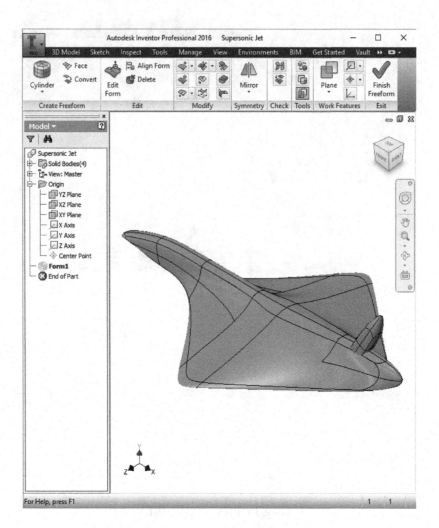

Supersonic

595

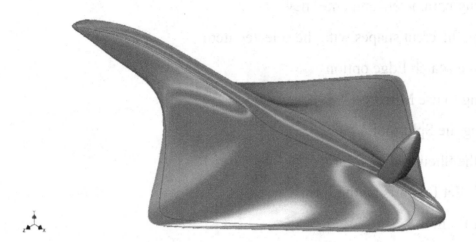

Take Off

Summary

In this chapters topics covered included but not limited to:

- Starting a new file and select a Freeform shape

- Changing parameters and enter new Data.

- Creating different shapes with the selected item

- Using the Match Edge option

- Learning to use Mirror

- Utilizing the Split tool

- Using the Shell tool on a form

- Using Fillet for parts on the form

- Editing Form

- Using the Plane form

- Using the Merge Edge tool

- Using thicken on planes

- Combining Shapes.

Chapter XIII

This chapter is set aside for the Final project in that, the student/designer is to re-create all the parts in the subsequent pages.

- Add materials to the parts with the Bushing as bronze and the rest Steel.
- Insert all the rubber O-Rings from the Content Center.
- Open up an assembly file and insert all the parts to form the Dual-Acting Air Cylinder.
- Insert Hex Head bolts from the Content Center
- Create Presentation using the saved assembly and add an exploded view.
- Set up drawing sheet, insert the presentation as well as the assembly and add bill of materials or parts list.
- Set up balloons to cross reference the parts in the B.O.M.
- Create Sections and Detail drawings to locate hidden holes as well as the weep holes.
- Detail the Weep holes.
- Add a Break feature to the long shaft to fit the drawing sheet.
- Create drawing sheet for each part with dimensions and details.
- Create an Analysis with the shaft and print the results.

Dual Acting Air Cylinder

1. Using the right plane create concentric circles of Ø0.50 and Ø0.750 and add a depth of 0.875.

2. Save as Bushing.

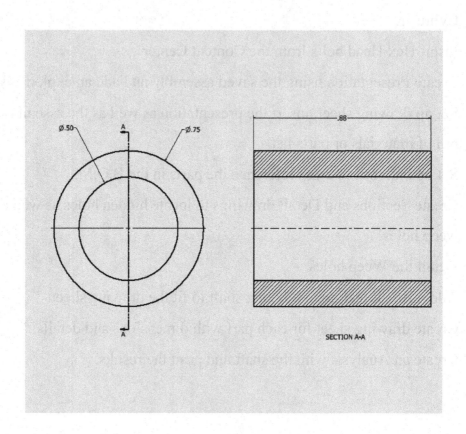

2D Sketch

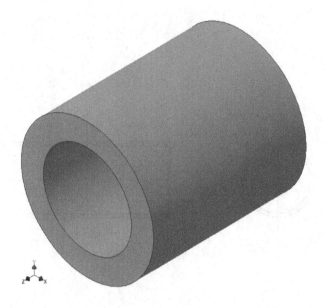

3D Model-Bushing

3. Start a new part in XY plane and add a concentric circle with Ø2.00 and Ø2.247 and use the extrude feature to add a depth of 5.625.

4. Add chamfer of 0.04 x 21° on the inner and outer edges.

5. Save it as Body.

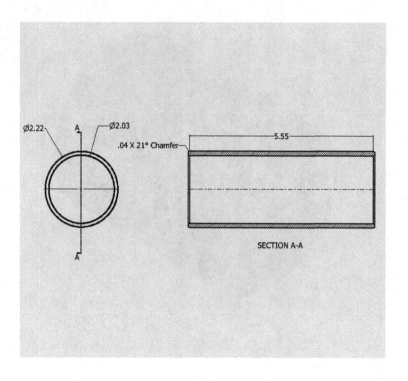

2D Sketch

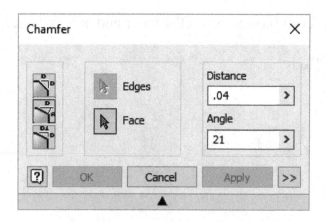

Chamfer dialogue box

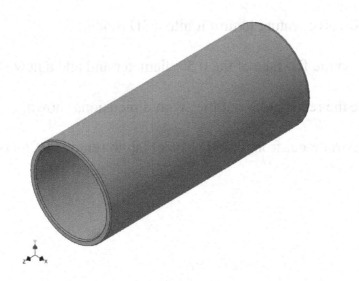

3D Model-Body

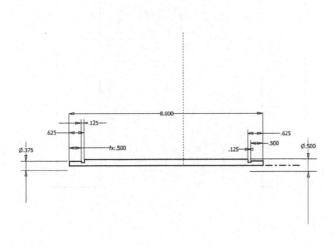

2D Sketch

1. Start a new part on the YZ plane and create the outline with all dimensions shown.

2. Use Revolve feature to turn it into a 3D model.

3. Click on the flat face of the 0.50 diameter and add a new sketch.

4. Create the rectangular outlines with dimensions shown.

5. Use Extrude-cut from the 3D Model tab to remove 0.250 of material and save.

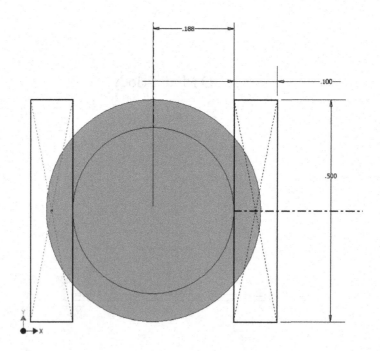

Rectangular Sketch

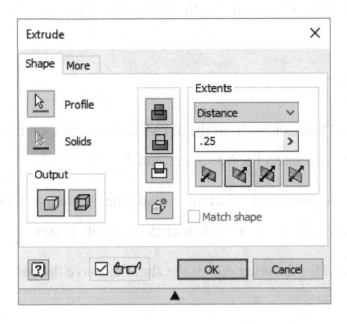

Extrude dialogue box

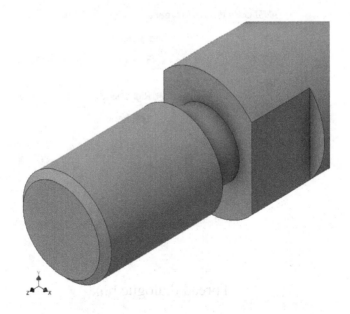

6. Add a 0.025 x 45° chamfer to the ends and save.

Adding Threads

1. Click on Threads icon from the 3D Model tab, click on the body of the extension and select the Specification tab.

2. Expand the arrow and select the thread type, move to Designation and select the required either 16 or 24 then click on Apply button.

3. Repeat this for the other end of the shaft and save the part.

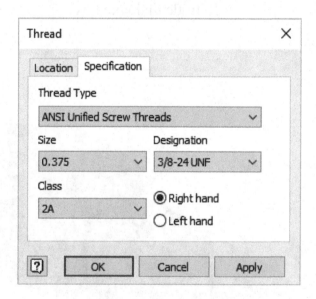

Thread dialogue box

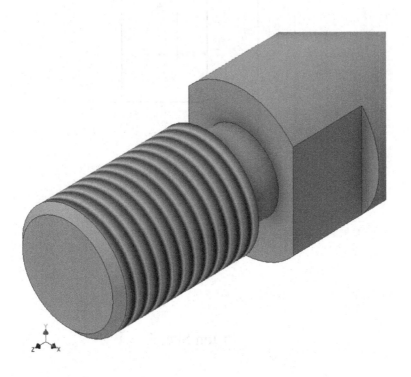

Threaded End

1. Start a new Part on YZ plane and create the shape with all dimensions and exit.

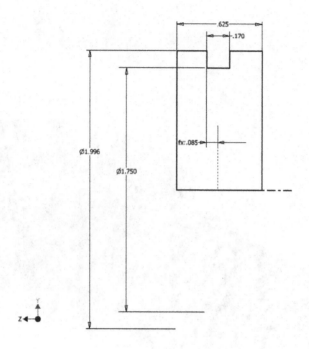

Piston Sketch

2. Use the revolve feature to turn it into a 3D model and save.

3. Add a new sketch on the flat face of the model, place a point from the sketch tool on the center and exit.

4. Select Hole icon under Modify tab make the changes shown and click on the check mark to place a hole on the center of the Piston.

5. Add threads to the inside of the hole and save.

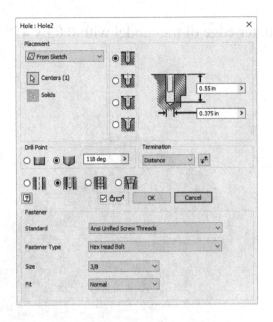

Hole dialogue box

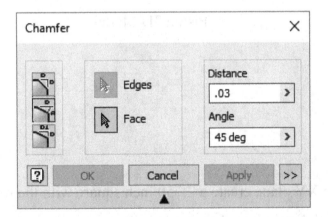

Chamfer dialogue box

6. Chamfer the outer edge of the model with 0.03 x 45°.

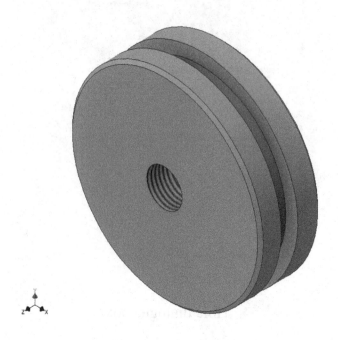

Piston 3D Model

Working End

1. Using the XY plane create a 2.750 inch square with the rectangular sketch and add all dimensions shown and exit.

2. Use the Extrude feature to add a depth of 1.375 and save the model.

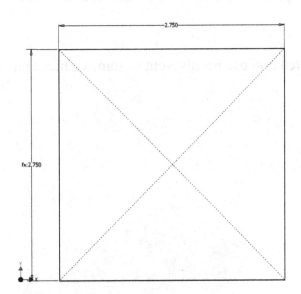

2D Sketch

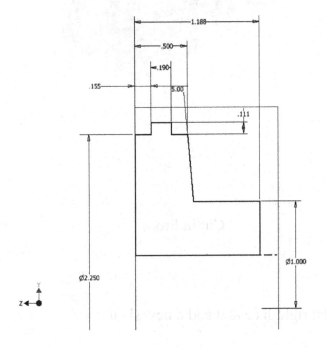

Hole Outline

3. Click on YZ plane add a new sketch and create the outline shown with a center line.

4. Exit the sketch and use revolve-cut to remove material as shown below.

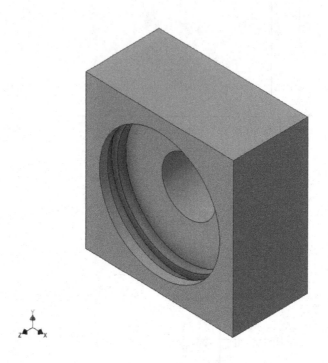

Cut in Front

5. Click on the flat right face and add a new sketch.

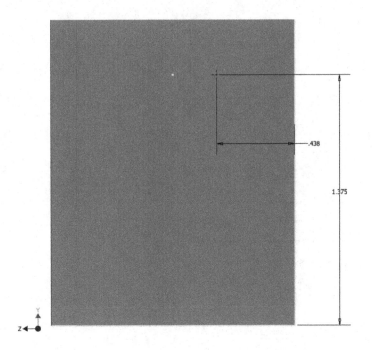

Point sketch

6. Place a point on the sketch and exit.

7. Select the hole feature and make changes in the dialogue box.

8. Click on Apply to add a hole to the box.

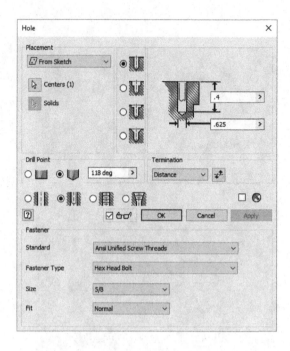

Hole dialogue box

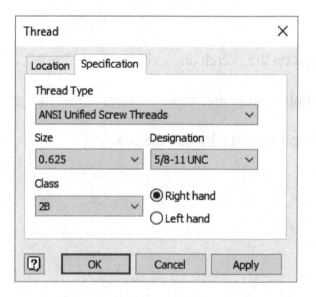

Thread dialogue box

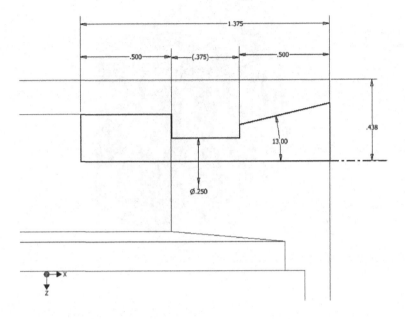

Hole sketch outline

1. Select the XZ plane and add the sketch shown.

2. Exit sketch and use the revolve cut option to remove material as shown and save.

3. Use the thread feature to add 0.625-11UNC thread in the inside of the side hole.

4. Click on the front flat face and add a new sketch and place 4 holes with dimensions shown.

5. Use Extrude cut to create holes through the model.

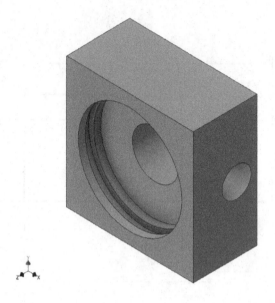

0.625-11UNC side hole

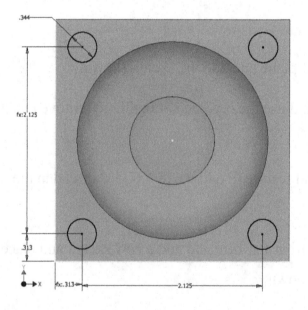

Four Holes

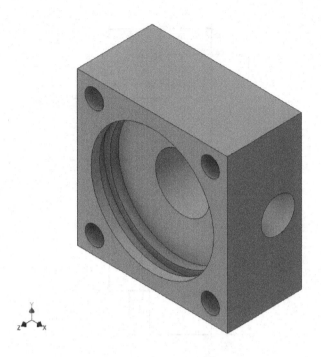

Finished Holes

Pressure End

1. Start a new part on YZ plane and add the sketch with all dimensions.

2. Exit the sketch and save.

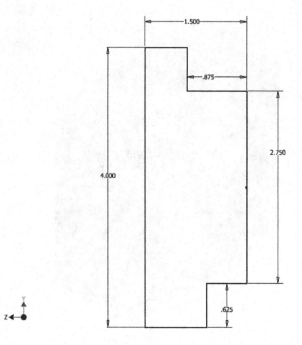

2D Sketch

3. Use the Extrude feature to add depth of 2.75 using the symmetry option.

4. Click on the front flat face of the model and add a new sketch.

5. Create a circle of Ø1.250 from the center of the model and exit the sketch.

6. Extrude the circle at a distance of 0.250 and save the model.

7. Select the YZ plane and add a new sketch.

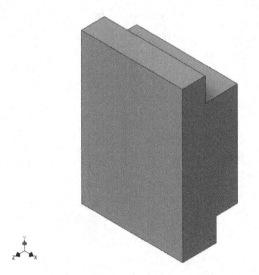

3D Model

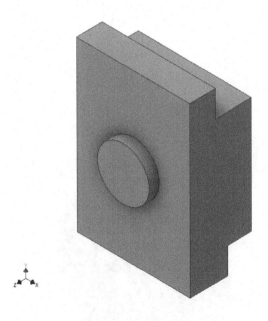

3D Model

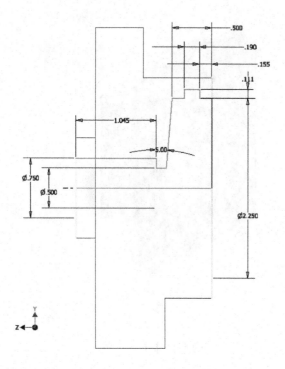

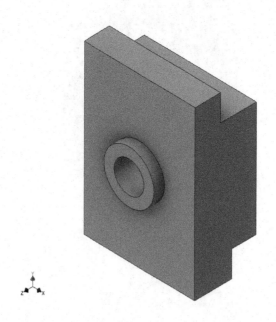

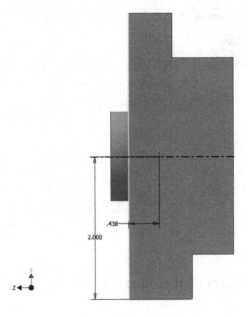

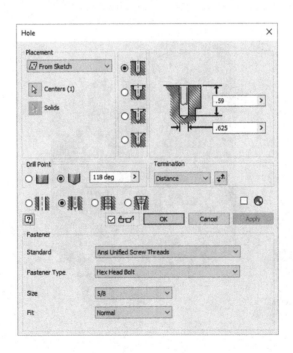

Hole dialogue box

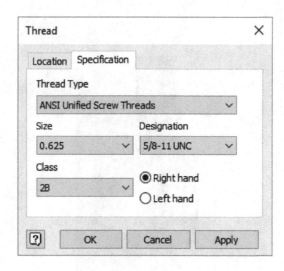

Thread dialogue box

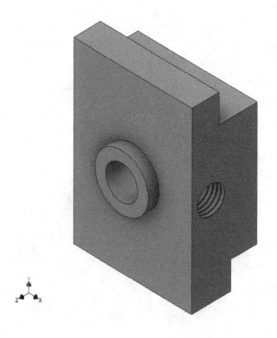

Side Hole

8. Place a WorkPlane 0.50 from the back face and add a new sketch.

9. Create a weep-hole of Ø.250 at a distance of 0.59 from the right edge of the positioned on the center.

10. Select the 3D model tab and click on Extrude with the cut option to remove material using a distance of 0.625 in.

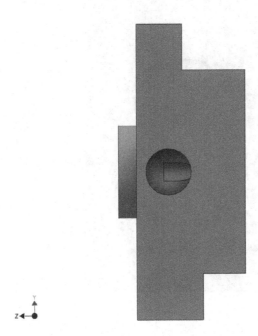

Weep-Hole

Back Hole

1. Click on the back flat face add a new sketch and position a points as shown add all dimensions.

2. Exit the sketch and select the hole feature from the Modify tab.

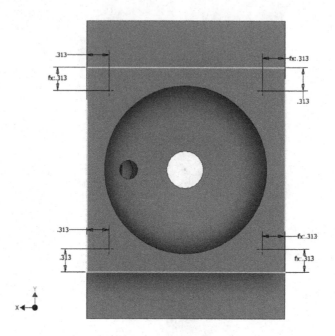

Points on back face

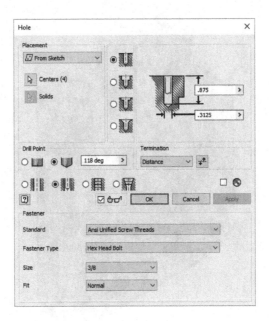

Hole Setup

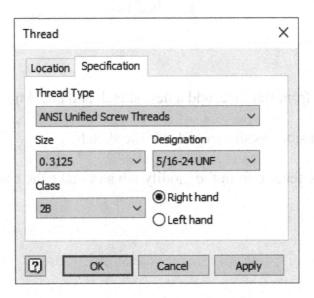

Thread Specification

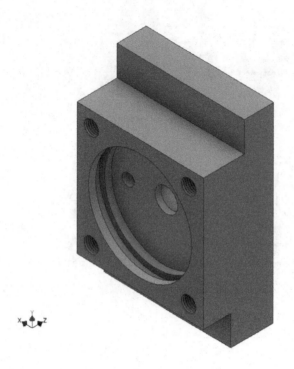

Finished Holes

1. Select the front flat face, add a new sketch and add 4 holes.

2. Add dimensions as shown and exit the sketch.

3. Select hole feature from the modify tab and make the changes in the dialogue box.

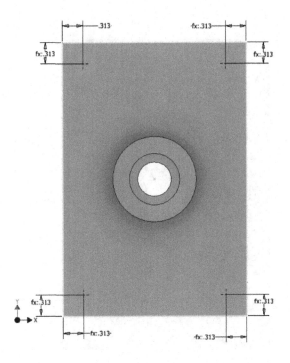

Points on Front face

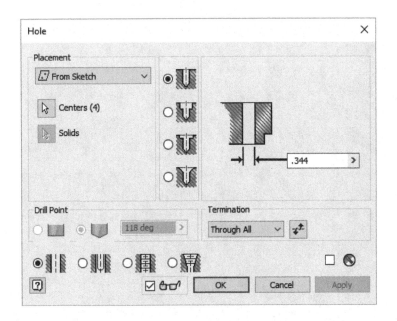

Hole dialogue box

Through Holes

Dual Acting Air Cylinder

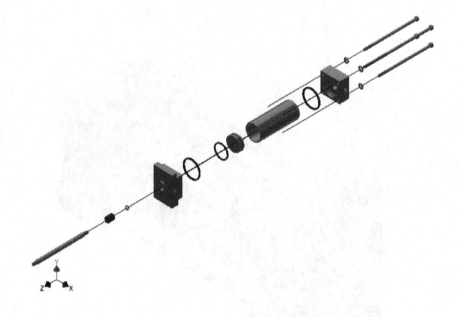

Presentation View

PARTS LIST			
ITEM	QTY	PART NUMBER	MATERIAL
1	1	Working End Model1b	Steel, Carbon
2	4	2-210-Skg-Ø=25,0 mm	Rubber
3	1	Body-1a	Steel, Carbon
4	1	Piston	Steel, Carbon
5	1	Pressure End Final model	Steel, Carbon
6	1	Bushing model	Bronze, Cast
7	1	Shaft Threads	Steel, Carbon
8	4	ASTM F436 - 5/16	Steel, Mild
9	4	ANSI/ASME B18.2.1 - 5/16-18 UNC - 7.5	Steel, Mild

Parts List / B.O.M.

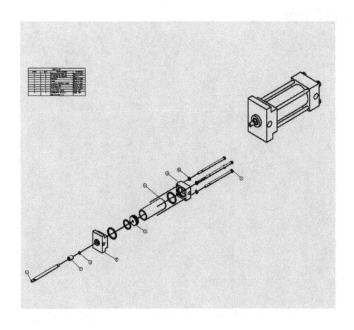

Drawing Views

Summary

This chapter was set aside for a Final Project to encompass all that was covered that included:

- Starting a new file and select a Freeform shape
- Changing parameters and enter new Data.
- Creating different shapes with the selected item
- Using the Match Edge option
- Learning to use Mirror
- Utilizing the Split tool
- Using the Shell tool on a form
- Using Fillet for parts on the form
- Editing Form
- Using the Plane form
- Using the Merge Edge tool
- Using thicken on planes
- Combining Shapes

632

HOW DO I?

Interacting with students with different backgrounds and disciplines has made me realize that, there is more to teaching than just imparting of information to the class. I have therefore come up with a section solely to answer repetitive questions that come up in class every other day that I teach. Thus the How Do I? Section is a Q & A Session.

Q. I just finished using the circular pattern in 2D sketch and accidentally entered 8. How do I change to 10 without starting all over again?

A. Hit the esc key on the keyboard to exit any tool, drag a window around the whole drawing to highlight it all and right-click on one of the circles to select edit Pattern. Change the value and click on OK button.

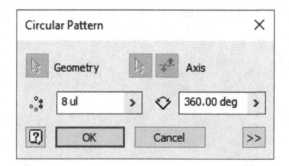

Circular Pattern

Q. How do I change the background color?

A. To change the background color do the following.

- Expand the arrow by *I_{PRO}* select Option and click on Colors tab.
- Select 1Color under Background and any color under Color scheme and click on Apply button.

Q. How do I know which icon is which?

A. Move the mouse pointer and rest it on any icon for a few seconds, a brief description of that particular icon will be displayed at the bottom.

Q. I picked the Top of the Model to add Project Geometry but the icon is grayed out why?

A. You must first click the top of the Model and add a Sketch for the Project Geometry to activate.

Q. How do I copy a Sketch?

A. Right-click on the Sketch from the Browser to highlight it hold down the ctrl-control key and click on 'c'. Open a new sketch and press down the ctrl-control key and hit the 'v' key on the keyboard.

Q. How do I add color to my model?

A. Right-click on the model, select Properties expand the arrow under Face Appearance and click to select color. Click on Ok button to exit.

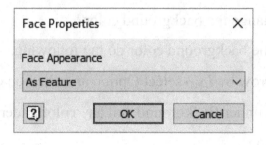

Face Properties

Q. I just finished drawing and added depth using Extrude, but all I can see is an Origin in the far distance on the graphics area. Where is the Model?

A. Click Home on the View cube.

Q. I sketched a rectangular-shaped part and added an Extrude. I would like to add a Flange from the Sheet Metal Tools how do I do it?

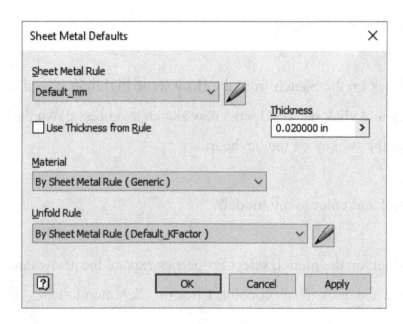

A. After finishing the Sketch, the Flange tool on the Sheet Metal Tools, should have been used instead of the Extrude. Alternatively click on Convert to Sheet Metal and click on Ok button.

Q. I have drawn two lines perpendicular to each other and would like to join them at the intersection. What do I do?

A. use the Extend tool to join the two.

Q. I just added an Extrude to my sketch, but do not remember what view I started my design in. How do I find out what view I started from?

A. Right-click on the Extrude icon and select Edit sketch and the view will be shown.

Q. I am trying to modify dimensions on my Model but when I click on the model with the dimension tool I only see a grayed-out value that cannot be changed, why?

A. You cannot add dimension in the Model view, but you can edit the dimensions. Right-click on the model on the Browser and select edit sketch. Change the dimensions and click on the check mark.

Q. How do I add an Angular dimension?

A. Click to select the dimension icon and click on two lines bordering the angle to place the value.

Q. I sketch a part and would like to add Extrude, but it is adding Surface output.
A. There is an open sketch or an extra Line on top of one of the lines. Track and

delete it or close the sketch to be able to add Extrude.

Q. I placed a Base Part in my assembly but realized that it is moving around freely. How do I set it as the base part so it does not move?

A. Right-click on the part in the Browser and select Grounded to stop it from moving.

Q. I drew a spline to be used as a path for a Sweep and a circle for a Profile. When I clicked on Sweep I got a message "Create sweep feature failed". What am I doing wrong?

A. The path might have sharp corners or the diameter of the circle is too large.

Q. How do I hide the Planes?

A. Right-Click on the WorkPlane in the Browser and select Visibility.

Q. How do I add a chamfer to a 2D sketch?

A. Expand the arrow by the Fillet icon on the Ribbon and select Chamfer. Select the required option and click on two intersecting lines then Ok button.

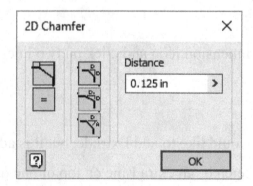

Q. How do I measure a distance in a model?

A. Click on Tools or Inspect tab on the Ribbon and use the Distance ruler to measure between two points.

Q. How do I send a copy of my drawing?

A. Expand the arrow by *I_{PRO}* select Export and click on Send DWF. Select one of the listed options and click on Publish button.

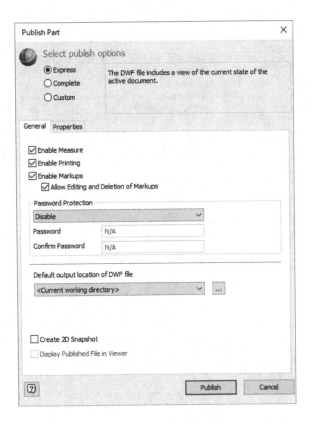

Select Publish Options dialogue box

Q. Finished a sketch using English.ipt how do I change it to millimeters?

638

A. right-click on the sketch under the Browser, start a new part select Metric under Templates and click on Standard (mm).ipt. Start a sketch on the XY plane right-click and paste a copy on the graphics area.

Q. How do I change the size of Text in the Drawing sheet?

A. With the part on the drawing sheet, select Styles Editor under the Manage tab expand the arrow under **A** Text, click on Label Text(ANSI) change the text height save and click on Done. Repeat this for Note and Standard.

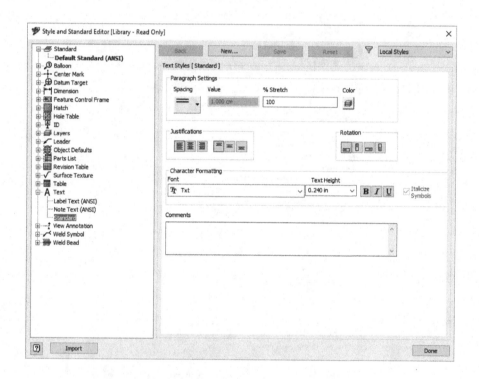

Style Editor

Q. How do I change the scale of the drawing?

A. Double-click on the Base part on the drawing to open up the Drawing View dialogue box and change the scale then OK button.

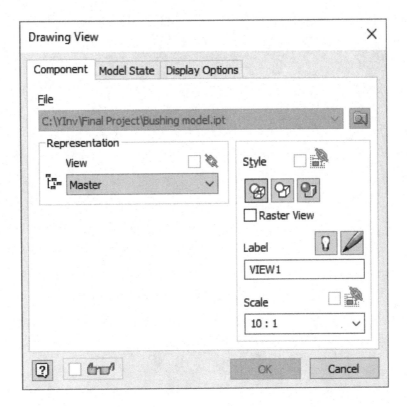

Drawing View

Q. How do I add center mark to a circle?

A. Select Annotate move to Symbols tab, click on the cross hair and click on the circumference of the circle.

Q. How do I sweep using spline?

A. Add a profile to one end of the spline using a WorkPlane perpendicular to the end line. Use the sweep icon from the 3D model and click on the spline.

INDEX

644

Printed in the United States
By Bookmasters